Learning C++

Neill Graham

Mc Graw Hill · Irwin
McGraw-Hill

Boston, Massachusetts   Burr Ridge, Illinois   Dubuque, Iowa
Madison, Wisconsin   New York, New York   San Francisco, California   St. Louis, Missouri

Irwin/McGraw-Hill

A Division of The **McGraw·Hill** Companies

This book was set in Bembo type by TBH Typecast, Inc.
Development and production management were provided by Cole and
Associates.
The editors were David M. Shapiro and Elliot Simon;
production coordination was done by Simon & Assocs.
The cover and interior were designed by Seventeenth Street Studios.
Illustrations were done by Advanced Presentations.
R. R. Donnelley & Sons Company was printer and binder.

This book is printed on acid-free paper.

LEARNING C++

7 8 9 0   DOC/DOC   9 0 9 8 7

ISBN 0-07-023983-5

Library of Congress Cataloging-in-Publication Data

Graham, Neill, (date).
    Learning C++ / Neill Graham.
        p.   cm.
    ISBN 0-07-023983-5
    1. C++ (Computer program language)   I. Title.   II. Title:
Learning C Plus Plus.
QA76.73.C153G73   1991
00513'3 — dc20   90-44655

Contents

PREFACE, VII

1
Elements of C++

HELLO, WORLD!, 1
Comments, 1
Source Files, 1
Header Files and `#include` *Directives,* 3
Functions and `main( )`, 4
Input and Output, 4
FUNCTION DECLARATIONS, DEFINITIONS,
 AND CALLS, 7
IDENTIFIERS, 9
VALUES, TYPES, AND CONSTANTS, 10
Integer Types, 10
Floating Types, 14
DATA OBJECTS, 15
Declaration, Initialization, and Assignment, 16
Constant Data Objects, 18
Scopes of Identifiers, 19
Lifetimes of Data Objects, 20
OPERATORS AND EXPRESSIONS, 21
Arithmetic Operators, 22
Assignment Operators, 23
Increment and Decrement Operators, 26
Equality, Relational, and Logical Operators, 27

Conditional Expressions, 29
The Comma Operator, 30
*Functions That Take Arguments and Return
 Values,* 31
Side Effects and Sequence Points, 33
TYPE CONVERSIONS, 35
Implicit Conversions, 36
Explicit Conversions, 37
EXAMPLE: COMPUTING DISCOUNTS, 39
CONTROL STATEMENTS: REPETITION, 42
The `while` *Statement,* 42
The `do` *Statement,* 43
Example: The Inverse Fibonacci Rabbit Problem,
 44
The `for` *Statement,* 46
Example: Computing Interest, 48
CONTROL STATEMENTS: SELECTION, 52
The `if` *and* `if-else` *Statements,* 52
The `switch` *Statement,* 56
EXERCISES, 59

2
Classes and Objects

OBJECT–ORIENTED PROGRAMMING, 61
Objects and Classes, 61
Methods, Messages, and Data Hiding, 63

CLASSES, 63
Classes Declared with `struct`, 64
Member Functions, 66
Constructors and Destructors, 70
Classes Declared with `class`, 73
Compiling and Linking, 74
Example: A Program Using Class `account`, 80
MORE ABOUT MEMBER FUNCTIONS, 81
Function Overloading, 81
Default Arguments, 87
Inline Expansion, 88
Constant Objects and Functions, 94
LINKAGE, 96
EXERCISES, 98

3
Arrays, Pointers, and References

ARRAYS, 102
POINTERS, 107
The Address-of Operator, 109
Pointers and Arguments, 110
Pointers to Class Objects, 112
ARRAYS AND POINTERS, 113
Array Names as Pointers, 113
Subscripting Pointers, 115
Pointer Arithmetic, 116
Using `const` *in Pointer Declarations,* 120
STRINGS, 122
FUNCTIONS FOR STRING PROCESSING, 125
REFERENCE TYPES, 131
MEMORY MANAGEMENT WITH `new` AND `delete`, 134
TYPE-NAME DEFINITIONS, 138
EXAMPLE: CLASS `table`, 139
Class Declarations, 140
Class Implementation, 142
EXAMPLE: A PROGRAM USING CLASS `table`, 149

Function Declarations, 149
Declaring and Setting `_new_handler`, 153
Reading Characters and Strings, 155
Using a Pointer to Constant Data, 158
EXERCISES, 158

4
Operators and Friends

OPERATOR OVERLOADING, 163
FRIEND FUNCTIONS AND OPERATORS, 168
CLASS `vector`, 171
Constant Definitions, 174
The Component Array, 174
Constructors, 175
Memberwise Initialization and Assignment, 175
Addition, Subtraction, and Multiplication, 179
Equality Operators, 181
Assignment Operators, 181
Subscripting Operator, 184
Conversion to a Scalar Magnitude, 185
Input and Output, 186
Demonstration Program, 187
DEFENDING AGAINST MULTIPLE INCLUSIONS, 189
CLASS `string`, 191
String Representation, 192
Copying and Reference Counts, 192
Construction, Destruction, and Assignment, 197
Concatenation, 205
Comparisons, 208
Function `pos( )`, 209
Function `length( )`, 210
Function `refs( )`, 210
Subscripting, 211
Substring Extraction, 212
Input and Output, 213
Demonstration Program, 214
EXERCISES, 218

5
Inheritance: Derived Classes

EXAMPLE: BANK ACCOUNTS, 221

Class account *and the Keyword* protected, 222

Class sav_acct, *Public Base Classes, and Constructors,* 227

Class chk_acct, 230

Class time_acct *and Redefining Inherited Functions,* 232

DEQUES, QUEUES, AND STACKS, 234

Implementation of Class deque, 238

LINKED LISTS, 243

Classes list *and* node, 244

Defining Derived Classes, 249

Using ilist *and* inode, 252

EXTENDING AN EXISTING CLASS, 254

MULTIPLE INHERITANCE, 257

Virtual Base Classes, 260

EXERCISES, 264

6
Polymorphism: Virtual Functions

POINTERS, REFERENCES, AND VIRTUAL FUNCTIONS, 267

Heterogeneous Lists, 269

Virtual Functions, 269

EXAMPLE: BREEDS OF DOGS, 273

ABSTRACT BASE CLASSES AND PURE VIRTUAL FUNCTIONS, 278

EXAMPLE: GRAPHICS FIGURES, 280

Using ANSI Escape Sequences, 282

Class figure, 283

Class block, 284

Class box, 288

Class triangle, 289

Class label, 290

Example Program: Heterogeneous Linear List, 292

Example Program: Heterogeneous Linked List, 295

EXAMPLE: EXPRESSION TREES, 299

Class Declarations: Structure of Expression Trees, 303

Class Declarations: Expression Evaluation, 304

EXAMPLE: STATE MACHINES, 305

Static Class Members: Class Variables and Functions, 309

Class state, 310

Classes state_S, state_W, *and* state_P, 315

Demonstration Program, 316

EXERCISES, 318

7
Case Study: Event-Driven Simulation

THE MACHINE–ADJUSTMENT PROBLEM, 323

Discrete, Event-Driven Simulations, 323

THE WORKINGS OF CHANCE, 326

The Geometric Distribution, 327

Class geometric, 328

ACTIVE OBJECTS, 334

Class active, 336

Class machine, 336

Class adjuster, 342

MANAGING AND COORDINATING RESOURCES, 345

Resource Coordinators, 346

Class manager, 347

THE SCHEDULER, 351

Class scheduler, 352

THE MAIN PROGRAM, 357

Sample Run, 362

EXERCISES, 363

8
More About Input and Output

THE BASIC INPUT–OUTPUT CLASSES, 367

FORMAT–STATE FLAGS, 369

FORMAT–STATE PARAMETERS, 372

SETTING FLAGS AND PARAMETERS, 372

FORMATTING EXAMPLES, 375

DETECTING ERRORS AND END–OF–FILE, 379

CLASSES FOR NAMED FILES, 381

INPUT AND OUTPUT WITH NAMED FILES, 382

USING COMMAND–LINE PARAMETERS, 387

DIRECT ACCESS, 389

EXERCISES, 392

Appendix 1
C++ KEYWORDS, 394

Appendix 2
OPERATOR PRECEDENCE AND ASSOCIATIVITY, 395

Appendix 3
TURBO C++, 397

GLOSSARY, 409

FOR FURTHER STUDY, 417

INDEX, 418

Preface

This book is an introduction to C++ and object-oriented programming for readers who know at least one programming language (which will probably be Pascal) but who are not necessarily familiar with C.

C++ and C

C++, an object-oriented extension of C, addresses the needs of two recent trends: the widespread use of C as a software implementation language, and the increasing interest in object-oriented programming.

C is by far the most popular language for professional software development on minicomputers and microcomputers. While offering all the known advantages of a higher-level language, C also provides the low-level access to hardware and system software that is characteristic of assembly language. Many microcomputer software packages that were originally written in assembly language have now been translated into C.

Object-Oriented Programming

Object-oriented programming allows a complex program to be built out of much simpler constructs called *objects*, which interact by exchanging messages. The following are characteristic of object-oriented programming:

- *Classes.* Objects are defined by means of classes; once a class has been defined, any number of objects of that class are easily created. Programmers are thus encouraged to reuse code by defining general purpose classes and using them in many different applications.

- *Abstraction.* To use an object, we need only know its public interface—what messages it understands and how it responds to each. We *do not* need to know anything about its internal workings, which are hidden from the object's users.

- *Inheritance.* A new class can be derived from one or more existing classes and can inherit some or all of their properties. This further encourages code reuse because classes derived from a general-purpose class can be customized as needed for each particular application.

- *Polymorphism.* Different kinds of objects can understand the same message, though they may respond to it in different ways. We can send such a message without knowing what kind of object is involved. For example, objects representing different geometrical figures might all respond to a message to draw the corresponding figure on the screen; we could send a `draw` message to any such object and be assured that the appropriate figure will be drawn.

About This Book

The background in C necessary for effective use of this book is provided in Chapter 1 (program structure, data types, expressions, and control statements) and in Chapter 3 (arrays, pointers, and strings).

The study of object-oriented programming begins in Chapter 2, which introduces the basic concepts and develops a simple bank account class as an example. Although Chapter 3 is devoted mainly to the elements of array and pointer manipulation, it does introduce the C++ `new` and `delete` operators, and it defines a class of dynamic lookup tables to illustrate all the material in the chapter.

Chapter 4 covers operator and function overloading as well as friend functions and operators. This chapter introduces a different approach to object-oriented programming, in which objects are passed as arguments to overloaded friend functions and operators rather than being sent messages via member functions.

In Chapters 5 and 6 we return to more conventional object-oriented programming. Chapter 5 develops inheritance; although multiple inheritance is introduced and illustrated, most of the discussion and examples focus on single inheritance, which beginners should master before going on to the more complicated multiple inheritance. Chapter 6 introduces polymorphism and its implementation via virtual functions; abstract base classes and pure virtual functions are also covered.

Chapter 7 develops a discrete-event simulation as a case study. Most examples in the preceding chapters have involved a conventional main program interacting with one or more objects; a major goal of Chapter 7 is to present a program whose computations proceed mainly via message passing between objects. This simulation *does not* use the C++ task library, which is not available in all implementations and which hides some details that it is instructive to work through.

Chapter 8 is devoted to further exploration of the input-output library. A complete discussion of this intricate library is beyond the scope of this book; instead, we focus on the following areas: the stream classes (which provide a good example of multiple inheritance); controlling the format of output and the expected format of input; detecting errors and end-of-file; using named files, such as disk files; using command-line parameters; and a brief introduction to direct access with `tellg()` and `seekg()`.

Appendix 1 provides a list of reserved words, and Appendix 2 provides a chart showing the precedence and associativity of operators. A comprehensive glossary defines important terms in C++ and object-oriented programming, and the "For Further Study" section suggests additional readings.

C++ was developed at AT&T, and for now the AT&T compiler and reference manual set the standard for the language. Most current software and books are based on AT&T Release 2.0, which was expected to be the final revision of the language prior to the development of an ANSI standard for C++.

To correct some problems with Release 2.0, however, a small number of changes were made. These resulted in Release 2.1, which appeared while this book was in the final stages of preparation. This book is based on Release 2.0; however, the most important changes in Release 2.1 are discussed briefly, mainly in footnotes.

The example programs in this book have also been tested with Turbo C++, which is compatible with AT&T Release 2.0. As the first C++ implementation from a major supplier of microcomputer software, Turbo C++ is expected to enjoy a substantial share of the market for MS-DOS C++ implementations. Appendix 3 is an introduction to Turbo C++ and its integrated development environment. Also discussed are a few problems in Version 1.00 of Turbo C++ that must be worked around in order to run some of the example programs.

Acknowledgments

For their helpful comments on various drafts of the manuscript, the author expresses his appreciation to J. Eugene Ball, University of Delaware; Krys J. Kochut, University of Georgia; Robert McCoard, California State University, Northridge; Tomasz Müldner, Acadia University; Roy Ogawa, University of Nevada, Las Vegas; and Steven Stepanek, California State University, Northridge.

1

Elements of C++

*T*HIS CHAPTER introduces the basic C++ constructions: variable declarations, arithmetic expressions, function calls and definitions, and input, output, and control statements. Because these constructions occur in many programming languages the concepts behind them will already be familiar, so we will be able to concentrate on how these concepts are expressed in C++.

HELLO, WORLD!

It is a tradition in C and C++ to begin any introductory text or programming course by discussing a program that prints the message "Hello, world!" Listing 1-1 shows the hello-world program; we will use an extended discussion of this program as a framework for introducing several C++ concepts.

Comments

The first two lines in Listing 1-1 are comments, although they will not seem to be such to readers familiar with C. Comments in C are enclosed between the symbols /* and */.

```
/* This is a comment */
```

Such a comment can extend over any number of lines.

```
/* Now is the time
   for all good programmers
   to put comments in their programs */
```

Listing 1-1

```
// File hello.cpp
// Program to print a greeting to the user

#include <iostream.h>

main()
{
    cout << "Hello, world!\n";
}
```

This style of comment is also allowed in C++. However, C++ also provides another style, in which a comment begins with // and extends to the end of the line. Since the comment always extends to the end of the line, no closing symbol (such as */) is needed:

```
// This is a comment
```

```
// Now is the time
// for all good programmers
// to put comments in their programs
```

The latter style is usually the easiest to write and is the style generally preferred by C++ programmers.

Source Files

The text of a program is stored on disk in one or more *source files*; each source file is printed in this book as a *listing*. At the beginning of each source file is a comment giving the name of the file; the name of the source file for the hello-world program is `hello.cpp`.

In this book we assume that the names of C++ source files end with .cpp; however, some C++ implementations use .c, .C, .cp, or .cxx. If the file-naming conventions for your computer system or C++ implementation differ from those assumed here, you will not be able to use the file names in this book unchanged. Nevertheless, they will still help you keep track of the source files listed here, particularly for programs having more than one source file.

FUNCTION DECLARATIONS, DEFINITIONS, AND CALLS

A *function declaration* gives the information necessary to call a function: it tells the number and types of values that must be passed to the function as arguments, and it describes the value (if any) that the function returns; a function declaration is also called a *function prototype*. A *function definition* gives the same information, but also gives the statements that are to be executed when the function is called. A function can be declared many times (in different source and header files, for example), but it can be defined only once. Declarations for the same function must agree with one another and with the definition.

A function must be declared or defined before it is used—that is, the definition or declaration must precede the first use of the function in the source file. We could try to arrange our source file so that all functions are defined before they are used, but this often would be inconvenient and in some cases would be impossible. Therefore, it is customary to declare at the beginning of a source file all the functions defined in the file. That done, we can arrange the definitions in any order we wish, without having to worry about whether a call to a function comes before or after its definition.

Declarations for functions defined in the library or in other source files are usually inserted in a program by including the appropriate header files.

Listing 1-2 shows a somewhat more elaborate greeting program in which `main()` does not print the greeting itself, but instead calls four functions, `wakeup()`, `hello()`, `welcome()`, and `goodbye()`, to do the work of the program. Because this program uses stream output, it includes the header file `iostream.h`.

Following the `#include` directive are declarations for the four functions called by `main()`—`main()` itself does not have to be declared because it is not called from within the program. In each declaration, the empty parentheses indicate that no argument values are to be passed to the function, and the keyword `void` indicates that the function does not return a value. Note that each declaration ends with a semicolon. As illustrated here, declarations are a good place to put comments describing the purpose and use of each function.

Next in Listing 1-2 is the definition of `main()`, which is called automatically when the program begins executing; `main()`, in turn, calls the functions `wakeup()`, `hello()`, `welcome()`, and `goodbye()`. A function is called by writing

Listing 1-2

```cpp
// File greet.cpp
// Program illustrating function declarations,
// definitions, and calls

#include <iostream.h>

// Function declarations

void wakeup();      // alert the user
void hello();       // say hello
void welcome();     // extend welcome
void goodbye();     // say goodbye

// Definition of function main

main()
{
    wakeup();       // call to function wakeup
    hello();        // call to function hello
    welcome();      // call to function welcome
    goodbye();      // call to function goodbye
}

// Definitions of functions called by main

void wakeup()
{
    cout << "\a\a\a\a";     // alert the user
}

void hello()
{
    cout << "Hello, user!\n";
}

void welcome()
{
    cout << "Welcome to the ranks of C++ programmers.\n";
}
```

```
void goodbye()
{
    cout << "Goodbye, for now.\n";
    cout << "Have a nice day.\n";
}
```

the name of the function followed by parentheses enclosing any argument values that are to be passed to the function. The parentheses must be present even if, as here, they are empty: the paired parentheses serve as an operator that causes the function to be called. A statement that calls a function is an expression statement, and so must end with a semicolon.

The definitions of `wakeup()`, `hello()`, `welcome()`, and `goodbye()` follow the definition of `main()`. Each function definition begins with a heading that is identical to the function declaration *except* that the heading does not end with a semicolon. As with `main()`, each heading is followed by a block giving the statements to be executed when the function is called.

The function `wakeup()` alerts the user by outputting four alert characters; `hello()` and `welcome()` each print one line, and `goodbye()` prints two lines. When the program is executed, the computer or terminal beeps and then displays the following:

```
Hello, user!
Welcome to the ranks of C++ programmers.
Goodbye, for now.
Have a nice day.
```

A function definition cannot occur within a block. Thus, unlike many other languages, C++ does not allow function definitions to be nested: the block that defines a function cannot itself contain function definitions.

IDENTIFIERS

The function names `wakeup`, `hello`, `welcome`, and `goodbye` are examples of *identifiers*, which are made up as needed by the programmer. An identifier consists of letters and digits; the underscore character, _, is considered to be a letter. No characters other than letters (including _) and digits are allowed. The first character must be a letter (including _). An identifier may not be the same as any of the C++ keywords, which are listed in Appendix 1. Some valid identifiers are

```
count COLUMN25 get_char _dos_call _DATE_
```

Some invalid identifiers are

```
124C41 hello.cpp $amount id_# get-char if
```

The first of these begins with a digit, the next four contain illegal characters, and `if` is a keyword.

C++ identifiers are case sensitive, so that `name`, `Name`, and `NAME` are three different identifiers. Avoid identifiers that begin or end with _ unless they are already defined by the C++ implementation; the implementation uses such identifiers to avoid conflict with identifiers created by the programmer.

VALUES, TYPES, AND CONSTANTS

Like most other languages, C++ classifies data values into *types* according to how they are stored in memory and what operations can be carried out on them. Types whose values represent numbers are called *arithmetic types*. The arithmetic types are divided into *integer types*, whose values represent whole numbers, and *floating types*, whose values can contain decimal points.

Integer Types

Most computers provide several different sizes of memory location for storing integer values. To accommodate this variety, C and C++ provide four basic integer types.

```
char
short
int
long
```

As we move down this list, the types get *larger* in two senses: (1) more memory is required to store a value of the type, and (2) the type can represent a wider range of values. The types in the list need not all be distinct; for example, it is common for type `int` to be the same as either type `short` or type `long`.

As its name implies, type `char` is used mainly for character codes. Type `int` (integer) is the type most commonly used for integer values, and the one on which arithmetic operations can be carried out most efficiently. Arithmetic is not carried out directly on values of types `char` and `short`; when a `char` or `short` value appears in an arithmetic expression, it is converted to type `int` before any arithmetic operations are applied to it.

An integer type can be *signed* (both positive and negative values can be represented) or *unsigned* (all the values are positive). For every signed type there is a corresponding unsigned type that can represent the same number of different values but interprets them as unsigned rather than signed numbers. For example, consider a very small type that can represent only eight different values. If the values are interpreted as signed numbers, four of the eight values must be used for negative numbers and the other four for positive numbers; thus the type can represent the following values:

$$-4, \ -3, \ -2, \ -1, \ 0, \ 1, \ 2, \ 3$$

If the values are interpreted as unsigned numbers, however, then all eight values are available for representing positive numbers:

$$0, \ 1, \ 2, \ 3, \ 4, \ 5, \ 6, \ 7$$

Thus going from a signed type to the corresponding unsigned type eliminates the negative values but doubles the number of available positive values.

Types `short`, `int`, and `long` all represent signed numbers; we can use the keyword `unsigned` to specify the corresponding unsigned types: `unsigned short`, `unsigned int` (which can be abbreviated to just `unsigned`), and `unsigned long`. For historical reasons, type `char` can be either signed or unsigned depending on the C++ implementation; to guarantee one or the other, we can specify `signed char` or `unsigned char`. Thus C++ has the following signed and unsigned integer types:*

---

* The AT&T Release 2.0 compiler does not implement the keyword `signed`; if `signed` is used, the compiler ignores it and issues a warning message.

```
char             int      unsigned int
signed char      short    unsigned short
unsigned char    long     unsigned long
```

In this book, our use of integer types will be confined mainly to char, int, and long.

Integer Constants

Integer constants are written as in ordinary arithmetic, except that commas are not allowed.

   325   7634   39876542   9989765

The value of a constant has type int unless the value is outside the range allowed for int, in which case it has type long or (if too large for long) type unsigned long. We can specify a type other than int by appending U for unsigned and L for long. Thus

   25U   10U   100000U   75U

have type unsigned int or (if too large for unsigned int) type unsigned long. Likewise,

   25L   10L   3000000000L   75L

have type long or (if too large for long) type unsigned long, and

   25UL   10UL   3000000000UL   75UL

have type unsigned long. The lowercase letters u and l can be used in place of U and L; however, l (ell) is best avoided because it is easily confused with the digit 1 (one).

There is one further restriction on integer constants: a number in decimal notation *must not begin with a zero*. A leading zero signals that the number is in the hardware-oriented octal notation. Thus, 0137 is an octal number whose decimal value is 95.

Character Constants

Characters are represented by their numerical codes, as given by a standard coding scheme such as ASCII or EBCDIC. Thus values of type char are integers, and type char can be included with the other integer types such as int and long. When values of type `char` appear in an arithmetic expression, they are converted to type `int`.

A character constant consists of a character enclosed in single quotation marks (apostrophes).

```
'A'    'b'    '0'    '1'    '$'    '%'
```

Escape sequences can be used in character constants.

```
'\a'    '\t'    '\n'    '\\'
```

Because a character constant is enclosed in single quotation marks, a single quotation mark or apostrophe must be represented by the escape sequence `\'`. On the other hand, the double quotation mark, which must be represented by an escape sequence in string literals, does not require an escape sequence in character constants.

```
'\''
```
  apostrophe

```
'"'
```
  double quotation mark

In C and in earlier versions of C++, character constants have type `int`. The problem with this is that operators and functions cannot distinguish characters from their integer codes; thus

```
cout << 'A';
```

unexpectedly prints the numerical code for the letter A (65 in ASCII) rather than the letter itself. In Release 2.0, therefore, character constants have type `char`, and the above statement prints the letter A, as expected.

The newline character, which occurs frequently in output statements, can be represented as either `"\n"` (a one-character string) or `'\n'` (a character constant). Thus the following two statements are equivalent:

```
cout << 25 << "\n";
cout << 25 << '\n';
```

Enumerations

Enumerations allow us to define integer types whose values are represented by identifiers; the identifiers make programs more readable by giving the significance of each integer value. For example, if we need to represent the colors red, yellow, green, and blue by integer codes, we can define an enumeration type color whose four values are represented by the constants RED, YELLOW, GREEN, and BLUE.

```
enum color { RED, YELLOW, GREEN, BLUE };
```

(It is a stylistic convention to use all capital letters for identifiers that represent constants.)

When we do not specify otherwise, enumeration constants are given integer values starting with zero; thus, RED represents 0, YELLOW represents 1, GREEN represents 2, and BLUE represents 3. If we wish, we can specify other integer values for the enumeration constants. Thus if we defined type color by

```
enum color { RED = 5, YELLOW = 3, GREEN = 7, BLUE = 9 };
```

then RED would represent 5, YELLOW would represent 3, and so on.

Enumeration types are like char and short in that no arithmetic operations are carried out on values of the type. When a value of an enumeration type appears in an arithmetic expression, it is converted to type int before any operation is carried out on it.

Floating Types

The floating types are used to represent floating-point numbers, which can contain a decimal point and can be written in scientific notation. There are three floating types, all of which represent signed numbers.

```
float
double
long double
```

As we go down the list, the amount of memory required for a value and the precision with which the value can be represented either increase or remain the same. For many implementations, the precision offered by type float is insufficient or marginal for many applications; therefore, type double is recommended unless there is a compelling need to save memory space or reduce computation time. Type long double will be needed only when extraordinary precision is demanded.

A floating-point constant must contain a decimal point

```
3.1416      25.75      19.99      100.      .005
```

or an exponent

```
25E4        7e-9        635E+10        84e-25
```

or both

```
3.5e+7        2.345E-15        28.9e10        25.0E3
```

An exponent, introduced by e or E, indicates the number of places the decimal point should be moved to the left (negative exponent) or to the right (positive exponent). If an exponent is present, the decimal point may be omitted, in which case it is assumed to occur just before the e or E.

A floating-point constant normally has type `double`; however, we can represent values of other floating types by appending F for `float` or L for `long double`. (The lowercase letters f and l can also be used.) Thus

```
3.1416F
3.1416
3.1416L
```

represent, from top to bottom, values of types `float`, `double`, and `long double`.

DATA OBJECTS

All programmers are familiar with the concept of a variable as a named memory location in which values can be stored. C++ generalizes this concept in that the location can have no name or several names, and the memory address of the location is available for use by the programmer. Such a generalized variable is called a *data object*.

A data object is a region of memory in which a value can be stored; it is characterized by its address, its names (if any), its type, and its value.

- The *address* is that of the region of memory the data object occupies. We are almost never interested in the numerical values of addresses, which are determined by the C++ implementation and the operating system. However, C++ has provisions for obtaining these system-assigned addresses, manipulating them, and using them to refer to the data objects they designate.

- A data object can have zero or more *names*. Names are not limited to simple identifiers such as x, y, and z; they can be any expressions that designate data objects. For example, a subscripted array name, such as a[i + 5], is a name expression that occurs in many languages, including C++. An expression that names a data object is called an *lvalue* because only such expressions can appear on the *left* side of an assignment operator. For the present, all lvalues will be simple identifiers such as x, y, and z; in later chapters, however, we will deal with more complicated lvalues such as a[i + 5].

- The *type* of a data object is the type of the values that can be stored in the object. The type determines the size of corresponding region of memory; for example, most computers store values of types char and int in memory locations of different sizes. The type also specifies how the stored bit pattern is to be interpreted. For example, some computers store values of types long and float in memory locations of the same size, but the meanings of the stored bit patterns are completely different for these two types.

- The *value* of a data object is the bit pattern that is stored in the corresponding region of memory. As indicated in the previous item, the type of the data object is essential to assigning meaning to the stored bit pattern. Unless the data object is declared to be a constant, the stored bit pattern can change during the execution of the program.

Declaration, Initialization, and Assignment

We use the common term *variable* for data objects whose stored values can be changed during the execution of the program. Variables must be declared before they are used; we declare a variable by giving its type and name.

```
int count;
long total;
float balance;
long double national_debt;
```

Note that each declaration ends with a semicolon. Declarations are considered to be statements in C++; a declaration can be used anywhere that a statement is allowed.

We can declare several variables in the same declaration:

```
int i, j, k;
float x, y, z;
```

The first statement declares three variables of type `int` and the second declares three variables of type `float`.

Normally, a variable declaration both *declares* an identifier (states its properties to the compiler) and *defines* it (creates the corresponding data object). Thus most variable declarations could just as well be called definitions; however, *declaration* is the customary term and hence the one that we usually will use.*

The assignment operator, =, assigns values to variables. After the following statements are executed, `count` will have the value 10 and `total` will have the value 100:

```
count = 10;
total = 100L;
```

A variable can be assigned an initial value when it is declared. For example, the declaration and initialization

```
int n = 25;
```

declares the variable n and initializes it to 25. Likewise,

```
double p = 7.8, q = 4.9, r = 25.35;
```

declares the variables p, q, and r and assigns them the respective initial values 7.8, 4.9, and 25.35.

Because declarations are statements in C++, they can be intermixed freely with other statements; they do not have to be grouped at the beginning of a block (as they must be in C). Rather than declaring a variable at the beginning of a block

```
float w;
```

and assigning it a value later,

```
w = 3.1416F;
```

we instead declare and initialize the variable at the point where the first assignment takes place.

* We will see in Chapter 3 how to declare a variable without defining it. Such declarations are used for accessing variables that are defined elsewhere, such as in the library.

```
float w = 3.1416F;
```

This procedure helps avoid the error of using an uninitialized variable — one that has been declared but to which no initial value has been assigned.

As in other languages, the value of a variable can be computed with an expression, which itself can contain variables.

```
i = j + k;
```

When a variable appears on the *right* side of an assignment operator, its *value* is used in computing the value to be assigned; when a variable appears on the *left* side of an assignment operator, its *name* is used to designate the variable that is to receive the computed result. The variable or expression on the left side of the assignment operator must be an lvalue — it must name a data object.

Constant Data Objects

In addition to designating literals such as 25, 3.5, and 'a', the term *constant* is also used for constant data objects — data objects whose values cannot be changed. Such a constant is declared by prefixing the declaration with the keyword const. A constant is given a value when it is declared, and that value cannot be later changed by an assignment statement. Thus

```
const double PI = 3.141592654;
```

defines the floating-point constant PI. (Recall that it is a stylistic convention to use all capital letters in the name of a constant.) Because the value of a constant cannot be changed, the assignment statement

```
PI = 3.5;   // Wrong
```

is invalid.

If no type is specified for a constant, then int is assumed. Thus

```
const int COUNT = 25;
```

can be abbreviated to

```
const COUNT = 25;
```

The names of both variables and constants are lvalues. To further distinguish variable names, we call them *modifiable lvalues*, because the corresponding values can be modified with assignment statements. Thus the lvalue on the left of an assignment operator must be a *modifiable* lvalue—it must name a data object to which new values can be assigned.

Scopes of Identifiers

The *scope* of an identifier is the portion of the program in which the identifier is defined and can be referred to. The scope of an identifier extends from its point of declaration to the end of the block containing the declaration. If the declaration is not inside a block, the scope extends from the point of declaration to the end of the source file. An identifier declared inside a block is said to be *local* to that block; an identifier whose declaration is not inside any block is said to be *global*.

For example, consider the block

```
{ ... int m = 25; ... }
```

where the ellipses, . . ., represent sequences of statements. The scope of m begins with the declaration and extends to the closing brace. The statements following the declaration can refer to m, whereas those that precede it cannot.

The same identifier can refer to different data objects in different blocks. For example:

```
{ ... int m = 1; ... }
{ ... int m = 2; ... }
```

The two declarations of m cause the identifier to refer to two different, unrelated data objects. The two declarations cannot conflict, because an identifier is inaccessible from outside the block in which it is declared. That is, statements in the first block cannot refer to the m declared in the second block, and vice versa.

Blocks can be nested, and a declaration in an inner block can hide a declaration of the same identifier in an enclosing block. For example:

```
{ int m = 1; { ... int m = 2; ... } }
```

Again, each declaration of m causes it to refer to a different data object. The declaration in the inner block hides the one in the outer block; anywhere within the scope of the inner declaration, a reference to m refers to the data object declared in the inner block. Thus in the inner block, any reference to m that precedes the declaration refers to the data object declared in the outer block, and any reference to m that follows the declaration refers to the data object declared in the inner block.

A global identifier is said to have *file scope* because it can be referred to from any point in the source file that follows its declaration and where its declaration is not hidden by a declaration of an identically named local identifier.

Lifetimes of Data Objects

The *lifetime* of a data object is the time that it remains in existence during the execution of the program. Note that an identifier has a scope (the part of the program in which it can be referenced) and a data object has a lifetime (the time it remains in existence); these two independent concepts should not be confused.

Normally, a data object declared within a block is created when its declaration is executed and destroyed when the end of the block is reached. For example, in the execution of

```
{ ... int m; ... }
```

the data object named by m is created when the computer comes to the declaration; the data object is destroyed when the computer reaches the closing }. If the block is executed more than once (as often happens), a new data object m is created for each execution. In particular, any value assigned to a data object during one execution of the block is lost when the end of the block is reached; the value is not preserved for succeeding executions of the block. Data objects with these properties are said to have storage class *automatic*.

A data object that is declared globally—outside of any block—remains in existence during the entire execution of the program. Such a data object is said to have storage class *static*.

A data object declared within a block can be explicitly declared as static (overriding the default of automatic):

```
{ ... static int m = 100; ... }
```

In that case, the data object named by m remains in existence for the entire duration of program execution. Its initial value is assigned before program execution begins, and it retains its current value from one execution of the block to the next. On the other hand, note that the scope of the identifier m is not affected. Although the data object remains in existence throughout the execution of the program, it can only be referred to by name from within the scope of m, which still extends from the declaration to the end of the block.

Static data objects that are not initialized in their declarations are given the initial value of zero. Automatic data objects that are not initialized in their declarations are not given any particular initial value; they contain garbage when created.

OPERATORS AND EXPRESSIONS

In an expression such as

```
3*4+5
```

the compiler must determine how the operands 3, 4, and 5 are to be grouped with the operators * and +; in particular, the compiler must determine whether 4 is an operand of * or +. As in other languages, we can use parentheses to specify this grouping. Thus in

```
(3*4)+5
```

3 and 4 are operands of *; the expression evaluates to 12 plus 5, or 17. On the other hand, in

```
3*(4+5)
```

the operands of + are 4 and 5; the expression evaluates to 3 times 9, or 27.

In the absence of parentheses, *precedence* and *associativity* determine the grouping that will be used for evaluating the expression. Appendix 2 shows all the C++ operators arranged according to precedence and associativity. The groups of operators are arranged in order of decreasing precedence; the associativity for each group of operators is given in the right-hand column of the table.

We can think of adjacent operators in an expression as competing for the operand between them, the operator with higher precedence winning the disputed operand. Thus in

```
3+4*5
```

operators + and * compete for the operand 4. Because the * has the higher precedence, it wins the 4, and the following grouping is used:

    3+(4*5)

Likewise, in

    3*4+5*6

the + loses the 4 and 5 to the higher precedence * on either side, so the expression is evaluated with the following grouping:

    (3*4)+(5*6)

Associativity determines whether operators with the same precedence will be grouped from left to right or from right to left. For example,

    10 – 5 + 3

is grouped as

    (10 – 5) + 3

because – and +, which have the same precedence, have left-to-right associativity. On the other hand

    x = y = z

is grouped as

    x = (y = z)

because = has right-to-left associativity.

Programming texts often state the rules for grouping in a way that implies a particular order of evaluation. For example, we may be told that "multiplications and divisions are performed before additions and subtractions" or that "parenthesized parts of an expression are evaluated before other parts." Such statements are not generally true for C++, where the compiler has considerable leeway in choosing the order in which different parts of an expression will be evaluated. Therefore, we have been careful to discuss parentheses, precedence, and associativity in terms of *grouping of operators with operands* rather than in terms of order of evaluation.

Arithmetic Operators

The C++ arithmetic operators are shown in Table 1-1. The operators in the left-hand column apply to values of integer

Table 1-1
Arithmetic Operators

INTEGER TYPES	FLOATING TYPES
+ addition	+ addition
− subtraction	− subtraction
* multiplication	* multiplication
/ integer division: quotient	/ floating-point division
% integer division: remainder	

types such as int and long; those in the right-hand column apply to values of the floating types such as float and double. The operators +, −, and * function in the same way for both integers and floating-point numbers. When / is applied to integers, it yields the integer quotient only (no remainder or fractional part); when applied to floating-point numbers, it yields a complete floating-point result with both whole-number and fractional parts. The remainder operator, %, applies only to values of integer types and yields the remainder of an integer division. For example, 7 / 2 yields 3 and 7 % 2 yields 1, whereas 7.0 / 2.0 yields 3.5.

The precedence of the arithmetic operators, from highest to lowest, is as follows:

```
unary +, unary −
*, /, %
+, −
```

The operators + and − are unary when they take only one operand, as in +x or −m*n. The unary + and − have higher precedence than the other arithmetic operators; thus −m*n is grouped as (−m)*n. The remaining arithmetic operators have the expected precedence: the multiplication and division operators *, /, and % have higher precedence than the addition and subtraction operators + and −.

Assignment Operators

An assignment, such as n = 10, is an expression and yields a value just like any other expression; the value returned is the same as the value assigned to the variable. Thus the statement

```
cout << (n = 10);
```

assigns the value 10 to n *and* prints 10, the value of the expression n = 10. The parentheses are necessary because = has a lower precedence than <<; without the parentheses, the meaningless grouping

```
(cout << n) = 10
```

would be used.

The statement

```
m = (n = 10);
```

first assigns 10 to n; the value of the assignment expression, 10, is then assigned to m. Thus both m and n are assigned the value 10. In this case the parentheses are unnecessary because assignment operators group from right to left. Thus

```
m = n = 10;
```

is equivalent to

```
m = (n = 10);
```

and assigns 10 to both m and n. Likewise,

```
w = x = y = z = 3.5;
```

is equivalent to

```
w = (x = (y = (z = 3.5)));
```

and assigns 3.5 to all four variables.

Statements such as

```
count = count + 10;
```

are common; the value of 10 is added to the value of count, and the result is stored back in count. The net effect of the statement is to increase the value of count by 10; if the value of count was 50 before the statement was executed, it will be 60 afterwards.

C++ allows such statements to be abbreviated as

```
count += 10;
```

by using the *add assign operator*, +=, which combines the operations of addition and assignment. C++ provides similar assignment operators for the other arithmetic operations, as shown in Table 1-2.

Like =, the other assignment operators yield a value as well as

Table 1-2

*Combined Assignment and
Arithmetic Operators*

ABBREVIATED STATEMENT	UNABBREVIATED FORM
m += n;	m = m + n;
m -= n;	m = m - n;
m *= n;	m = m * n;
m /= n;	m = m / n;
m %= n;	m = m % n;

perform an assignment; the value yielded is the value assigned. For example, the statement

```
m = (n -= 5);
```

subtracts 5 from the value of n and assigns the resulting difference to both n and m. The parentheses could be omitted in this statement, since all the assignment operators have the same precedence and group from right to left. For the sake of readability, however, the parentheses should probably be retained.

For all forms of assignment operators, the identifier or expression on the left must be a modifiable lvalue, that is, the name of a data object whose value can be changed by assignment. A constant—either a literal constant such as 25 or the name of a constant data object—can never appear on the left side of an assignment operator.

An expression is said to have *side effects* if its evaluation changes the contents of memory or of a file. Expressions such as 3+4 and 5*7 have no side effects because they merely compute a result without storing any value in memory. On the other hand, assignment expressions such as m = 10 and n += 25 do have side effects because each alters the contents of memory by assigning a new value to a variable.

When an expression statement is executed, the value of the expression is ignored, but any side effects are carried out. Thus when

```
n = 10;
```

is executed, the expression n = 10 is evaluated. Its value (10) is ignored, but its side effect (assigning 10 to n) is carried out.

If an expression has no side effects, the corresponding expression statement has no effect on the computation. For example,

```
3*4;
```

is a valid expression statement, but it has no effect because the

	INCREMENT	DECREMENT
Table 1-3	++n	--n
Increment and Decrement	n += 1	n -= 1
Operators	n = n + 1	n = n - 1

value of the expression is ignored and there are no side effects to carry out. Some compilers will give a warning message if the programmer writes an expression statement that has no effect.

Increment and Decrement Operators

Incrementing (increasing by 1) and *decrementing* (decreasing by 1) the value of a variable are so common that C++ provides two special operators for this task: the increment operator ++ and the decrement operator --. For a variable n, ++n and --n are expressions with side effects: ++n increments the value of n and returns the incremented value; --n decrements the value of n and returns the decremented value. In Table 1-3, expressions in the same column are equivalent.

When the increment and decrement operators precede the variable name, the values of the variables are changed before being returned as values of the expression. Thus the values of ++n and --n are the new incremented or decremented values. If ++ and -- follow the variable name, the value of the variable is returned *before* the value is incremented or decremented. For example, if the value of n is 20, then both ++n and n++ change the value of n to 21. The value of the expression ++n is 21, the new incremented value of n; the value of the expression n++ is 20, the value of n before the incrementation took place. Similar remarks apply to --n and n--.

We recall that when an expression is used as a statement, its value is ignored; only its side effects are important. Therefore the statements

```
++n;
n++;
```

have the same effect, as do the statements

```
--n;
n--;
```

When used as expressions, however, as in

```
m = n++;
```

or

```
cout << --n;
```

++n yields a value that is one greater than the value of n++, and --n yields a value that is one less than the value of n--.

The identifier or expression to which ++ or -- is applied must be a modifiable lvalue because it must represent a data object whose value can be incremented or decremented.

We now can see how C++ got its name. The "++" in C++ is the increment operator, which suggests that C++ is an incremental improvement of C, or perhaps the next step beyond C.

Equality, Relational, and Logical Operators

C++ does not have a separate logical or Boolean type for representing the values *true* and *false*; instead, type int is used for this purpose, with the integer value 0 representing *false* and any nonzero value representing *true*. In discussing logical operations and expressions, we will sometimes use *false* to refer to 0 and *true* to refer to any nonzero value. The operators described in this section yield 1 for *true* and 0 for *false*.

The *equality operators*, shown in Table 1-4, determine whether or not two values are equal. Each operator yields *true* if the corresponding relation is true and *false* if the relation is false. Thus 3 == 3 yields *true* (that is, 1) and 3 == 5 yields *false* (that is, 0). Likewise, 3 != 3 yields *false* and 3 != 5 yields *true*.

A very common mistake is to write the assignment operator = when the equality operator == is intended. The compiler often cannot catch this mistake because both operators are allowed at

	OPERATOR	RELATION
Table 1-4		
Equality Operators	==	*is equal to*
	!=	*is not equal to*

Table 1-5
Relational Operators

OPERATOR	RELATION
<	*is less than*
<=	*is less than or equal to*
>	*is greater than*
>=	*is greater than or equal to*

the point in the program where the mistake occurs. Nevertheless, the effects of the two operators are completely different, and a program has no chance of working as intended if the programmer inadvertently writes = where == is needed.

The *relational operators*, shown in Table 1-5, determine whether or not one value precedes another in numerical order. For example, 3 < 5 and 3 <= 5 both yield *true*, whereas 3 > 5 and 3 >= 5 yield *false*; 3 < 3 and 3 > 3 yield *false*, whereas 3 <= 3 and 3 >= 3 yield *true*.

The equality and relational operators have lower precedence than the arithmetic operators. Therefore, expressions such as

```
m + 5 <= 2 * n
```

are grouped as

```
(m + 5) <= (2 * n)
```

The two arithmetic expressions are evaluated first, after which their values are compared using the equality or relational operator.

The *logical NOT* operator, !, yields *false* if its operand is *true* (that is, nonzero) and vice versa. The *logical AND* operator, &&, yields *true* only if both its operands are *true* (nonzero); if either operand is *false*, && yields *false*. The *logical OR* operator, ||, yields *true* if either of its operands is *true* (nonzero); it yields *false* only if both its operands are *false*.

For example, the expression

```
m < n && i > j
```

yields *true* when the value of m is less than the value of n *and* the value of i is greater than the value of j; the expression

```
m == 5 || n != 10
```

yields *true* if the value of m is equal to 5 *or* the value of n is not equal to 10. On the other hand, the expression

```
!(m == 5 || n != 10)
```

yields *true* if *it is false that* "the value of m is equal to 5 *or* the value of n is not equal to 10."

Operators && and || have lower precedence than the equality and relational operators, so that expressions such as

```
m == 5 || n != 10 || p < 25
```

can be written without parentheses; however, many programmers prefer to parenthesize such expressions for clarity:

```
(m == 5) || (n != 10) || (p < 25)
```

Operator ! has higher precedence than &&, which in turn has higher precedence than ||. Parentheses are particularly recommended for clarity when different logical operators occur in the same expression.

The left operand of && or || is always evaluated first; if the value of the left operand determines the value of the expression, the right operand is not evaluated. Specifically, if the left operand of && yields *false* or the left operand of || yields *true*, the right operand is not evaluated. This property, called *short-circuit evaluation*, is useful if there are circumstances in which evaluating the right operand could cause an error. For example, it is an error to apply the library function sqrt() to a negative number. But the expression

```
(x >= 0.0) && (sqrt(x) <= 2)
```

can never cause an error: if the value of x is negative, the left operand of && will yield *false*, and the right operand will never be evaluated.

Conditional Expressions

A conditional expression has the following form:

expression-c ? *expression-t* : *expression-f*

The condition is represented by *expression-c*, which is evaluated first, and whose value (zero for *false*, nonzero for *true*) determines which of the other two expressions will be evaluated. If the condition is *true*, *expression-t* is evaluated and its value becomes the value of the conditional expression. If the condition is *false*, *expression-f* is evaluated and its value becomes the value of the conditional expression.

For example, the expression

```
n >= 0 ? 1 : -1
```

yields 1 if the value of n is nonnegative and -1 if the value is negative. The expression

```
m >= n ? m : n
```

yields the larger of the values of m and n. The expression

```
x >= 0.0 ? x : -x
```

yields the absolute value of x: the value of x changed, if need be, to a positive number.

The precedence of ? and : is less than that of any of the other operators we have considered; therefore, no parentheses are required in the preceding expressions. Nevertheless, parentheses are often used for readability; in particular, the condition is often enclosed in parentheses.

```
(n >= 0) ? 1 : -1
(m >= n) ? m : n
(x >= 0.0) ? x : -x
```

The Comma Operator

Occasionally, we may wish to write two or more expressions where only a single expression is called for. The comma operator allows us to combine two or more expressions into a single expression. For example, we can use the comma operator to combine the expressions i++ and j++ into the following single expression:

```
i++, j++
```

The expression to the left of the comma is evaluated first, then the expression to the right. Thus the preceding expression increments the value of i first, then the value of j. The comma operator returns the value of the rightmost expression; thus the value of the preceding expression equals the value of j before it was incremented.

The comma operator associates from left to right, so if several expressions are separated by comma operators, they will be evaluated from left to right. Thus

```
i++,  j++,  k++,  m++
```

causes i, j, k, and m to be incremented in that order. The value of the entire expression is the value of the rightmost constituent expression, which in this case is the value of m before it is incremented.

The comma operator has lower precedence than any other C++ operator; this means that the expressions joined by a comma operator never have to be enclosed in parentheses, and each such expression is evaluated exactly the same as if it were not joined to another expression with the comma operator.

There are several places in C++ where commas are used to separate items on a list; the items separated may even be expressions. Commas that separate items on a list are not comma operators; a comma represents a comma operator only if it cannot be interpreted as separating items on a list.

Functions That Take Arguments and Return Values

As in other languages, functions can be passed argument values and can return a value. When we define or declare a function, we must specify the types of the arguments and return values. For example, the following function takes two double-precision floating-point arguments and returns a double-precision floating-point result:

```
double area( double length, double width )
{
    return length * width;
}
```

The double preceding the function name area indicates that this function returns a result of type double. The doubles preceding the argument names length and width declare both arguments to be of type double.

The spaces between the parentheses and the argument list are optional and are intended to improve readability. The use of spaces in this way is an increasingly common C and C++ style.

The function area() would normally be used in an expression, for example:

```
2.0 * area( 5.0, 7.0 ) + 25.0
```

The argument values that are passed to a function—5.0 and 7.0 in the example—are its *actual arguments*. The argument variables in the function definition are its *formal arguments*. When a function is called, the formal arguments are declared and initialized to the values of the actual arguments. Thus, when `area()` is called in the preceding expression, `length` and `width` are declared and initialized as if the following statements had been executed:

```
double length = 5.0;
double width = 7.0;
```

The scope of the formal arguments is the block that defines the function. The lifetime of the formal arguments is the duration of the function call—that is, the time during which the statements that define the function are being executed.

Notice that the commas separating arguments—actual or formal—are not comma operators, but just serve to separate items on an argument list.

After the formal arguments have been declared and initialized, the statements that define the function are executed. A statement of the form

```
return expression;
```

terminates function execution and returns the value of *expression* as the value of the function. In our example, the computation of the return value can be carried out entirely in the `return` statement:

```
return length * width;
```

The return value is used in evaluating the expression from which the function is called. Thus when

```
2.0 * area( 5.0, 7.0 ) + 25.0
```

is evaluated, `area()` returns the value 35.0—the product of its two argument values—and the value of the entire expression is 95.0.

We recall that a function must be declared before it can be called; declarations for all the functions called in a source file are usually placed near the beginning of the file. We can get a declaration for any function by taking the heading from the function definition and putting a semicolon after it. Thus `area()` can be declared by

```
double area( double length, double width );
```

The names of the formal arguments are optional in the declaration (they are required in the definition). Thus the declaration of `area()` can be simplified to

```
double area( double, double );
```

By indicating the significance of the arguments, well-chosen argument names can help a human reader understand the declaration. If the argument names do not accomplish this purpose, they are probably best omitted.

Side Effects and Sequence Points

We have seen that the compiler has considerable leeway as to the order in which the operators in an expression are applied. If some operators have side effects, the compiler has further leeway as to when the side effects will take place—when the newly computed values will be stored in memory. Unfortunately, uncertainties as to when operators will be applied and when side effects will take place make it possible for us to write expressions whose values and effects are unpredictable.

For example, we cannot predict the value of

```
++i + i
```

because we do not know whether the value of i will be incremented before or after it is accessed as the right operand of +. If the initial value of i is 100, the expression can be evaluated as either

```
101 + 100
```

or

```
101 + 101
```

depending on when the value of i is updated. Thus the value of the expression can be either 201 or 202.

Likewise, we cannot predict the effect of the statement

```
i = ++i + 25;
```

Both the = and ++ operators produce side effects, and we cannot predict the order in which the two side effects will be carried out. If the initial value of i is 100, the ++ operator assigns i the value of

```
100 + 1
```

and the = operator assigns i the value of

```
100 + 1 + 25
```

Because we cannot predict the order in which these assignments are carried out, we cannot predict which one will determine the final value of i. Thus, after the statement has been executed, the value of i can be either 101 or 126.

To help us manage side effects, certain points in the execution of the program are designated as *sequence points*. At a sequence point we can determine what side effects have taken place and which still remain to take place.

There is a sequence point at the end of each expression statement; all side effects produced by the expression take place before the end of the statement is reached. Thus, because of the sequence point at the end of each statement, we can be sure that the assignments in

```
m = 10;
n = m + 5;
p = m + n;
```

will be carried out in the order shown.

When an expression occurs in any other kind of statement, such as the control statements discussed later in this chapter, there is a sequence point at the end of the expression.

The order in which operands are evaluated is specified for only four operators: , (comma operator), &&, ||, and ?: (conditional operator); in each case the leftmost operand is evaluated first. Each operator has a sequence point after the evaluation of the left-most operand; any side effects produced by the left-most operand will take place before any other operand is evaluated. For example, in

```
i++, i + 10
```

we can be sure that the incrementation is carried out before the value of i + 10 is calculated.

For all other operators, the operands can be evaluated in any order, and we cannot predict when during the evaluation any side effects will take place. Thus, we cannot predict the values of expressions such as

```
++i * i
```

and

```
(m += 10) / m
```

There is also a sequence point just prior to each function call. Thus any side effects produced by the expressions representing the function and its arguments will take place before the function is called. For example, in

```
f( n++ )
```

the value of n will be incremented before the function f() is called.

Between sequence points, we should not assign more than one value to the same variable. Nor should we both assign a value to a variable and access the value of the same variable, unless we can be sure of the order in which the assignment and the access take place.

One principle that we *can* sometimes use to determine order of evaluation is that an operator cannot be applied until its operands have been evaluated. This principle assures us that statements such as

```
i = 2*i + 5;
```

are safe even though the statement both accesses the value of i and assigns i a new value. The assignment operator cannot be applied until its right operand (which gives the value to be assigned) is evaluated; therefore, we can be sure that a new value will be assigned to i only *after* 2*i + 5 has been evaluated.

TYPE CONVERSIONS

A given numerical value, such as 2, could belong to a number of different types, such as char, short, int, unsigned int, long, and so on. For this reason, we sometimes need to convert a value from one arithmetic type to another without changing the number that the value represents.

Converting to a type with a wider range of values or a greater degree of precision presents no problems. Such harmless conversions include converting from char to int, from int to long, and from float to double. Unfortunately, converting in the opposite direction, such as from int to char, and from long to int, can turn a meaningful value into meaningless garbage if it is outside the range of values allowed for the type to which it is being converted. Conversions such as from long double to double or from `double` to `float` will generally result in a loss of precision because the smaller type will represent numbers less accurately than the larger type.

Type conversions can be *implicit* (carried out automatically) or *explicit* (specifically requested by the programmer).

Implicit Conversions

Arithmetic and other operations are not carried out directly on values of types `char` and `short` or on values of enumeration types. When a value of one of these types appears in an expression, it is converted to type `int` before any operation is carried out on it; such conversions are called *integral promotions.*[*]

The machine instructions that implement arithmetic operations take operands of the same type and produce a result of that type. For example, there may be an instruction for adding two values of type `int` to produce a result of type `int`, an instruction for adding two values of type `long` to produce a result of type `long`, and so on.

In contrast, C++ allows *mixed mode expressions*, in which the operands have different types. Thus we can add a value of type `int` to a value of type `long`, a value of type `float` to a value of type `double`, and so on. Before such an operation can be carried out, however, one operand must be converted to the type of the other, so that both operands will have the same type as required by the machine instructions. Of the two possible conversions, we wish to select the one (if either) that will not turn a value into garbage or even cause a loss of accuracy.

Integral promotions are done first: if either operand has type `char`, type `short`, or an enumeration type, it is converted to type `int`. If the operands still have different types, the following list of types determines which operand will be converted:

```
int
unsigned int
long
unsigned long
float
double
long double
```

---

* Types `char`, `unsigned char`, and `signed char` are all converted to type `int`. Type `unsigned short` is converted to type `int` if the latter can represent all the values of type `unsigned short`; otherwise, `unsigned short` is converted to `unsigned int`.

The type that comes first in this list is converted to the type that comes second. For example, if the operand types are int and long, the int operand would be converted to type long. If the operand types are long and long double, the long operand would be converted to type long double, and so on.

There is one possible exception to the use of the list. On some systems, type long cannot represent all values of type unsigned int; for example, this will be true on systems where int and long have the same range. On such systems, if one operand is unsigned int and the other is long, both will be converted to unsigned long.

Conversions are performed as needed during initialization and assignment, without regard for whether a conversion can cause problems. Thus in

```
char c = 65;
```

the integer value 65 is converted from type int to type char and stored in the variable c (if the ASCII code is in use, c will now represent the letter A, whose ASCII code is 65). Unfortunately, C++ also allows us to write

```
char c = 10000;
```

This statement will probably store garbage in c, because in most implementations 10000 is outside the range of values allowed for type char.

Explicit Conversions

Indicating explicitly where conversions take place helps readers understand a program. In addition, some conversions that are not performed implicitly can be requested explicitly.

C++ provides two means for requesting type conversions. One uses a *type cast*, which is a type designation enclosed in parentheses, as in (int), (long), and (double). The type cast serves as a unary operator that converts a value to the indicated type. For example, the expression

```
(double) 25
```

converts the value 25 from int to double. Note that safe as well as unsafe conversions can be indicated with type casts. Thus

```
(char) 10000
```

will yield garbage on most systems.

Listing 1-3

```
// File discount.cpp
// Program to compute discount and sales tax

#include <iostream.h>

double round( double );   // round positive amount to cents

const double SALES_TAX_RATE = 0.06;

main()
{

// Get input data from user

    double regular_price;
    double percent_discount;

    cout << "Regular price: ";
    cin >> regular_price;

    cout << "Percent discount: ";
    cin >> percent_discount;

// Compute results

    double discount_rate = percent_discount / 100.0;
    double discount = round( regular_price * discount_rate );
    double discounted_price = regular_price - discount;
    double sales_tax = round( discounted_price *
                            SALES_TAX_RATE );
    double amount_due = discounted_price + sales_tax;

// Print results

    cout << "Discount = $" << discount << '\n';
    cout << "Sales tax = $" << sales_tax << '\n';
    cout << "Amount due = $" << amount_due << '\n';
}
```

```
double round( double amount )
{
    long cents = long( 100.0 * amount + 0.5 );
    return double( cents ) / 100.0;
}
```

Type-cast operators, which are designated by (*type*) in Appendix 2, have the same precedence as other unary operators, such as unary +, unary −, and !.

C++ (but not C) also allows type conversions to be indicated using function-call notation: a type name behaves as if it were a function for converting values to the designated type. Thus

```
double( 25 )
```

yields the `double` value 25.0, and

```
char( 10000 )
```

yields garbage. Function-call notation usually leads to the simplest expressions. It can only be used, however, for types designated by identifiers. As we will see later, some types are designated by a sequence of symbols, such as `char (*)()`; such a sequence must be enclosed in parentheses, so only type-cast notation is permitted.

EXAMPLE: COMPUTING DISCOUNTS

Listing 1-3 shows a simple program for computing discounts and sales tax, as might be done by an electronic cash register. The program illustrates input; variable declaration and initialization; function definition, declaration, and call; and explicit type conversion.

The program uses type `double` for all numerical values. A function `round()` is used to round results to two decimal places; the declaration

```
double round( double );
```

indicates that `round()` takes a `double` argument and yields a `double` result. `SALES_TAX_RATE` is defined as a `double` constant with the value 0.06, representing a 6 percent rate.

Via the header file `iostream.h`, the C++ library provides a standard input stream `cin` and an *extraction operator*, `>>`, for extracting values from the stream and storing them in variables. If `cin` is not explicitly redirected, the input will come from the user's keyboard. The type of a variable determines the type of the input value. Thus

```
int n;
cin >> n;
```

read an `int` value into the variable n, and

```
double x;
cin >> x;
```

read a `double` value into the variable x. Note that the extraction and insertion operators >> and << each point in the direction of data flow, either away from or toward the stream.

The program declares two `double` variables, `regular_price` and `percent_discount`, to hold values obtained from the user. One of the few situations in C++ where we declare a variable without initializing it is when the initial value is to be read from an input stream.

The statement

```
cout << "Regular price ";
```

prompts the user to enter the regular price of an item of merchandise. The statement

```
cin >> regular_price;
```

reads the value that the user entered into the variable `regular_price`. Likewise, the statements

```
cout << "Percent discount: ";
cin >> percent_discount;
```

obtain the value of `percent_discount` from the user. Note that the prompt strings do not end with \n; this allows the responses to be typed on the same line as the prompts, as in

```
Regular price: 999.99
Percent discount: 23
```

The next section of `main()` carries out the discount and sales-tax computations; variables are declared as needed to hold computed results. The variable `discount_rate` holds the discount rate expressed as a decimal, which is equal to the percentage rate divided by 100. The function `round()` is used to round off products, which generally will have more than two decimal places.

The final section of `main()` prints the computed results. These statements also illustrate the use of the character `'\n'` instead of the string `"\n"` for terminating a line; as mentioned earlier, either the character or the string can be used to insert a newline into a stream. A complete run of the program looks like this:

```
Regular price: 999.99
Percent discount: 23
Discount = $230
Sales tax = $46.2
Amount due = $816.19
```

The function `round()` rounds an amount to two decimal places. To do this, we first multiply the amount to be rounded by 100.0 to convert it to cents. Adding 0.5 increases the number of cents by one if the amount to the right of the decimal point is 0.5 or more. We then discard everything to the right of the decimal point by converting the number of cents to a long integer.

```
long cents = long( 100.0 * amount + 0.5 );
```

The type conversion would have been carried out implicitly if we had just written

```
long cents = 100.0 * amount + 0.5;
```

Stating the conversion explicitly, however, makes it easier for a human reader to see what is going on.

To compute the value to be returned, we convert the value of `cents` back to type **double** and divide by 100.0 to get a double-precision dollars-and-cents amount.

```
return double( cents ) / 100.0;
```

Again, the type conversion would have been carried out implicitly (because the constant `100.0` has type **double**, the first operand of / would also be converted to **double**); making the conversion explicit, however, helps the reader figure out what the programmer is up to.

CONTROL STATEMENTS: REPETITION

Control statements govern how other statements of the program will be executed. A *repetition* (or *iteration*) *statement* causes the statements it controls to be executed zero or more times.

The while *Statement*

The while statement has the following form, in which *expression* represents the control expression and *statement* represents the controlled statement:

```
while ( expression ) statement
```

The controlled statement is executed repeatedly as long as the value of the control expression is not zero. If we think of the control expression as a condition, with a zero value representing *false* and a nonzero value representing *true*, then the controlled statement will be executed while the condition is true. Specifically, before each possible execution of the statement, the control expression is evaluated. If the value is zero (*false*), the controlled statement is not executed and the computer goes on to the next statement in the program, the one following the while statement. If the value of the control expression is nonzero (*true*), the controlled statement is executed, after which the control expression is evaluated again, and so on.

For example, the following statements read integers from the input stream until a value greater than 1000 is read:

```
int n;
cin >> n;
while ( n <= 1000 )
    cin >> n;
```

Here the controlled statement is an expression statement; note that it ends with a semicolon just as it would if it were not part of a while statement.

The controlled statement can also be a block, in which case all the statements of the block are executed repeatedly as determined by the control expression. For example, the following statements print the numbers from 1 through 100:

```
int count = 1;
while ( count <= 100 ) {
    cout << count << "\n";
    count++;
}
```

Here the controlled statement is the block

```
{ cout << count << "\n"; count++; }
```

Note that the block is enclosed in braces, exactly as if it were not part of a `while` statement. The opening brace of the block is usually placed either on the same line as `while` (as above) or on a line by itself (as follows):

```
int count = 1;
while ( count <= 100 )
{
    cout << count << "\n";
    count++;
}
```

The do Statement

The `do` statement has the following form:

`do` *statement* `while ( ` *expression* ` );`

The `do` statement works just like the `while` statement, except that the value of the control expression is tested after each execution of the controlled statement rather than before. Thus the controlled statement is always executed at least once; after each execution, the control expression is evaluated and its value tested to see whether any further executions will take place.

The `do` statement is useful when the controlled statement must be executed before the control expression can be evaluated. For example, in our code for reading and testing input values, we had to use an extra input statement to read the first value so that n would have a valid value the first time the control expression was evaluated.

```
int n;
cin >> n;
while ( n <= 1000 )
    cin >> n;
```

With a do statement, the extra input statement is not needed.

```
int n;
do
    cin >> n;
while ( n <= 1000 );
```

Some repetitions can be written equally well with a `while` or a `do` statement. For example, our code for printing the numbers from 1 through 100 could be written as

```
int count = 1;
do {
    cout << count << "\n";
    count++;
} while ( count <= 100 );
```

Note the controlled statement is a block.

Example: The Inverse Fibonacci Rabbit Problem

The Fibonacci rabbit problem concerns pairs of rabbits that reproduce in a peculiarly regular manner. Each fertile pair produces exactly one pair of offspring each month, and each newly born pair becomes fertile after exactly one month. Given the current number of pairs and the number that are fertile, how many pairs will there be after the rabbits have reproduced for a given number of months? Listing 1-4 shows a program for solving the inverse problem: if we need a given number of pairs, for how many months must the rabbits reproduce to meet that need?

Let `current` be the total number of pairs at the beginning of the current month and `fertile` the number of those that are fertile. Each fertile pair will have one pair of offspring this month; therefore the number of pairs at the beginning of next month is `current + fertile`. Also, each newly born pair becomes fertile after one month. Therefore, the number of pairs alive at the beginning of this month (`current`) will be the number of fertile pairs (`fertile`) at the beginning of next month. Thus for each month that the rabbits reproduce, the variables `current` and `fertile` are updated as follows:

```
long next = current + fertile;
fertile = current;
current = next;
```

Listing 1-4

```cpp
// File rabbits.cpp
// Program for inverse Fibonacci rabbit problem

#include <iostream.h>

main()
{

// Get input from user

    long current;     // number of pairs this month
    long fertile;     // number of fertile pairs
    long needed;      // number of pairs needed

    cout << "Starting number of pairs: ";
    cin >> current;

    cout << "Starting number of fertile pairs: ";
    cin >> fertile;

    cout << "Number of pairs desired: ";
    cin >> needed;

// Compute number of months rabbits must reproduce

    int months = 0;
    while ( current < needed ) {
        long next = current + fertile;   // pairs next month
        fertile = current;               // update fertile
        current = next;                  // update current
        months++;                        // count this month
    }

// Print result

    cout << "After " << months << " months there will be ";
    cout << current << " pairs\n";
}
```

Let the value of `needed` be the number of pairs that we need. The following code counts the number of months the rabbits must reproduce to yield at least the needed number of pairs:

```
int months = 0;
while ( current < needed ) {
    long next = current + fertile;
    fertile = current;
    current = next;
    months++;
}
```

The `for` Statement

The `for` statement has the following form:

for (*statement-i expression-c* ; *expression-s*)
    statement

It is equivalent to the following statements:

statement-i
while (*expression-c*) {
    statement
    expression-s ;
}

Statement-i is the initialization statement, which is executed before any other actions are taken. *Expression-c* is the control expression whose value determines whether repetitions will continue. *Expression-s* is used to step a control variable through a series of values; frequently, the value of the variable is incremented with ++ or decremented with --.

If *statement-i* is an expression statement

expression-i ;

the `for` statement then takes the following form:

for (*expression-i* ; *expression-c* ; *expression-s*)
    statement

This is the general form of the `for` statement in C. By allowing the initialization part to be a statement rather than an expression, C++ allows declarations (which are statements) rather than just assignments (which are expressions). If *statement-i* is a declaration, the scope of the declared variable or variables extends to the end of the block containing the `for` statement.

Our code for printing the numbers 1 through 100

```
int count = 1;
while ( count <= 100 ) {
    cout << count << "\n";
    count++;
}
```

can be written as the following `for` statement:

```
for ( int count = 1; count <= 100; count++ )
    cout << count << "\n";
```

Note that the initialization part is a declaration statement. By reserving special places for the initialization statement, the control expression, and the step expression, the `for` statement clarifies the structure of a repetition without losing any of the power or generality that was available with the `while` statement.

If not needed, *expression-c* and *expression-s* can be omitted, and *statement-i* can be the null statement, which consists of only a semicolon. If *expression-c* is omitted, the repetition will not terminate. Thus

```
for ( ;; ) {
    // controlled statements
}
```

is the C++ idiom for an infinite loop — a repetition that (as far as the `for` statement is concerned) continues indefinitely.

The initialization statement will be the null statement when the control variable has already been declared and initialized. For example, if `count` had already been declared and its value set to 1, the code for printing numbers would have been written as

```
for ( ; count <= 100; count++ )
    cout << count << "\n";
```

With the aid of the comma operator, a `for` statement can step more than one variable through a series of values. If `i` and `j` have been declared as `int` variables, then the statement

```
for ( i = 0, j = 10; i < 5; i++, j++ )
    cout << "i = " << i << " j = " << j << "\n";
```

prints

```
i = 0   j = 10
i = 1   j = 11
i = 2   j = 12
i = 3   j = 13
i = 4   j = 14
```

Here *statement-i* is an expression statement consisting of the two expressions i = 0 and j = 10 joined by a comma operator; thus i is initialized to 0 and j is initialized to 10. Likewise, *expression-s* consists of the two expressions i++ and j++ joined by a comma operator; thus both i and j are incremented after each execution of the controlled statement.

If i and j had not been declared previously, we could declare and initialize them both in the for statement:

```
for ( int i = 0, j = 10; i < 5; i++, j++ )
    cout << "i = " << i << " j = " << j << "\n";
```

However, the comma in

```
int i = 0, j = 10;
```

is not a comma operator, but just a separator in a list of variables to be declared, as in

```
int i, j, k, m;
```

In such a list, every variable can be given a separate initial value.

```
int i = 5, j = 10, k = 15, m = 20;
```

Example: Computing Interest

Listing 1-5 shows a program for computing the amount in a bank account after a given number of months; we assume that interest is compounded monthly and a fixed amount is deposited at the beginning of each month. We are given the starting balance (initial value of balance), the monthly deposit (deposit), the interest rate (annual_pcnt_rate), and the number of months (months) for which deposits will be made and interest compounded. In our calculations we will use the monthly decimal rate (rate), which is equal to the annual percentage rate divided by 1200.

We update the balance each month by adding the deposit to the balance, computing the interest for the month, and adding

Listing 1-5

```
// File balance.cpp
// Compute amount in bank account

#include <iostream.h>

double round( double );   // round positive amount to cents

main()
{

// Get input data from user

    double balance;                 // current balance
    double deposit;                 // monthly deposit
    double annual_pcnt_rate;        // annual percentage rate
    double interest;                // monthly interest payment
    int months;                     // number of months

    cout << "Starting balance: ";
    cin >> balance;

    cout << "Monthly deposit: ";
    cin >> deposit;

    cout << "Annual percentage rate: ";
    cin >> annual_pcnt_rate;

    cout << "Number of months: ";
    cin >> months;

// Compute new balance

    double rate = annual_pcnt_rate / 1200.0;   // monthly
                                               // decimal rate
    for ( int m = 0; m < months; m++ ) {
       balance += deposit;                      // make deposit
       interest = round( balance * rate );  // compute interest
       balance += interest;                     // deposit interest
    }
```

(continued)

```
// Print balance

    cout << "Balance after " << months << " months = $";
    cout << balance << endl;
    cout << "Final interest payment = $" << interest << endl;
}

double round( double amount )
{
    long cents = long( 100.0 * amount + 0.5 );
    return double( cents ) / 100.0;
}
```

the interest to the balance. We use the function round() to round the interest to two decimal places.

```
    balance += deposit;
    interest = round( balance * rate );
    balance += interest;
```

These calculations must be repeated for each month in question.

```
    for ( int m = 0; m < months; m++ ) {
        balance += deposit;
        interest = round( balance * rate );
        balance += interest;
    }
```

Notice that m is stepped from 0 through months − 1 rather than from 1 through months. Counting from 0 rather than from 1 is common in C++. The reason (as we will see later) is that array indexes in C++ start at 0 rather than 1. However, this method of counting is often used in problems (such as the one at hand) that have nothing to do with array indexes. For example, the C++ idiom for getting something done count times is

```
    for ( int i = 0; i < count; i++ ) {
        // do it once
    }
```

The program prints the balance after the specified number of months, as well as the final interest payment. The following is a typical interaction between the user and the program:

```
Starting balance: 1000
Monthly deposit: 150
Annual percentage rate: 7.5
Number of months: 48
Balance after 48 months = $9767.26
Final interest payment = $60.67
```

This program illustrates yet another way to terminate a line of output. In

```
cout << balance << endl;
```

the *manipulator* endl outputs a newline character after the value of balance has been printed. Manipulators are used with << and >> exactly as if they represented data for output or variables to receive input. As the name implies, however, manipulators can carry out arbitrary operations on the input and output streams.

For example, endl has another effect besides outputting a newline. The output stream cout is *buffered* — values inserted in cout are not written directly to an output device; instead, the output is stored temporarily in a memory area called a *buffer*. When the buffer is full, its contents are outputted in a single operation, which is much more efficient than outputting each character separately. After inserting a newline the manipulator endl *flushes* the buffer — outputs its contents even if it is not full. Thus we can use endl to assure that a program's messages will be presented to the user in a timely fashion. There is also a manipulator flush, which flushes the buffer without first outputting a newline.

It might seem that we would have to use flush or endl when printing prompts, to assure that each prompt would appear immediately on the user's display. We do not have to do so, however, because of a special tie between cin and cout. Before attempting to read an input value, cin first flushes the buffer for cout, thus assuring that any request for input will be printed *before* cin attempts to read the requested input.

CONTROL STATEMENTS: SELECTION

Selection (or *alternation*) *statements* select from among one or more alternatives the action that the computer is to carry out; the selection is based on the value of a control expression. We have already encountered selection in the form of conditional expressions such as

```
m >= n ? m : n
```

C++ also has three selection statements: the `if` statement, the `if-else` statement, and the `switch` statement.

The `if` and `if-else` Statements

The `if` statement has the form

if (*expression*) *statement*

As with the `while` statement, the control expression is often interpreted as representing a condition. If the value of the control expression is nonzero (*true*), the controlled statement is executed; if the value of the control expression is zero (*false*), the controlled statement is skipped. Consider the following example:

```
if ( count > MAX_COUNT )
    cerr << "Overflow\n";
```

If the value of `count` exceeds that of `MAX_COUNT`, the message `Overflow` is printed on `cerr`, a standard output stream used for error messages. If the value of `count` does not exceed that of `MAX_COUNT`, no message is printed. As with other control statements, the controlled statement can be a block.

```
if ( count > MAX_COUNT ) {
    cerr << "Overflow\n";
    count = 0;
}
```

Adding an `else` part to the `if` statement gives us the `if-else` statement:

if (*expression*) *statement-1* else *statement-2*

Listing 1-6

```
double round( double amount )
{
    long cents;
    if ( amount >= 0.0 )
        cents = long( 100.0 * amount + 0.5 );
    else
        cents = -long( 100.0 * (-amount) + 0.5 );
    return double( cents ) / 100.0;
}
```

If the value of the control expression is nonzero (*true*), *statement-1* is executed; if the value of the expression is zero (*false*), *statement-2* is executed. For example, the following statement increments the value of a counter if its maximum count has not been reached; if the maximum count has been reached, the statement resets the counter to 0 and prints an error message:

```
if ( count < MAX_COUNT )
    count++;
else {
    cerr << "Overflow\n";
    count = 0;
}
```

Listing 1-6 shows an improved version of the rounding function `round()`, which we have been using to round `double` values to two decimal places. The version in Listings 1-4 and 1-5 can be used only with positive numbers; the version in Listing 1-6 can also round negative numbers. The easiest way to round a negative amount is to change its sign to positive, convert it to an integer number of cents, as we did before, and then change its sign back to negative. The function in Listing 1-6 uses an `if-else` statement to carry out the proper calculation for the value of `cents` depending on whether the value of `amount` is positive or negative. We could have used a conditional expression to calculate the value of `cents`, but the required expression would be long and cumbersome.

The controlled statement in an `if` or `if-else` statement can itself be an `if` or `if-else` statement. We say that statements are *nested* when a controlled statement is the same kind of state-

ment as the control statement in which it is embedded. Nested
if-else statements allow us to construct multiway selection
statements, such as the following:

```
if ( expression-1 )
    statement-1
else if ( expression-2 )
    statement-2
else if ( expression-3 )
    statement-3
else if ( expression-4 )
    statement-4
else
    statement-5
```

There can be as many else if parts as we wish. Only one of
the statements is selected for execution. The expressions are
evaluated in the order shown; the first expression to yield a nonzero value (*true*) causes the corresponding statement (and only
that statement) to be executed. If all the expressions yield zero
(*false*), the statement in the else part is executed. If there is no
else part, then no statement is executed when all the expressions yield *false*.

Nested if-else statements are illustrated in Listing 1–7 by a
dummy command interpreter. A command interpreter is a part of
a program that accepts and carries out user commands. The command interpreter in Listing 1–7 is a dummy one because it doesn't
carry out any commands, except Quit, but just informs the user
that each command hasn't yet been implemented. Often an inter-
active program starts out as a dummy command interpreter; once
the command interpreter is working, the programmer turns to
implementing the commands one by one.

The user is prompted to enter the first letter of a command,
and (the code for) the letter entered is read into the char variable cmd. We allow the user to enter each letter in either uppercase or lowercase; both possibilities must be tested for. The
multiway selection construction formed by the nested if-else
statements executes the proper expression statements according
to the value of cmd.

The variable running is used as a flag to indicate whether
the program should continue. To clarify the use of running,
an enumerated type Boolean and constants TRUE and FALSE
are declared; running is declared as a Boolean variable at

Listing 1-7

```cpp
// File command1.cpp
// Dummy command interpreter using nested if-else statements

#include <iostream.h>

enum Boolean { FALSE, TRUE };   // truth values

main()
{
    Boolean running = TRUE;
    char cmd;

    do {
        cout << "\nCommands: Insert, Find, Delete, Quit\n";
        cout << "Enter first letter of command: ";
        cin >> cmd;

        if ( (cmd == 'i') || (cmd == 'I') ) {
            cout << "You have selected the Insert command\n";
            cout << "The Insert command is not implemented\n";
        }
        else if ( (cmd == 'f') || (cmd == 'F') ) {
            cout << "You have selected the Find command\n";
            cout << "The Find command is not implemented\n";
        }
        else if ( (cmd == 'd') || (cmd == 'D') ) {
            cout << "You have selected the Delete command\n";
            cout << "The Delete command is not implemented\n";
        }
        else if ( (cmd == 'q') || (cmd == 'Q') ) {
            cout << "You have selected the Quit command\n";
            cout << "Goodbye!\n";
            running = FALSE;
        }
        else
            cout << "Invalid command: please try again\n";
    } while ( running );
}
```

the beginning of the program and initialized to TRUE. The Quit command sets running to FALSE, causing the program to terminate.

Because `running` is initialized at the beginning of the program, we could use either a `while` or a `do` statement to control the repetition. The use of a `do` statement, however, emphasizes that the most conceptually meaningful place to test `running` is *after* the execution of a command (which could have been a Quit command).

The `switch` *Statement*

Another approach to multiway selection is the `switch` statement, which corresponds to the `case` or `select` statements in other languages. The `switch` statement has the following general form:

`switch (` *expression* `)` *statement*

The controlled statement is normally a block, one or more of whose statements are preceded by *case labels*. Each case label represents a possible value for the control expression; for example, the case label

```
case 25:
```

represents the value 25 and

```
case 'A':
```

represents (the integer code for) the letter A. If the value of the control expression is equal to the value given in one of the case labels, the computer begins execution of the block immediately after the case label rather than at the beginning of the block. No two of the case labels can represent the same value.

In the following examples, each ellipsis (. . .) represents any number of statements. In

```
switch ( 2 ) { case 1: ... case 2: ... case 3: ... }
```

execution of the block begins immediately after the label `case 2:`, rather than at the beginning of the block. In

```
switch ( 3 ) { case 1: ... case 2: ... case 3: ... }
```

execution of the block begins immediately following the label `case 3:`.

If none of the case labels corresponds to the value of the control expression, then none of the statements in the block are executed. Thus in

```
switch ( 5 ) { case 1: ... case 2: ... case 3: ... }
```

the entire block is skipped.

The case label `default:` corresponds to any value of the control expression that is not represented by another case label. Thus in

```
switch ( 5 ) { case 1: ... case 2: ... default: ... }
```

execution will begin following the label `default:` because none of the other case labels corresponds to the value of the control expression.

The control expression determines only where execution of the block begins. If we do not specify otherwise, all the statements between the selected case label and the end of the block will be executed. Generally, this is not what we want. Instead we want a separate set of statements executed for each case; after executing the statements for the selected case, we want to leave the block and continue with the rest of the program. We accomplish this with a `break` statement, which directs the computer to exit a `switch` or a repetition statement and carry on with the rest of the program.

Listing 1-8 shows a `switch` statement version of our dummy command interpreter. The first statement for each case has two case labels: one for the lowercase version of the corresponding command and one for the uppercase version. The statements for each case end with a `break` statement. The `break` statement could be omitted for the last case in the block, but since omitting a `break` statement is a very common error, it is well to form the invariable habit of ending the statements for *every* case with a `break` statement.

Listing 1-8

```cpp
// File command2.cpp
// Dummy command interpreter using switch statement

#include <iostream.h>
```

(continued)

```
enum Boolean { FALSE, TRUE };   // truth values

main()
{
    Boolean running = TRUE;
    char cmd;

    do {
        cout << "\nCommands: Insert, Find, Delete, Quit\n";
        cout << "Enter first letter of command: ";
        cin >> cmd;

        switch ( cmd ) {
        case 'i':
        case 'I':
            cout << "You have selected the Insert command\n";
            cout << "The Insert command is not implemented\n";
            break;
        case 'f':
        case 'F':
            cout << "You have selected the Find command\n";
            cout << "The Find command is not implemented\n";
            break;
        case 'd':
        case 'D':
            cout << "You have selected the Delete command\n";
            cout << "The Delete command is not implemented\n";
            break;
        case 'q':
        case 'Q':
            cout << "You have selected the Quit command\n";
            cout << "Goodbye!\n";
            running = FALSE;
            break;
        default:
            cout << "Invalid command: please try again\n";
            break;
        }
    } while ( running );
}
```

EXERCISES

The following are common programming exercises with which you are probably already familiar. Writing the solutions in C++ and running them on your computer will give you experience with the elements of the language and with your C++ compiler.

1. The inventor of chess asked the king for the following reward: "Give me one grain of wheat for the first square of my chessboard, two grains for the second square, four grains for the third, and so on for all 64 squares." Write a program to determine how many grains the inventor requested. *Hint*: Use `float` or `double` for the arithmetic; the numbers become too large for even `long` on most machines.

2. A weather station records the temperature every hour; write a program to read the 24 temperatures recorded during one day-night period and print the low, high, and average temperatures for the period. *Hint*: In the input data, the temperatures should be separated by spaces or line breaks. You can arrange the data into lines in any way that you please; the extraction operator will go from line to line as needed.

3. A triangle is equilateral if all three sides are equal, isosceles if any two (but no more than two) sides are equal, and scalene if no two sides are equal. Write a program to input the three sides of a triangle and classify it as equilateral, isosceles, or scalene.

4. The factorial of 0 is 1; the factorial of any other positive integer is the product of all integers from 1 through the integer in question. Write a function

   ```
   long factorial( int n );
   ```

   that returns the factorial of a positive integer n. Write a program that uses the function to print a short table of factorials.

5. Fibonacci numbers, which are important in mathematics and computer science, can be defined in terms of Fibonacci's rabbit problem as follows: Suppose that there are zero rabbits present during month zero and a single,

newly born pair is introduced at the beginning of month one. Then for any positive number n, the nth Fibonacci number is the number of pairs present at the beginning of month n. Write a function

```
long fibonacci( int n );
```

that returns the nth Fibonacci number. Take care that fibonacci(0) and fibonacci(1) return the correct values. Write a program that uses the function to print a short table of Fibonacci numbers.

2 *Classes and Objects*

W ITH THE elements of C++ in hand, we can now turn our attention to the central theme of this book: object-oriented programming. This chapter introduces the basic concepts of object-oriented programming and shows how they are realized in C++. As our first exercise in object-oriented programming, we will see how to create bank-account objects that can be used in the interest program described in Chapter 1.

OBJECT-ORIENTED PROGRAMMING

Object-oriented programming encourages programmers to assemble complex programs out of simpler components that can be designed and tested independently of the program that will use them. Preferably, many of the components will be of sufficiently general purpose that they can be reused in other programs.

Objects and Classes

In object-oriented programming, a program running on a computer is made up — in large part, at least — of interacting components called *objects*. Typically, each object corresponds to some person, place, or thing with which the computer must deal. Some objects may correspond to real-world entities such as bank accounts, employees, and inventory items. Others may correspond to computer hardware and software components, such as a communications port, a video-display window, or a mouse.

Still others may correspond to data structures such as stacks, queues, and lists.

As a program executes, the objects interact by sending messages to one another and receiving replies. For example, the program can make a withdrawal from a simulated bank account by having a customer object send a withdrawal message to a bank-account object. If the customer object needs to know the current balance in the account, it can send a message requesting the bank-account object to reply with this information. An object never needs to know anything about the internal workings of the objects with which it interacts; it only needs to know what kinds of messages they will accept and what kinds of replies to expect from them.

Many of the objects that a program uses may have the same structure. For example, a program that simulates the operation of a bank will need many account objects and many customer objects. Once we have decided on the structure of an object, we need a way to produce as many copies of it as needed. This is accomplished with a *class*, which contains a complete description of one kind of object. We can think of a class as a factory for manufacturing a particular kind of object. The objects manufactured by a class are called *instances* of that class.

Object-oriented programming languages vary in how classes are implemented; in some languages, for example, classes are themselves objects that can send and receive messages. In C++, however, *classes are user-defined data types*, which are used in the same way as such built-in data types as `int` and `float`. The instances of a C++ class are those objects (such as variables) that have been declared with the class as their data type.

Chapter 1 introduced the term *data object* for a region of memory in which values of a given type can be stored. However, only a data object declared with a class as its data type is an object in the sense of object-oriented programming; we distinguish such data objects by calling them *class objects*. Throughout this book we will frequently abbreviate *class object* to just *object*, so when the term *object* occurs without further qualification, it refers to a class object.

We can define a new class from scratch or we can create it by extending and modifying one or more existing classes. The latter capability is known as *inheritance*, because the new class inherits many of its properties from the existing class or classes (much as C++ inherits many of its features from C). Inheritance makes it easy to customize a class for a particular purpose, and it encourages us to organize our class definitions into "family trees" of related classes.

Methods, Messages, and Data Hiding

Few people would ever learn to operate a camera, a TV set, or a microwave oven if doing so meant understanding the device's internal workings. Fortunately, such machines usually provide users with a simple set of controls and data displays that conceal the device's complex internal structure and operation.

Likewise, an object can be manipulated only through an interface that responds to a limited number of different kinds of message; the object's internal structure is hidden from the user. This property of objects is called *data hiding*; alternate terms are *encapsulation* and *data abstraction*.

Data hiding simplifies the use of objects because users — that is, programmers who use objects in their programs — do not have to understand the objects' internal structure and operation. As long as the external interface remains unchanged, the internal structure of an object can be changed (during program maintenance or upgrade, for example) without affecting those parts of the program that use the object. Indeed, an important feature of object-oriented programming is *polymorphism* (literally, the ability to have many forms), whereby objects with very different internal structures can share the same external interface and so can be used in the same way.

The external interface is implemented by providing a set of *methods*, each of which accepts and responds to a particular kind of message. The methods are defined for an object's class and are the same for all objects that belong to the same class. In C++, methods are implemented with *functions* and *operators*, and we will usually use those terms rather than the more general *method*.

CLASSES

In Chapter 1 we wrote a program to compute the current balance in a bank account; the program worked by simulating the monthly process by which deposits are made and interest is computed for an actual account. As an ongoing example for the rest of this chapter, we will carry this simulation even further by defining a class of objects to represent bank accounts. The current-balance program can then work by first creating a bank-account object with a certain initial balance and interest rate, then repeatedly sending the object messages to accept deposits and compute interest, and finally sending a message asking the object to reply with its current balance.

Every instance of a bank account must keep track of two values: the current balance in the account and the interest rate. The interest rate will be expressed as a decimal rather than a percentage, and it will apply to the period (such as a day, a month, or a year) for which interest is compounded. These values could be stored in two variables:

```
double balance; // current balance
double rate; // decimal periodic interest rate
```

These variables are called *instance variables* because a separate set of them is needed for each instance of a bank-account class—that is, for every bank-account object. What we need is a mechanism for declaring the instance variables of each object and making these variables accessible to the methods—the functions and operators—that will manipulate the instance variables in response to incoming messages.

C++ provides two keywords for declaring classes: `struct` and `class`. Although `class` will turn out to be the more useful of the two, we will start with `struct`, which yields a direct generalization of the structures or records found in other languages such as C and Pascal.

Classes Declared with `struct`

Standard C allows several variables to be packaged together as a *structure,* which is very similar to a Pascal record. We can declare a structure for a bank account as follows:

```
struct account {
   double balance;
   double rate;
};
```

The objects declared within a structure are called its *members*; their names are *member names.* Thus the structure `account` has two members, the instance variables `balance` and `rate`. The

Figure 2-1

Two class objects, or instances, of class `account`*. Each is composed of the two instance variables,* `balance` *and* `rate`*, that were declared for the class.*

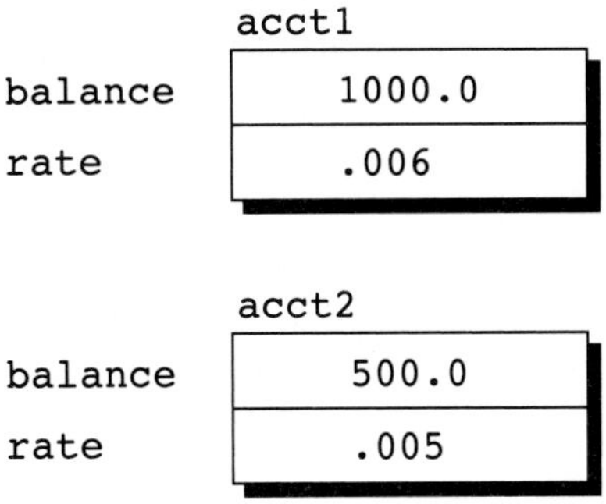

scope of the member names is the declaration itself; there are, however, special operators that allow the member names to be used for specific purposes outside the structure declaration.

Because instance variables are declared as members of a class, they are also known as *member variables* and as *data members.*

We can use the structure name to declare objects representing accounts. In standard C, we can declare bank-account variables `acct1` and `acct2` as follows:

```
struct account acct1;
struct account acct2;
```

C++ allows us to omit the keyword `struct` in such declarations; structure names can be used like any other type names, such as `int` and `double`. In C++, then, our declarations can be written

```
account acct1;
account acct2;
```

In C++, a class is a type and can be used just like any other type to declare variables; the variables are class objects and are instances of the class.

As illustrated in Figure 2-1, each instance of `account` is composed of two instance variables, `balance` and `rate`, which were declared as member variables of class `account`. C++ provides an operator, `.` (dot or period), for referring to class members associated with a class object. Thus `acct1.balance` refers to the instance variable `balance` of `acct1`, `acct2.rate` refers to the instance variable `rate` of `acct2`, and so on. We say that member names such as `balance` and `rate` are *qualified* by the name of a particular object. In the table of operators in Appendix 2, note that the dot operator associates from left to right and has higher precedence than most other operators, including all arithmetic, logical, and assignment operators.

We can use qualified names in statements and expressions just as we would use any other variable names. For example, the statement

```
acct1.balance = 1000.0;
```

makes an initial deposit of $1000 in `acct1`, the statement

```
acct2.balance += 100.0;
```

makes a $100 deposit in `acct2`, and the statement

```
if ( acct2.balance >= 500.0 )
    acct2.balance -= 500.0;
```

withdraws $500 from `acct2` provided that doing so will not overdraw the account.

Member Functions

With the aid of `struct` declarations, we can declare bank-account objects and use qualified names to access and manipulate their instance variables. But such direct access to the internal structures of objects violates the principle of data hiding. Instead of manipulating instance variables in arbitrary and uncontrolled ways, we want to send objects messages to do particular meaningful things, such as accepting a deposit or replying with the current balance. In C++, messages are sent with functions and operators; for now, we will consider only functions.

C structures are generalized to C++ classes by allowing them to contain functions as members. These *member functions* are used to send messages and receive replies from objects declared using a class.

For example, we can generalize our bank-account structure to a bank-account class by providing declarations for member functions:

```
struct account {
    double balance;
    double rate;
```

```
    void deposit( double amt );
    double withdraw( double amt );
    void compound();
    double get_balance();
};
```

The member functions `deposit()`, `withdraw()`, compound(), and `get_balance()` can be used to manipulate objects of type `account`. Note that the instances of `account` still have the form shown in Figure 2-1; the member functions are not actually stored in the class objects. Rather, the function declarations in the class definition tell the compiler which functions can be applied to objects of the class. It is up to the compiler to provide a member function with access to the object to which it is applied.

We use the dot operator to apply a member function to a particular object. For example, if `acct1` and `acct2` are account objects, the statements

```
    acct1.deposit( 100.0 );
    acct2.deposit( 500.0 );
```

deposit $100 in `acct1` and $500 in `acct2`. The statement

```
    cout << acct1.withdraw( 500.0 );
```

attempts to withdraw $500 from `acct1` and prints the amount that is actually withdrawn. The statement

```
    acct1.compound();
```

computes and deposits interest for `acct1`, and

```
    cout << acct2.get_balance();
```

prints the current balance for `acct2`. Each of these statements sends a message to an object; the value returned, if any, is the object's reply.

Although we have declared the member functions of `account`, they have yet to be defined. We can define the function `deposit()` as follows:

```
    void account::deposit( double amt )
    {
        balance += amt;
    }
```

The notation `account::deposit` indicates that the function name is the identifier `deposit` that was declared in the class declaration for `account`. By indicating the scope in which an identifier was declared, the *scope resolution operator*, `::`, distinguishes between occurrences of the same identifier in different scopes and allows access to an identifier from outside its scope. The scope resolution operator associates from left to right and has higher precedence than any other operator.

Be careful not to confuse the operators `.` and `::`. We use the dot operator to associate an identifier with a particular *object*, whereas the scope resolution operator designates an identifier declared in a particular *class*. Thus `acct1.balance` and `acct1.rate` are instance variables of the *object* `acct1`, and the function call

```
acct2.deposit( 250.95 );
```

applies the member function `deposit()` to the *object* `acct2`. On the other hand, `account::balance`, `account::rate`, `account::deposit`, and so on, are all identifiers declared in *class* `account`.

When a member function is called for a particular object, the name of that object qualifies all the member names in the statements that define the function. For example, the function call

```
acct1.deposit( 100.0 );
```

has the same effect as the statements

```
double amt = 100.0;
acct1.balance += amt;
```

Likewise, the function call

```
acct2.deposit( 500.0 );
```

has the same effect as

```
double amt = 500.0;
acct2.balance += amt;
```

Thus the first call updates the balance of `acct1`, and the second call updates the balance of `acct2`.

The function `withdraw()` is defined as follows:

```
double account::withdraw( double amt )
{
    if ( amt <= balance ) {
        balance -= amt;
        return amt;
    }
    else
        return 0.0;
}
```

The function returns the amount actually withdrawn. If the amount requested is less than the current balance, that amount is withdrawn; otherwise, the transaction is rejected, and no amount is withdrawn. Note that the statement

```
cash = acct1.withdraw( 500.0 );
```

is equivalent to the statements

```
double amt = 500.0;
if ( amt <= acct1.balance ) {
    acct1.balance -= amt;
    cash = amt;
}
else
    cash = 0.0;
```

Again, notice that the member names—two occurrences of balance—are qualified with the name of the object to which the function was applied.

The function compound(), which computes and deposits the interest for one period, is defined as follows (round() is the rounding function that was discussed in Chapter 1):

```
void account::compound()
{
    double interest = round( balance * rate );
    balance += interest;
}
```

The statement

```
acct1.compound();
```

is equivalent to

```
double interest = round( acct1.balance * acct1.rate );
acct1.balance += interest;
```

Note that both `balance` and `rate` are qualified with `acct1`. The function `get_balance()` is defined by

```
double account::get_balance()
{
    return balance;
}
```

Thus the statement

```
cash = acct1.get_balance();
```

is equivalent to

```
cash = acct1.balance;
```

Constructors and Destructors

We have yet to consider how to initialize `account` variables such as `acct1` or, more generally, how to create a value of type `account`. One approach is to assign values to `acct1.balance` and `acct1.rate`:

```
account acct1;
acct1.balance = 0.0;
acct1.rate = 0.006;
```

However, these statements directly manipulate the instance variables of an object, in defiance of data hiding. When we use the `class` keyword to enforce data hiding, assignments such as these will be disallowed.

C and C++ allow `struct` variables to be initialized as follows:

```
account acct1 = { 0.0, 0.006 };
```

The values listed in braces are assigned to member variables in the order in which they appear in the `struct` declaration; thus 0.0 is assigned to `acct1.balance` and 0.006 is assigned to `acct1.rate`. However, because this also involves assignments to instance variables, it will be disallowed when data hiding is strictly enforced.

To allow convenient initialization while preserving data hiding, C++ provides for *constructors*, member functions that return initialized objects. A constructor function that returns objects of class `account` is itself named `account`. We can add a constructor to the class declaration of `account` as follows:

```
struct account {
   double balance;
   double rate;

   account( double bal, double pcnt );
   void deposit( double amt );
   double withdraw( double amt );
   void compound();
   double get_balance();
};
```

Notice that no return type is specified for the constructor `account()`. Because the constructor `account()` will always return an object of type `account`, no return type need be (nor can be) specified.

Constructors are defined much as are other member functions:

```
account::account( double bal, double pcnt )
{
   balance = bal;
   rate = pcnt / 100.0;
}
```

Again, note that no return type is specified. The constructor initializes an object of type `account` by assigning values to member variables. There is no return statement; the object initialized by the constructor is returned automatically.

The most common use of constructors is for initializing variables:

```
account acct1 = account( 1000.0, 0.6 );
account acct2 = account( 500.0, 0.5 );
```

The first statement declares `acct1` as an account object with a balance of 1000.0 and a periodic percentage rate of 0.6; the second statement declares and initializes `acct2` in similar fashion.

C++ allows the preceding statements to be abbreviated as follows:

```
account acct1( 1000.0, 0.6 );
account acct2( 500.0, 0.5 );
```

The arguments for the constructor are listed directly after the name of the object being declared.

When a constructor is declared for a class, initialization of class objects becomes mandatory. The constructor is always called when a class object is declared, and the programmer must always provide appropriate arguments for the constructor. Thus `acct1` and `acct2` must be declared using one of the forms just given. The declarations

```
account acct1;
account acct2;
```

are illegal because no arguments are provided for the constructor. Declarations in this form are allowed only when there is no constructor or when the constructor takes no arguments.

We will see presently that more than one constructor can be declared for a class, allowing several options for initialization.

A *destructor* is the complement of a constructor; just as the constructor is called immediately after an object is created, a destructor is called when an object is about to be destroyed. If an object is declared in a block (and is not declared as `static`), the destructor is called when the object *goes out of scope,* that is, when the computer reaches the end of the block in which the object was declared.

The name of a destructor is the name of the class preceded by a tilde, or "squiggle" character, ˜. A class can have only one destructor, which cannot take any arguments. Thus if `account` needed a destructor (which it doesn't), the destructor would be declared in the class declaration by

```
˜account();
```

The corresponding definition would have the form

```
account::˜account()
{
    // Statements for destructor
}
```

Destructors are used mainly in connection with the memory-management techniques discussed in Chapter 3. Another application is to output some of the data stored in an object before the object is destroyed. Exercise 5 illustrates this use of a destructor.

By default—that is, unless we explicitly specify otherwise—all the members of a `struct` are *public*. This means that all the member variables and functions can be accessed with the dot operator. Thus we can refer to `acct1.balance` and `acct1.rate` as well as calling `acct1.deposit()` and `acct1.get_balance()`. Under these circumstances, true data hiding is impossible, since users can access an object's instance variables as well as the functions that are intended for receiving and replying to message.

The keyword `class` can be used in place of `struct` to declare a class. When `class` is used, all members are *private* by default. Aside from certain exceptions, such as access from within the definition of a member function, all the member variables and member functions of an object are hidden and cannot be accessed even with the dot operator.

However, this situation is also unsatisfactory because the member functions—which are supposed to provide a user interface to objects of the class—are themselves hidden. Thus, calls such as

```
acct1.deposit( 100.0 );
```

and

```
cout << acct1.get_balance();
```

are disallowed.

The keywords `private` and `public` allow us to declare some members private and others public. All declarations following one of these keywords will be private or public, respectively, until another such keyword is encountered. Because the default for `class` is private, we need only use the keyword `public`. Thus, a version of `account` that enforces data hiding can be declared as follows:

```
class account {
    double balance;
    double rate;
public:
    account( double bal, double pcnt );
    void deposit( double amt );
    double withdraw( double amt );
    void compound();
    double get_balance();
};
```

With this declaration, the instance variables `balance` and `rate` are private; attempts to manipulate their values directly, such as

```
acct1.balance += 500.0;
```

are disallowed. Member functions, on the other hand, are public, so they can be called as usual:

```
acct1.deposit( 500.0 );
```

All member names, public and private, are still accessible from within the definitions of member functions. Therefore, the definitions of member functions do not change when we go from a `struct` to a `class` or when we use the keywords `public` and `private`.

With the `public` and `private` keywords we can declare public and private members with either `struct` or `class`. Thus it does not matter whether we use `struct` or `class` as long as we use `public` and `private` appropriately inside the declaration. Nevertheless, we will hereafter follow the usual practice of using `class` for classes with member functions and reserving `struct` for C-style structures that do not have member functions and whose member variables are all public.

Compiling and Linking

We want to use classes in our programs in the same way that we use function libraries. We would like to include a header file for each class that we wish to use. Doing so would give us full use of each class: we could use the class name to declare and initialize objects, and we could manipulate the declared objects using any public members of the class. To see how classes can be used in this way, we must look in more detail at how C++ programs are compiled.

Although compiling a C++ program can involve four or five distinct steps, your implementation probably provides a single command that will compile a C++ source file to an *executable file*—a machine-language program that the computer can execute. Such a compilation takes place in two stages, however. In the first stage, the *source file* (which contains the program) is compiled to a machine-coded file called an *object file* (this traditional name has nothing to do with object-oriented programming). The object file contains the machine code for the program statements in the source file; it does not, however, contain the code for the library functions called by the source program. Therefore, a second stage, called *linking*, is needed. Linking combines the user's object file with object files from the library, yielding an executable file that contains all the machine code needed to execute the program.

A C++ program can consist of any number of source files. Each source file is compiled separately into an object file. The resulting object files are then linked with one another and with any needed library files to yield a single executable file.

Now let's apply these considerations to our class `account`. The class declaration contains all the information that a program needs to use the class or any of its member functions. Therefore, we place the class declaration in a header file, `account.h`, which is shown in Listing 2-1. Any program that uses the class `account` will include this header file with the statement

```
#include "account.h"
```

Note the quotation marks: the names of header files written by the user are enclosed in quotation marks rather than angle brackets. The reason is that user-written header files are usually placed in a different disk directory than the header files that came with the C++ implementation. The quotation marks or angle brackets indicate where the preprocessor should look for the file to be included.

Listing 2-1

```
// File account.h
// Header file for class account
```

(continued)

```
class account {
   double balance;              // current balance
   double rate;                 // decimal periodic interest rate
public:
   account( double bal, double pcnt );   // open new account
   void deposit( double amt );           // make deposit
   double withdraw( double amt );        // attempt withdrawal
   void compound();                      // compute interest
   double get_balance();                 // return balance
};
```

The definitions of the member functions are placed in the source file account.cpp, which is shown in Listing 2-2. Note that this file includes account.h; the declarations in the header file are needed to compile the member functions. We now compile account.cpp to an object file, say account.obj. We can diagram this step as follows:

compile

account.cpp ————————————> account.obj

Naming conventions for object and executable files vary; we will use the MS-DOS conventions because they employ the obvious abbreviations .obj and .exe.

Listing 2-2

```
// File account.cpp
// Source file for class account

#include "account.h"

double round( double amt );   // round to two decimal places

// Open account with starting balance bal and
// periodic percentage rate pcnt

account::account( double bal, double pcnt )
{
   balance = bal;
   rate = pcnt / 100.0;
}
```

```
// Deposit amount amt

void account::deposit( double amt )
{
    balance += amt;
}


// Attempt to withdraw amount amt;
// return amount actually withdrawn

double account::withdraw( double amt )
{
    if ( amt <= balance ) {
        balance -= amt;
        return amt;
    }
    else
        return 0.0;
}


// Compute interest for current period and add to balance

void account::compound()
{
    double interest =  round( balance * rate );
    balance += interest;
}


// Return current balance

double account::get_balance()
{
    return balance;
}


// Round amt to two decimal places

double round( double amt )
{
    long cents = long( 100.0 * amt + 0.5 );
    return double( cents ) / 100.0;
}
```

Now suppose we want to use the class `account` in the program `balance`, whose source file `balance.cpp` is shown in Listing 2-3. Note that this program also includes the header file `account.h`. The program that uses a class must also be compiled to an object file:

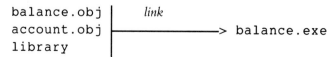

The resulting object file, `balance.obj`, must be linked with `account.obj` and any needed library files to produce the final executable program:

```
balance.obj |     link
account.obj |————————————> balance.exe
library     |
```

Unfortunately, the commands for actually carrying out these compiling and linking operations vary enormously among different computer systems and C++ implementations. For information on compiling and linking commands, you must depend on an instructor, a reference manual, or a local expert.

Separate compilation saves time because, when changes are made in a program, only the source files that have been changed need to be recompiled. Indeed, many implementations provide a utility program called `make`, which manages all the compilation and linking for a programming project; `make` recompiles only those source files that have been changed since the most recent previous compilation. Also, separate compilation encourages programmers to create generally useful object files and libraries that they can reuse in their own programming and share with other programmers. Code reuse and sharing are major themes of object-oriented programming.

Listing 2-3

```
// File balance.cpp
// Compute amount in bank account

#include <iostream.h>
#include "account.h"

main()
{
```

```cpp
    // Get input data from user

        double balance;                 // current balance
        double deposit;                 // monthly deposit
        double annual_pcnt_rate;        // annual percentage rate
        int months;                     // number of months

        cout << "Starting balance: ";
        cin >> balance;

        cout << "Monthly deposit: ";
        cin >> deposit;

        cout << "Annual percentage rate: ";
        cin >> annual_pcnt_rate;

        cout << "Number of months: ";
        cin >> months;

    // Compute new balance

        account acct( balance, annual_pcnt_rate / 12.0 );

        for ( int m = 0; m < months; m++ ) {
            acct.deposit( deposit );
            acct.compound();
        }

    // Print balance

        cout << "Balance after " << months << " months = $";
        cout << acct.get_balance() << endl;
    }
```

Although separate compilation of classes is the norm for professional programming, it is not always convenient for simple examples and exercises. If we don't want to bother with multiple source files and compilations, we can put class declarations, member function definitions, and a program into a single source file and compile everything with a single command. Put the class declarations at the beginning of the source file and follow each class declaration with the definitions of its member functions; the program that uses the classes comes last. In this book we will usually use separate compilation but will occasionally use a single source file for short examples.

Example: A Program Using Class account

The program in Listing 2-3 is a version of the program `balance` that we studied in Chapter 1; this version, however, uses an object of class `account` to accept deposits and compound interest.

This version of the program, like the original, uses variables named `balance` and `deposit`; however, the class `account` also has members named `balance` and `deposit`. Because the scope of member names is the class declaration, no conflict between the variable names and the member names can occur. Although using the same name for different things in the same program is not a recommended programming style, we do it in this example to illustrate the restricted scope of member names.

As in the original version, this program begins by obtaining input data from the user. It then uses the starting balance and the interest rate to declare an `account` object:

```
account acct( balance, annual_pcnt_rate / 12.0 );
```

The variable `balance` is the one declared in this program and used to hold the starting balance; it has nothing to do with the member variable `balance` in the declaration for `account`. Because interest will be compounded monthly, the annual percentage rate is divided by 12 to get the monthly percentage rate that is required by the constructor.

A `for` statement calls `acct.deposit()` to make each month's deposit and `acct.compound()` to compound the interest each month:

```
for ( int m = 0; m < months; m++ ) {
    acct.deposit( deposit );
    acct.compound();
}
```

In the statement

```
acct.deposit( deposit );
```

the compiler cannot confuse the two uses of the identifier `deposit`. The qualified name `acct.deposit` must refer to the member function of `account`; the unqualified name `deposit` must refer to the variable `deposit` declared in the program. Although the compiler has no trouble with this statement, it may still be confusing to human readers, which is why using the same name for different entitites should be avoided when possible.

After the deposits have been made and interest has been compounded for the required number of months, the function `acct.get_balance()` is called to get the final balance, which is printed for the user.

MORE ABOUT MEMBER FUNCTIONS

In this section we look at four more properties of member functions. *Function-name overloading* and *default arguments* can increase the convenience of writing C++ programs; *inline functions* can increase the speed with which those programs execute. *Constant functions* allow us to specify which member functions can be applied to constant objects.

Although our focus here will be on member functions, we note that overloading, default arguments, and inlining can also be used with functions that are not a member of any class.

Function Overloading

C++ allows function names and operator symbols to be *overloaded*. That is, the same function name or operator symbol can be given several different definitions; the types and number of arguments supplied to a function or operator determine which definition will be used.

The arithmetic operators +, −, *, and / are good examples of overloading: these operators can be applied to values of types `int`, `long`, `float`, `double`, and `long double`, although different machine instructions or library routines are required for each type. The insertion and extraction operators, << and >>, are also overloaded, because a different definition is required for each type that is to be read or written. For example, each of the following statements invokes a different definition of <<:

```
cout << 250;
cout << 3.1416;
cout << '\n';
cout << "Now is the time";
```

We can provide additional overloading for << and >> by providing additional definitions for user-defined types; for example, we could provide such a definition for type account, so that << and >> would input and output values of type account in some format of our choosing.

What's more, all uses of << and >> for input and output are made possible by overloading, because according to the built-in definitions of << and >>, these operators shift bits to the right or left within an integer value. The built-in definitions are invoked when both operands belong to integer types. Thus the expression

```
175 << 5
```

yields the result of taking the binary code for 175 and shifting all the bits five places to the left. (The use of << and >> for bit shifting is discussed further in Chapter 8.)

We will confine our attention here to functions; operator overloading will be taken up in Chapter 4. Consider a function square() that returns the square of its argument. If the argument is long, we want the function to carry out the computation using long-integer arithmetic and return a long result; if the argument is double, we want the function to carry out the computation using double-precision floating-point arithmetic and return a double result. To accomplish this, we need two versions of the function, which we declare as follows:

```
long square( long );       // long version
double square( double );   // double version
```

We must provide a separate definition for each declaration:

```
long square( long n )
{
    return n * n;
}
```

for the long-integer version and

```
double square( double x )
{
    return x * x;
}
```

for the double-precision floating-point version. The similarity of the two definitions is due in part to the fact that the operator * is already overloaded, so that the `long` multiplication and the `double` multiplication are represented by the same operator. Of course, the definitions could be completely different, if that were appropriate for our purpose.

When an overloaded function name appears in a function call, the types and number of the actual arguments determine which definition will be used. A series of rules governs how the compiler matches the types of actual and formal arguments. The rules given in the Release 2.0 reference manual are rather complex and involve aspects of C++ that we have not yet studied; the following simplified rules will suffice for most purposes:

1. The compiler first tries to find an exact match in which the types of the actual and formal arguments are the same. Thus `square( 25L )` yields a `long` result and `square( 25.0 )` yields a `double` result.

2. If an exact match fails, the compiler applies any possible promotions to the actual argument. The promotions in question are the integral promotions (such as from `char` to `int`) and a special promotion from `float` to `double` that is used only in argument matching. Because of the promotion from `float` to `double`, the expression `square( 3.14F )` is valid; the float argument will be converted to type `double` and the `double` version of the function will be called.

3. If the preceding steps fail, the compiler will try to use the standard conversions (the implicit conversions that can take place during an assignment) to convert each actual argument to the type of a corresponding formal argument. Any conversion that is found must be unique; if more than one conversion is possible, the compiler will give an error message. For example, `square( 100 )` will cause an error message because the `int` argument can be converted to either `long` or `double`, leaving the compiler in doubt as to which version of `square()` should be used.

4. If all else fails, the compiler will try user-defined conversions, such as those discussed later in this section. User-defined conversions can be combined with promotions and standard conversions; however, any sequence of conversions can contain at most one user-defined conversion. As in rule 3, the sequence of conversions that is found must be unique; the compiler will give an error message if more than one sequence of conversions is possible.

For example, amounts of money are often stored as an integral number of cents to avoid the inaccuracies inherent in floating-point arithmetic (thus $12.95 would be stored as 1295). Let us rewrite class `account` so that `deposit()` and `withdraw()` will accept an amount either as a double-precision dollars-and-cents value or as a long-integer number of cents; `withdraw()` will return its result in the same form as its argument. We include declarations for the alternative versions of each function in the class declaration:

```
class account {
    double balance;
    double rate;
public:
    account( double bal, double pcnt );
    void deposit( double amt );     // overloaded
    void deposit( long amt );
    double withdraw( double amt );   // overloaded
    long withdraw( long amt );
    void compound();
    double get_balance();
};
```

The double-precision versions of `deposit()` and `withdraw()` are the same as before. The `long` version of `deposit()` can be defined as follows:

```
void account::deposit( long amt )
{
    balance += double( amt ) / 100.0;
}
```

The `long` version of `withdraw()` is defined similarly:

```
long account::withdraw( long amt )
{
    double amt_d = double( amt ) / 100.0;
    if ( amt_d <= balance ) {
        balance -= amt_d;
        return amt;
    }
    else
        return 0L;
}
```

We can also overload the constructor name, and doing so is particularly useful because it allows us to provide several options for initializing objects. For example, we might provide `account` with three constructors:

```
account();
account( double bal );
account( double bal, double pcnt );
```

We can define the first two constructors by assuming that, in the absence of information to the contrary, an account will be opened with a balance of zero and an interest rate of 0.005 (6 percent annually):

```
account::account()
{
    balance = 0.0;
    rate = 0.005;
}
```

```
account::account( double bal )
{
    balance = bal;
    rate = 0.005;
}
```

We now have three ways to declare an object of type `account`. The declaration

```
account acct1;
```

invokes the constructor with no arguments; `acct1` is created with a balance of zero and a rate of 0.005. (Note that no parentheses are necessary in the declaration when the constructor message is sent with no arguments.) The declaration

```
account acct2( 500.0 );
```

invokes the constructor with one argument; `acct2` is created with a balance of 500.0 and a rate of 0.005. Finally, the declaration

```
account acct3( 1000.0, 0.6 );
```

uses the constructor with three arguments; `acct3` is created with a balance of 1000.0 and a rate of 0.006 (recall that the constructor divides its second argument by 100).

A constructor with one argument may be taken to define a type conversion; this is the user-defined conversion referred to earlier. Thus

```
account acct2 = account( 500.0 );
```

is on the same footing as

```
double x = double( 100 );
```

In each case a type name is used to convert an argument value to the named type.

Type conversions defined by constructors can be applied implicitly in initializations and assignments. For example, we could declare `acct2` by

```
account acct2 = 500.0;
```

and later assign it a different value by

```
acct2 = 1000.0;
```

In each case, the constructor with one argument would be called to convert from type `double` to type `account`.

A user-defined conversion can be combined with promotions and standard conversions. Thus the preceding declaration and assignment can be written as follows:

```
account acct2 = 500;
acct2 = 1000;
```

In each case, the `int` value is converted to `double` (by a standard conversion) before the constructor is applied.

It is illegal for two functions to differ only in their return type, as in

```
long square( long );
double square( long );    // invalid
```

When an overloaded function is called, the types of the arguments (and only the arguments) determine which definition will be used; the return type plays no role in this process. If functions differing only in their return type were allowed it would be impossible to determine which definition to use when the overloaded function was called.

Default Arguments

In many cases we can obtain the benefits of overloading without the use of multiple definitions by providing default arguments in a function declaration. For example, our three declarations for the constructor `account()` could all be replaced by

```
account( double bal = 0.0, double pcnt = 0.5 );
```

with the corresponding definition

```
account::account( double bal, double pcnt )
{
    balance = bal;
    rate = pcnt / 100.0;
}
```

The values following the = signs in the declaration are *default arguments*; each is used when no corresponding actual argument is supplied. Note that the default arguments are specified in the *declaration*, not the *definition*.

For example,

```
account()
```

is equivalent to

```
account( 0.0, 0.5 )
```

and

```
account( 500.0 )
```

is equivalent to

```
account( 500.0, 0.5 )
```

Thus the declaration

```
account acct2;
```

is equivalent to

```
account acct2( 0.0, 0.5 );
```

and

```
account acct2( 500.0 );
```

is equivalent to

```
account acct2( 500.0, 0.5 );
```

Default values do not have to be supplied for all the arguments of a function. For example, the declaration

```
account( double bal, double pcnt = 0.5 );
```

allows the second argument of `account()` to be omitted, but not the first. In C++, only trailing arguments can be omitted when a function is called. That is, we can omit arguments only by dropping them off the end of the argument list; we cannot omit an argument without omitting all those that follow it. For this reason, only a series of trailing arguments can be given default values. Thus the declaration

```
account( double bal = 0.0, double pcnt );
```

is invalid because there is no way to call `account()` with the first argument omitted but the second present.

For the same reasons, the declaration

```
int three( int m, int p = 0, int q = 0 );
```

is valid and allows either the third argument or both the second and third arguments to be omitted. However, the declaration

```
int three( int m = 0, int p, int q = 0 );
```

is invalid because there is no way to omit the first argument without omitting the second.

Inline Expansion

Object-oriented programming uses functions to control access to the instance variables of an object. Consequently, an object-oriented program contains many function calls, and many function definitions consist only of the few statements needed to access the values of one or more private variables. For example, the definitions of `account::deposit()` and `account::get_balance()` contain only a single statement each.

Unfortunately, a certain amount of computational overhead is associated with each function call and return. A memory area has to be allocated for the called function's arguments and local variables, and argument values have to be copied to the proper locations in the called function's memory area. If a function accomplishes a substantial task, then the time required for call and return will be small in comparison to the time spent doing useful work. But if each called function executes only a statement or two, then a substantial percentage of the computer's time may be spent calling and returning from functions.

A solution to this problem is *inline expansion*, which replaces each function call by the statements that define the function, modified as needed to simulate argument passing and value return. For example, the function call

```
acctl.deposit( 100.0 );
```

might be replaced with the inline expansion

```
acctl.balance += 100.0;
```

and the function call

```
double cash = acctl.get_balance();
```

might be replaced with the inline expansion

```
double cash = acctl.balance;
```

Because inline expansions are derived from the definitions of member functions, they are allowed access to both the private and public members of an object.

The following are the pros and cons of inline expansion:

- *Pro:* Inline expansion can make a program run faster because the overhead of function call and return is eliminated.

- *Con:* Inline expansion can make a program take up more memory because the statements that define the function are reproduced at each point where the function is called.

For functions with very short definitions, inline expansion wins because it eliminates function call-and-return overhead without appreciably increasing the size of the program. For functions with long definitions, inline expansion loses because the time saved is small compared to the time required for function execution, and the size of the program is increased substantially.

C++ provides two ways to request inline expansion of functions. One way is to precede the function definition with the keyword `inline`. Thus, we could define `deposit()` and `get_balance()` as inline functions as follows:

```
inline void account::deposit( double amt )
{
    balance += amt;
}

inline double account::get_balance()
{
    return balance;
}
```

The `inline` keyword is merely a request that inline expansion be used with this function; the compiler can ignore this request if the function definition is too long or too complicated. Note, however, that the *semantics*, or meaning, of a function call or definition is exactly the same whether or not inline expansion is requested and whether or not the compiler chooses to grant the request. Inline functions can always be used exactly like conventional functions.

Listings 2-4 and 2-5 show the header and source files for a version of class `account` in which inline expansion has been requested for the functions `deposit()` and `get_balance()`. Note that the definitions of the inline functions have been placed in the header file, *not* in the source file. Because each call to an inline function is replaced with the function's definition, every source file that calls an inline function needs the full text of its definition, not just its declaration.

Listing 2-4

```
// File account1.h
// Header file for class account

class account {
    double balance;                        // current balance
    double rate;                           // interest rate
public:
    account( double bal, double pcnt );    // open new account
    void deposit( double amt );            // make deposit
    double withdraw( double amt );         // attempt withdrawal
    void compound();                       // compute interest
    double get_balance();                  // return balance
};

// Deposit amount amt

inline void account::deposit( double amt )
{
    balance += amt;
}

// Return current balance

inline double account::get_balance()
{
    return balance;
}
```

Listing 2-5

```
// File account1.cpp
// Source file for class account

#include "account1.h"

double round( double amt );   // round to two decimal places
```
(continued)

```cpp
// Open account with starting balance bal and
// periodic percentage rate pcnt

account::account( double bal, double pcnt )
{
    balance = bal;
    rate = pcnt / 100.0;
}


// Attempt to withdraw amount amt;
// return amount actually withdrawn

double account::withdraw( double amt )
{
    if ( amt <= balance ) {
        balance -= amt;
        return amt;
    }
    else
        return 0.0;
}


// Compute interest for current period and add to balance

void account::compound()
{
    double interest =  round( balance * rate );
    balance += interest;
}


// Round amt to two decimal places

double round( double amt )
{
    long cents = long( 100.0 * amt + 0.5 );
    return double( cents ) / 100.0;
}
```

Listing 2-6

```
// File account2.h
// Header file for class account

class account {
    double balance;                          // current balance
    double rate;                             // interest rate
public:
    account( double bal, double pcnt );   // open new account
    void deposit( double amt )            // make deposit
        { balance += amt; }
    double withdraw( double amt );           // attempt withdrawal
    void compound();                         // compute interest
    double get_balance()                     // return balance
        { return balance; }
};
```

Listing 2-6 shows the second way to declare an inline function: placing the complete definition of the function in a class declaration. Any function that is defined (not just declared) inside a class declaration is considered to be an inline function; the keyword `inline` is not needed:

```
class account {
    double balance;
    double rate;
public:
    account( double bal, double pcnt );
    void deposit( double amt )
        { balance += amt; }
    double withdraw( double amt );
    void compound();
    double get_balance()
        { return balance; }
};
```

Because definitions for `deposit()` and `get_balance()` are included in the class declaration, calls to these functions (most likely) will be expanded inline. Listings 2-6 and 2-4 are equivalent; either header file can be used with the source file in Listing 2-5.

To save space in class declarations, the block that defines an inline function is often written on a single line, which can be the same line that contains the function heading. Thus the definitions of `deposit()` and `get_balance()` could be written even more compactly as follows:

```
void deposit( double amt ) { balance += amt; }
double get_balance() { return balance; }
```

When we include the definition of an inline function in a class declaration, the definition also serves as a *declaration* for the function. It can, therefore, specify default arguments, which are specified in declarations. Thus if we define (and declare) `deposit()` by

```
void deposit( double amt = 100.0 )
    { balance += amt; }
```

the call

```
acct1.deposit();
```

is valid and equivalent to

```
acct1.deposit( 100.0 );
```

Constant Objects and Functions

Chapter 1 introduced constant data objects whose values cannot be changed. Class objects can also be declared as constant data objects; for example,

```
const account acct4( 10000, 0.5 );
```

declares `acct4` as a constant `account` object. The identifier `acct4` is an unmodifiable lvalue and so cannot appear on the left side of an assignment operator.

Class objects, however, are usually modified not by assignment but by applying member functions. Thus statements such as

```
acct4.deposit( 100 );
```

and

```
acct4.compound();
```

must also be forbidden because they modify `acct4` — that is, they change the values of some of its instance variables. Yet a blanket prohibition against applying any member function to a constant object goes too far. For example, the statement

```
cout << acct4.get_balance();
```

does not change any instance variables of `acct4` and so should be allowed.

C++ allows us to specify which member functions can be applied to constant objects by including the keyword `const` in the function declarations and definitions. Member functions not declared as `const` cannot be applied to constant objects. Member functions that are declared as `const` cannot modify any of the instance variables of an object; such a function treats all the instance variables as if they were constant objects.

The only member function of class `account` that can be declared as `const` is `get_balance()`, which does not modify any instance variables. Attempting to declare `deposit()`, `withdraw()`, or `compound()` as constant would produce a compiler error message because each of those functions modifies the instance variable `balance`.

The keyword `const` appears after the function heading in both the declaration and the definition of a `const` function. To declare `get_balance()` as `const`, its declaration in class `account` is changed from

```
double get_balance();
```

to

```
double get_balance() const;
```

The definition of `get_balance()` is likewise changed to include `const`:

```
double account::get_balance() const
{
    return balance;
}
```

Inline definitions are changed in the same way. Thus an inline definition of `get_balance()` would be changed to

```
double get_balance() const
    { return balance; }
```

or (if the definition is written on a single line) to

```
double get_balance() const { return balance; }
```

Because of these changes, get_balance() is declared as const, whereas deposit(), withdraw(), and compound() are not. Thus, for the constant object acct4, statements such as

```
double b = acct4.get_balance();
```

and

```
cout << acct4.get_balance();
```

are valid, whereas statements such as

```
acct4.deposit( 1000 );
acct4.withdraw( 500 );
acct4.compound();
```

are invalid and produce compiler error messages.

LINKAGE

This section provides additional information about identifiers that, courtesy of the linking process, can be used in source files other than the one in which they were defined. Note, however, that almost all our uses of separately compiled source files will follow the simple patterns already illustrated; therefore this section can be skimmed on a first reading.

Just as the *scope* of an identifier governs its accessibility within a single source file, so its *linkage* governs its accessibility in all the source files that are compiled and linked to form a C++ program. An identifier with *internal linkage* is accessible only within the source file in which it is declared; it has no connection with any identifier in any other source file. An identifier with *external linkage* is accessible from all the source files that make up a program.

If an identifier is declared with external linkage in several source files then all such declarations refer to the same entity (data object, function, or class), which can be accessed via the identifier from each source file. Release 2.0 of C++ imposes an additional restriction known as *type-safe linkage*: all the declarations for an identifier must specify the same kind of entity and must specify the same types. For example, if one declaration specifies a function, all other declarations of the same identifier must specify a function with the same argument and return types.

The following are the default linkages for several kinds of identifiers; these defaults will apply unless the programmer explicitly specifies a different linkage in the identifier declaration:

- Local identifiers have internal linkage.

- The names of global variables—those declared with file scope—have external linkage.

- Constant identifiers declared with `const` have internal linkage.

- The names of non-inline functions have external linkage.

- The names of inline functions have internal linkage.

We can override these defaults by using the keyword `static` to force internal linkage and the keyword `extern` to force external linkage. Thus

```
static int fctn( int, int );
```

declares a function whose name, `fctn`, has internal linkage. Likewise,

```
extern const MAX_COUNT = 25;
```

defines a constant identifer, `MAX_COUNT`, which has external linkage.

Normally, a class name has external linkage. A class name will have internal linkage only in the unusual situation where all three of the following conditions are met: (1) all member functions are inline, (2) the class is not used to declare any data object or function with external linkage, and (3) the class has no static members (static members are discussed in Chapter 6).

Type names other than class names always have internal linkage. Specifically, the names of enumeration types have internal linkage.

Among all the *declarations* of a data object or function with external linkage, there must be exactly one *definition*. If there is no definition, or if there is more than one, the linker—the system program that combines object files—will give an error message. Note that the compiler does not consider a missing definition to be an error if the identifier has external linkage, because the definition may be in another source file. Only the linker can determine that an identifier is not defined in any of the object files being linked.

Header files often contain *declarations* of identifiers with external linkage; this assures that the corresponding identifiers will be declared in the same way in every source file that includes the header file. On the other hand, *definitions* for identifiers with external linkage must not be placed in header files; doing so would cause the identifier to be defined in more than one source file, which would cause the linker to give a "multiple definitions" error message. Identifiers with internal linkage can be safely defined in header files; for example, constant identifiers, inline functions, and enumerated types are frequently defined in header files.

EXERCISES

1. Chapter 1 presented a program for Fibonacci's rabbit problem. As we did with the bank-interest program, let's modify the rabbit program to use object-oriented techniques. Define a class `farm`, each of whose instances represents a rabbit farm where the rabbits reproduce according to Fibonacci's rules. The external interface for a `farm` object consists of the following three functions:

```
farm( long fertile, long nonfertile );
void next_month( );
long pairs( );
```

The constructor `farm( )` creates an object with given numbers of fertile and nonfertile pairs. The function `next_month( )` updates the object's instance variables to reflect the passage of one month's time. The function `pairs( )` returns the current number of pairs. Use this class to write programs for solving the original rabbit problem (how many pairs after a given number of months) and the inverse problem (how many months to get a given number of pairs).

2. Define a class `counter` whose instances represent hand-held counting devices of the kind sometimes used for taking inventory. Each `counter` object has the following external interface:

```
counter( int max_count );
void increment();
void reset();
int get_count();
int check_for_overflow();
```

The constructor creates a counter with a given maximum count. For example,

```
counter cnt( 9999 );
```

creates a counter that can count through 9999; a newly created counter has a reading of 0. The function incre-ment() increases the current count by one; if the current count equals the maximum count, the count is set to 0 and the counter remembers that an overflow took place. The function reset() sets the counter to 0 and clears the overflow indicator; get_count() returns the current count; and check_for_overflow() returns 1 (*true*) if an overflow has occurred and 0 (*false*) if it has not. Write a program that counts the number of A's, B's, and so on, in set of student grades. The program should use a separate counter for each possible letter grade, and it should print an error message if any of the counters overflows.

3. Define a class clock for representing digital clocks. Each clock object has the following public interface:

```
clock();
void set_hours( int hours, int am_or_pm );
void set_minutes( minutes );
void set_seconds( seconds );
void tick();
void display();
```

The constructor creates a clock with the reading 12:00:00 A.M. The three set_ functions set hours, minutes, and seconds; the value of hours ranges from 1 through 12, and the value of am_or_pm is 0 for A.M. and 1 for P.M. The function tick() advances the time by one second, and the function display() prints the current time on cout. Write a program to test this class. A good test for tick() is to verify that it changes 11:59:59 A.M. to 12:00:00 P.M. and 11:59:59 P.M. to 12:00:00 A.M.

4. Define a class `robot` for robots with the following properties. The location of a robot is given by two integer coordinates: `x` for its east-west position and `y` for its north-south position (`x` increases as the robot moves east and `y` increases as the robot moves north). The robot can face in any of four directions defined by

```
enum direction { EAST, NORTH, WEST, SOUTH };
```

The public interface for a robot is as follows:

```
robot( int x, int y, direction d );
void move( int distance );
void left_face();
void right_face();
int x_position();
int y_position();
direction orientation();
```

The constructor creates a robot in a given location and facing in a given direction. The function `move()` moves the robot a given distance in the direction it is facing; this is done by adding or subtracting the distance from the appropriate coordinate. The functions `left_face()` and `right_face()` turn the robot to the left or right by 90 degrees; `x_position()`, `y_position()`, and `orientation()` return the robot's current location and the direction in which it is facing. Write a program that lets the user create a robot and move it about at will. After each user command, the program will print the current location and orientation of the robot.

5. An object is often used to represent and communicate with some system component, such as a piece of hardware or software. In this spirit, let us make our bank-interest program even more object-oriented by employing an object to represent the user. When this object is created, it will obtain the required input data from the user. The rest of the program will access this data and update the balance via the user-object's public interface. When the end of its lifetime is reached, the object will write the number of months and the updated balance to the user's display.

Specifically, define a class `user` with the following public interface (note that `~user` is a destructor):

```
user();
~user();
double get_balance();
double get_deposit();
double get_apr();
int get_months();
void put_balance( double bal );
```

The constructor `user()`, which is called when a `user` object is declared, will obtain the starting balance, monthly deposit, annual percentage rate, and number of months from the user and store these in instance variables.

The destructor `~user()`, which is called just before a `user` object is destroyed, will print (in the same form used by the existing balance program) the number of months and the current value of balance.

During execution of the balance program, the `get_` functions will be used to access the input data. The program will start by creating both a `user` object and an `account` object:

```
user u;
account acct( u.get_balance(), u.get_apr() / 12.0 );
```

The user object must be created first because some of the input data is used in initializing the account object. The `get_` functions are called as needed. For example, the `for` statement that governs the deposit and interest calculations has the following form:

```
for ( int m = 0; m < u.get_months(); m++ ) {
    // deposit and interest calculations
}
```

When the calculation is complete, the program will transfer the result from `acct` to u:

```
u.put_balance( acct.get_balance() );
```

This value will be printed automatically when u goes out of scope—when the computer reaches the end of the block in which u is declared.

3 Arrays, Pointers, and References

W E C A N refer to data objects by either their addresses or their names (lvalues). So far, we have not had occasion to refer to data objects by their addresses, and for names we have used only simple and qualified identifiers such as `acct` and `acct.balance`. This chapter focuses on more flexible means of designating data objects, means that involve names, addresses, and the relationships between the two.

A second theme of this chapter is *dynamic memory allocation*, which gives the programmer complete control of the lifetimes of data objects. Dynamically allocated data objects are created when they are needed and remain in existence until they are explicitly destroyed; this behavior is in contrast to the preordained lifetime rules that apply to data objects with storage classes static and automatic.

Designating data objects and allocating memory are not unrelated because we need powerful and flexible means for referring to individual data objects within the blocks of memory that we allocate.

ARRAYS

As in other programming languages, a C++ array is a series of data objects all of which have the same type; these data objects are called the *elements* of the array. We declare an array by giving the type of its elements, the name of the array, and the number of elements. For example,

```
int a[ 5 ];
```

declares a as an array of five int data objects; that is, as a series of five memory locations, each capable of holding a value of type int. Likewise,

```
double x[ 100 ];
```

declares an array of 100 data objects of type double.

We can initialize an array when it is declared by listing the initial values for its elements, as follows:

```
int a[ 5 ] = { 75, 25, 100, -45, 60 };
```

This array is illustrated in Figure 3-1. If the number of initial values given is less than the number of elements in the array, the remaining elements are initialized to zero. Thus

```
int b[ 5 ] = { 75, 25 };
```

is equivalent to

```
int b[ 5 ] = { 75, 25, 0, 0, 0 };
```

If we do not specify the number of elements for an initialized array, the number of initial values supplied determines the number of elements. Thus

```
int a[] = { 75, 25, 100, -45, 60 };
```

declares a as an array of five elements.

Static arrays—those declared outside of any block or declared with the keyword static—are initialized to zeros if no other initialization is specified by the user. Non-static uninitialized arrays contain garbage.

As illustrated in Figure 3-1, the elements of the array a are designated by a[0], a[1], a[2], and so on, through a[4]. The integers in brackets are *subscripts* and range from 0 through one less than the number of elements in the array. Thus if an array has 10 elements, the subscripts range from 0 through 9; if the array has 50 elements, the subscripts range from 0 through 49. Subscripts can be expressions as well as constants. Thus a[i + j] refers to the element of a designated by the value of the integer expression i + j.

Subscripted array identifiers are modifiable★ lvalues that can

---

★ The lvalue referring to an array element is modifiable *unless* the array elements have been declared constant.

Figure 3-1

The array a has five elements,
which are numbered 0 through 4.
The elements, which are them-
selves data objects, are named by
the lvalues a [0] *through*
a [4], *which can be used to*
refer to the values of the elements
or to assign new values to them.

a

a[0]	75
a[1]	25
a[2]	100
a[3]	−45
a[4]	60

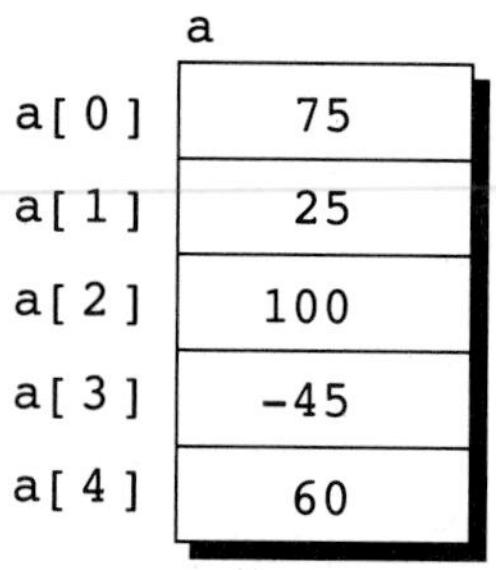

be used just like any other variable names to access the values of array elements and to assign new values to them. Thus

```
cout << a[ 2 ];
```

prints the value of element 2 of a, and

```
a[ 3 ] = 39;
```

assigns 39 to element 3 of a.

Consider the array c declared by

```
const SIZE = 1000;
int c[ SIZE ];
```

Subscripts for c range from 0 through SIZE − 1. A for state-ment for processing all the elements of c has the form

```
for ( int i = 0; i < SIZE; i++ ) {
    // Process element c[ i ]
}
```

Because the less-than sign, < (rather than the less-than-or-equal-to sign, <=), is used, the values of i will range from 0 through SIZE − 1. For example, the statement

```
for ( int i = 0; i < SIZE; i++ )
    c[ i ] = 50;
```

sets all the elements of c to 50.

Assignment for an entire array is *not* allowed. Thus we cannot write

```
b = a;    // invalid
```

to assign the elements of a to the corresponding elements of b.

Instead, we must use a `for` statement to carry out the assignment for each pair of corresponding elements:

```
for ( int i = 0; i < 5; i++ )
    b[ i ] = a[ i ];
```

Expressions such as `c[ i++ ]` and `c[ i-- ]` are frequently used in array processing. After the current value of `i` is used as an array subscript, the value of `i` is incremented or decremented; thus the next time `i` is used as a subscript it will refer to the next (for ++) or previous (for --) array element.

For example, the statement

```
c[ i++ ] = 50;
```

assigns 50 to `c[ i ]` and increments the value of `i`; if the statement is executed repeatedly, 50 will be assigned to successive elements of `c`. Thus the statements

```
i = 101;
for ( j = 0; j < 10; j ++ )
    c[ i++ ] = 50;
```

assign 50 to elements 101 through 110 of array `c`.

There is one pitfall we must beware of. As discussed in Chapter 1, we cannot predict the order in which parts of an expression will be evaluated. Therefore, a variable to which ++ or -- has been applied should not be used elsewhere in the same expression, because we cannot be sure when its value will be incremented or decremented. For example, to copy the value of `a[ i ]` to `b[ i ]` and then increment the value of `i`, we might be tempted to write

```
b[ i ] = a[ i++ ];   // wrong
```

Unfortunately, we cannot predict the effect of this statement because we do not know whether the value of `i` will be incremented before or after `i` is used as a subscript of `b`. Therefore, we should instead write

```
b[ i ] = a[ i ];
i++;
```

The elements of an array can be class objects. We recall that if a class defines constructors, then every declaration of a class object *must* initialize the object with one of the constructors; the declaration is invalid if none of the constructors can be applied.

The same is true of arrays of class objects; if the class defines constructors then they *must* be used to initialize the elements of the array.

Let us use the class `account` from Chapter 2 as an example. The declaration

```
account acct[ 3 ];
```

is valid only if (1) class `account` does not define any constructors or (2) class `account` defines a constructor that can be called with zero arguments (either because the constructor has no arguments or because default values are provided for all arguments). When there is a constructor that can be called with zero arguments, the above declaration is an abbreviation for

```
account acct[ 3 ] = { account(),
                      account(),
                      account() };
```

in which the constructor is called with zero arguments to initialize each element.

If class `account` defines a constructor with one `double` argument, the following declaration is valid:

```
account acct[ 3 ] = { account( 1000.0 ),
                      account( 250.75 ),
                      account( 599.83 ) };
```

This can be abbreviated to

```
account acct[ 3 ] = { 1000.0, 250.75, 599.83 };
```

Because the one-argument constructor is treated as a type conversion, it will be applied automatically to convert each of the initial values from type `double` to type `account`.

If some initializers (expressions for initial values) are omitted, the constructor is called with zero arguments to initialize the corresponding array elements. Thus

```
account acct[ 3 ] = { 1000.0 };
```

is equivalent to

```
account acct[ 3 ] = { account( 1000.0 ),
                      account(),
                      account() };
```

Clearly, initializers can be omitted only if there is a constructor that can be called with zero arguments.

If `account` also defines a constructor with two `double` arguments, we can use the following declaration, which illustrates calling several different constructors in the same declaration:

```
account acct[ 3 ] = { account( 575.98, 0.65 ),
                      account(),
                      account( 100.0 ) };
```

POINTERS

A pointer is the address of a data object *of a particular type*. The type is essential for using the data object designated by the address. The address merely gives the beginning of the memory area that contains the data object. The type determines the size of the data object, the functions and operators that can be applied to it, and which definitions should be used for overloaded functions and operators. Thus we do not have a single pointer type for all addresses. Instead, we have type pointer-to-`int` for addresses of `int` data objects, type pointer-to-`double` for addresses of `double` data objects, and so on.

Figure 3-2 illustrates a pointer variable `p` and the data object pointed to by the value of `p`. In diagrams, a pointer is represented by an arrow that begins in the pointer variable and terminates on the *target data object*—the data object that is pointed to by the pointer variable. The expression `*p` refers to the data object pointed to by `p`; `*p` is a modifiable* lvalue, so it can be used both to refer to the value of the target data object and to assign new values to it. For example, if `p` points to an `int` data object, then

```
cout << *p;
```

prints the stored value, and

```
*p = 25;
```

assigns a new value to the data object.

The unary operator `*` is called the *indirection operator* because it allows a data object to be referred to indirectly, via an identifier naming a pointer variable, rather than directly, via an identifier naming the data object itself. Do not confuse the unary operator

---

* The lvalue `*p` is modifiable *unless* the object pointed to by p has been declared constant.

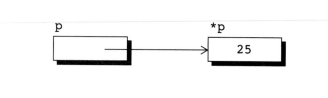

* with the binary operator *, which is the multiplication operator. In Appendix 2, note that the precedence and associativity of the unary operator * is the same as that of most other unary operators.

The term *pointer* is applied to both pointer variables and to the addresses they contain; the context in which the word is used determines whether a pointer variable or a pointer value (an address) is meant.

We declare a pointer variable by declaring the type of the target data object:

```
int *p;
double *q;
```

Because *p names an `int` data object, p must point to such an object; we say that p has the type pointer-to-`int`. Likewise, because *q names a `double` data object, the type of q must be pointer-to-`double`.

The preceding example illustrates the style in which pointer declarations are usually written in C. Many C++ programmers use a slightly different style:

```
int* p;
double* q;
```

In this style, we think of `int*` as designating the type pointer-to-`int` and of `double*` as designating the type pointer-to-`double`. Note that the difference between the two sets of declarations is purely a matter of style: spaces before and after an operator are optional, so the compiler processes the two sets of declarations in exactly the same way. In fact,

```
int*p;
double*q;
```

and

```
int * p;
double * q;
```

are also valid. The first of these is too hard to read, but the second is popular with some programmers.

In this book we will generally use the C++ style for pointer declarations. One pitfall needs to be mentioned, however. If you want to declare three pointer-to-int variables in the same declaration, you might be tempted to write

```
int* p, q, r;    // wrong
```

This does not work as intended; the * operator is applied only to the first variable, so the declaration is interpreted as

```
int *p, q, r;
```

Only p is declared as a pointer variable; q and r are declared as ordinary int variables. If we want to declare three pointer-to-int variables in one declaration, we must use the C style and write:

```
int *p, *q, *r;
```

The Address-of Operator

At this point you may be wondering where we get the addresses that are stored in pointer variables. Normally, the addresses of data objects are not known when a program is written. Not only does the address of a data object depend on the computer system and the C++ implementation, it can vary between runs of the same program on the same computer. If pointers are to be used effectively, we need operators and expressions that will yield the current addresses of data objects.

One such operator is the *address-of operator*, &. When & is applied to an lvalue, it returns a pointer to the designated object.* Thus if count is an integer variable, &count is a pointer con-

---

* The address-of operator can be applied to almost any lvalue; the two exceptions are lvalues that designate machine registers and bitfields.

stant that points to `count` and has type pointer-to-`int`. We can use the address-of operator to initialize and assign values to pointer variables. For example, after the declarations

```
int n;
int* p = &n;
```

the pointer variable p points to the integer variable n. Therefore, *p is an *alias* of n — an alternate name for the data object named by n. An assignment to *p will also change the value of n, and an assignment to n will also change the value of *p. We recall that a data object can have more than one name; here, both *p and n are alternate names for the same data object.

We can make *p the alias of another variable name by assigning another value to p. If m is also an integer variable, then

```
p = &m;
```

assigns the address of m to p. After the assignment, *p will be an alias for m, so that assigning a new value to *p will also assign that value to m, and referring to the value of *p will be the same as referring to the value of m.

Pointers and Arguments

We can use pointers to give a function access to variables passed to it as arguments. For example, suppose we wish to write a function `swap` to exchange the values of two integer variables. That is, after the statement

```
swap( i, j );
```

is executed, i will have the previous value of j, and j will have the previous value of i. At first thought, we might try to declare swap like this:

```
void swap( int m, int n );   // wrong
```

But there is no way that this can work, regardless of how `swap()` is defined. C and C++ pass arguments *by value* — only the *values* of the actual arguments are transmitted to the function. The function is not given access to the variables in which the actual arguments are stored.

On the other hand, pointers are values and can be passed to functions. If we provide `swap()` with pointers to the variables in question, it can use the pointers to access the variables and hence to swap their values. Therefore, we declare `swap()` to take two pointer-to-`int` values as its arguments:

```
void swap( int* p, int* q );
```

When we call the function, we must pass it pointers to the variables whose values we wish swapped. We can do this with the aid of the address-of operator. The statement

```
swap( &i, &j );
```

calls the function and passes it the addresses of `i` and `j`. The formal arguments are initialized by

```
int* p = &i;
int* q = &j;
```

so that `p` points to `i` and `q` points to `j`. Thus `*p` and `*q` become aliases of `i` and `j`, respectively, and can be used to exchange their values. Here is the definition of `swap()`:

```
void swap( int* p, int* q )
{
    int temp = *p; // save value of *p
    *p = *q;       // set *p to value of *q
    *q = temp;     // set *q to saved value
}
```

Variables passed to a function in this way are said to be passed *by reference* because references to the variables (that is, pointers to them) are passed instead of the variables' values. The technique just discussed is the only way to pass variables by reference in C. Its main drawback is that users are prone forget the `&` that must precede each variable passed by reference. We will see later that C++ provides another technique, using *reference types*, that allows us to eliminate the `&`s in the function call and the `*`s in the function definition.

Consider a simple class, date, defined as follows:

```
struct date {
    int day;
    int month;
    int year;
};
```

Let us declare a date variable dt and a pointer pdt to dt, as follows:

```
date dt;
date* pdt = &dt;
```

We can refer to the member variables of dt directly, as follows:

```
dt.day
dt.month
dt.year
```

We can also refer to the member variables indirectly, via the pointer pdt. Because *pdt is an alias of dt, we can write

```
(*pdt).day
(*pdt).month
(*pdt).year
```

The parentheses are necessary because the dot operator has higher precedence than the indirection operator. Because such expressions occur frequently, C++ provides an indirect access operator, ->, to simplify them. The expression

```
pdt->day
```

is defined to be equivalent to

```
(*pdt).day
```

Thus the following expressions provide indirect access to the member variables of dt:

```
pdt->day
pdt->month
pdt->year
```

The arrow operator can also be used to invoke member functions. For example, suppose we define an `account` object `acct` and a pointer `pa` to it, as follows:

```
account acct( 1000.0, 0.6 );
account* pa = &acct;
```

Then

```
pa->deposit( 500 );
```

is equivalent to

```
acct.deposit( 500 );
```

Both statements deposit 500 dollars in `acct`. Likewise,

```
cout << pa->get_balance();
```

is equivalent to

```
cout << acct.get_balance();
```

Both statements print the current balance of `acct`.

To summarize, if we are given a class object such as `dt` or `acct`, we use the dot operator to access its member variables and functions. If we are given a pointer to a class object, such as `pdt` or `pa`, we use the arrow operator to access the member variables and functions.

ARRAYS AND POINTERS

Arrays and pointers are closely related in C and C++: almost any processing that can be carried out using the name of an array can also be accomplished via a pointer to the first element of the array. Arrays can be passed to functions as arguments by reference only, never by value. Any function that receives an array as an argument must access it via pointers.

Array Names as Pointers

Array names behave differently from the names of any other kinds of data objects.* As mentioned earlier, we cannot use an

---

* Because array names differ so greatly from other data-object names, they were not considered to be lvalues in early versions of C. In modern ANSI C, on which C++ is based, an array name is considered to be an unmodifiable lvalue.

array name to refer an entire array nor to assign the array a new value. Instead, when an array name appears in an expression, it is converted to the address of the first element (element 0) of the array. For example, consider the integer arrays a and b declared by

```
int a[ 100 ], b[ 100 ];
```

In any expression, a behaves like &a[0], a pointer value designating the first element of array a. Likewise, b behaves like &b[0], a pointer to the first element of array b.

What we *can* use an array name for is to initialize a pointer to the address of the first element of an array or to assign the address of the first element to an existing pointer. For example, in

```
int* pa = a;
int* pb;
pb = b;
```

pa is initialized with the address of the first element of a and pb is assigned the address of the first element of b.

Suppose we wish to define a function sum( ) so that, for example, the expression

```
sum( a, 50 )
```

returns the sum of the first 50 elements of the integer array a. Because a acts like a pointer to the first element of an integer array, the corresponding formal argument must have type int*, pointer-to-int:

```
int sum( int* p, int n );
```

When the function is called, p will be initialized with the address of the first element of array a; all processing of the array by the function must be accomplished via this pointer. In the function call, note that the array argument is *not* preceded by the address-of operator, &, because the array name already represents the address of the array.*

We say that a pointer *points to an array* when it points to the first element of the array. We may sometimes use the names of such pointers to refer to the arrays to which they point. For example, if p points to one array and q points to another, we may refer to the two arrays as "array p" and "array q."

---

* If the address-of operator is applied to an array name, the address of the array will be returned. But the address-of operator is never necessary because the array name will be converted automatically to the address of the array.

Figure 3-3

The pointer variable p *points to the first element of array* a; *we can use either* a *or* p *to name the elements of the array. The first element of the array can be referred to as* a[0], p[0], *or* *p. *The remaining four elements can be referred to using* a[1] *through* a[4] *or* p[1] *through* p[4].

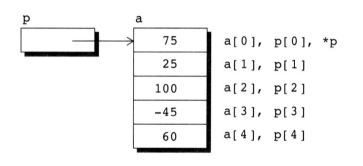

75	a[0],	p[0], *p
25	a[1],	p[1]
100	a[2],	p[2]
-45	a[3],	p[3]
60	a[4],	p[4]

Subscripting Pointers

The correspondence between pointers and arrays works both ways: if array names can behave like pointers, then pointers — like array names — can be subscripted. For example, suppose that p has been set to point to array a:

```
int* p = a;
```

As illustrated in Figure 3-3, we can apply the subscript operator to either p or a to refer to the elements of the array. Thus p[0] and a[0] are both names for element 0 of the array, p[1] and a[1] are both names for element 1 of the array, and so on. For each value of i, p[i] and a[i] are lvalues that can be used both to refer to the value of the designated element and to assign it new values.

For example, let's use pointer subscripting to define the function sum( ) that computes the sum of the first n elements of an integer array:

```
int sum( int* p, int n )
{
    int total = 0;
    for ( int i = 0; i < n; i++ )
        total += p[ i ];
    return total;
}
```

The function call

```
sum( a, 50 )
```

sets n to 50 and p to the address of a [0]. Thus p[i] is an alias of a [i], and

```
total += p[ i ];
```

adds to total the value of element i of array a.

As another example, we can make up for the lack of array assignment by writing a function copy() such that the statement

```
copy( b, a, 75);
```

copies the values of the first 75 elements of array a to the corresponding elements of array b:

```
void copy( int* p, int* q, int n )
{
    for ( int i = 0; i < n; i++ )
        p[ i ] = q[ i ];
}
```

After the function call, p points to array b and q points to array a. Therefore, the statement

```
p[ i ] = q[ i ];
```

has the same effect as

```
b[ i ] = a[ i ];
```

Each statement assigns to an element of b the value of the corresponding element of a.

Pointer Arithmetic

Although we can always use subscripting to refer to array elements via a pointer, there are alternative techniques that are sometimes more efficient. These alternative techniques make use of *pointer arithmetic*—arithmetic involving integers and pointers.

We can add an integer to a pointer with the following effect: if p points to element 0 of an array, then p + 1 points to element 1, p + 2 points to element 2, and so on. Thus, *p is an alias for p[0], *(p + 1) is an alias for p[1], *(p + 2) is an alias for p[2], and so on.

If p points to an array element other than the first, then subtracting an integer from p is also useful. For example, if p points to a[10], then p − 1 points to a[9], p − 2 points to a[8], and so on.

LEARNING C++

Figure 3-4

The pointer variable p points to an array element; the element pointed to can be designated by either *p or p[0]. The two array elements following *p can be designated by either *(p + 1) and *(p + 2) or by p[1] and p[2]. Likewise, the two array elements preceding *p can be designated by either *(p – 1) and *(p – 2) or p[–1] and p[–2]. The negative subscripts are valid as long as the referenced array elements actually exist; it is invalid for either positive or negative subscripts to refer to elements outside the bounds of the array.

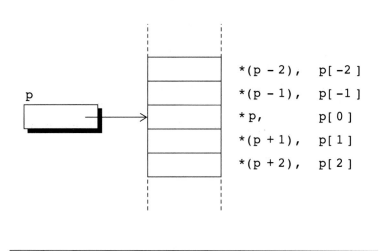

Figure 3-4 illustrates the general case, where p points to some element within an array. The lvalues *p, *(p + 1), *(p + 2), and so on refer to successive array elements starting with the element pointed to by p. Likewise, *(p – 1), *(p – 2), and so on, refer to successive array elements preceding the element pointed to by p. The expressions *(p + i) and p[i] refer to the same array element. Note that negative subscripts are allowed provided the corresponding array elements actually exist, which will be the case only if p *does not* point to the first element of the array.

When carrying out pointer arithmetic, C++ takes into account the sizes of the array elements. Thus expressions such as *(p + 1) and *(p – 1) will work as expected regardless of how much memory is taken up by each array element.

With subscripting, we leave the pointer on the first element of the array and use the subscript operator to designate the element that we actually wish to access. An alternative is to use pointer arithmetic to move the pointer through the array so that it always points to the element that we wish to access, eliminating the need for subscripts. For example, after

```
int* p = a;
```

p points to element 0 of a, and we can use *p to refer to a[0]. If we execute

```
p = p + 1;
```

p now points to element 1 of a, and we can use *p to refer to
a[1]. Likewise, if we again execute

```
p = p + 1;
```

p will refer to element 2 of a, and we can use *p to refer to
a[2]. Proceeding in the same way, we can step through the
elements of a and at each step use *p to refer to the element currently pointed to by p.

The assignment operators += and -= also can be used with
pointers. For example,

```
p += 5;
```

is equivalent to

```
p = p + 5;
```

Both statements move the value of p forward in the array by five
elements. Likewise,

```
p -= 7;
```

is equivalent to

```
p = p - 7;
```

Both statements move the value of p backwards in the array by
seven elements.

The increment and decrement operators work with pointers
just as they do with numbers. The expression p++ moves the
value of p forward in the array by one element; the value of p++
is the old value of p, the value before the increment operator was
applied. Likewise, ++p also moves the value of p forward in the
array by one element, but the value of ++p is the new value of
p. The decrement operator, --, works similarly, except that it
moves backward instead of forward.

The expression

```
*p++
```

occurs frequently and can confuse the unwary. Postfix ++ has
higher precedence than *, yielding the following grouping:

```
*(p++)
```

Thus the increment operator is applied to the pointer p, *not* to
*p, the target data object. The subexpression p++ increments p
so that it points to the next element of the array. The value of
p++, however, is the value of the pointer *before* it was in-

cremented. Applying the indirection operator, *, yields the element that p pointed to before it was incremented. Thus *p++ increments p and, at the same time, names the element that p pointed to before it was incremented. Prefix ++ and * have the same precedence and associate from right to left. Therefore *++p, which groups as *(++p), increments the value of p and, at the same time, names the element that p points to after it is incremented.

For example, if we execute

```
*p++ = *q++;
```

then (1) the value of *q will be assigned to *p, and (2) p and q will each be incremented to point to the next array element. Executing this statement repeatedly will step p and q through their respective arrays, at each step assigning the value of *q to *p. Thus our copy function can be defined as follows:

```
void copy( int* p, int* q, int n )
{
    for ( int i = 0; i < n; i++ )
        *p++ = *q++;
}
```

Likewise, we can define the summation function by

```
int sum( int* p, int n )
{
    int total = 0;
    for ( int i = 0; i < n; i++ )
        total += *p++;
    return total;
}
```

In the statement

```
total += *p++;
```

*p++ returns the value of *p and increments p so that it points to the next element of the array.

In most cases it is more efficient (though sometimes only marginally so) to apply the increment operator than to apply the subscript operator. Therefore, the versions of copy() and sum() that use pointer arithmetic are at least marginally more efficient than those that use subscripting.

We can also subtract pointers that point to elements of the same array; the result is an integer equal to the difference of the corresponding array subscripts. For example, if p points to a[10] and q points to a[15], then q – p has the value 5, the result of subtracting 10 from 15. The value of q – p is the number of array elements from *p up to but not including *q. If we include *q in the count, then the count must be increased by one. Thus the number of array elements from *p through *q, including both *p and *q, is given by q – p + 1.

Pointers can be compared with the equality and relational operators. The equality operators indicate whether two pointers point to the same data object. The expression p == q yields 1 (*true*) if p and q point to the same data object and yields 0 (*false*) if they do not. Likewise, p != q yields 1 if p and q *do not* point to the same object and 0 if they do.

There is a *null pointer* that does not point to any object; it is frequently used to indicate the absence of a valid pointer. C++ will convert between the null pointer and the integer constant 0 (zero) as needed; we can use 0 to represent the null pointer and can consider the null pointer to have the value 0. Thus the expression p == 0 yields 1 if the value of p is the null pointer and yields 0 otherwise; likewise, p != 0 yields 1 if the value of p is not the null pointer and yields 0 otherwise.

The relational operators, such as < and >=, can be used to compare pointers that point to elements of the same array; the result is the same as if the corresponding array subscripts were compared. Thus if p points to a[5] and q points to a[6], then p < q and p <= q both yield 1, because 5 is less than 6. For the same reason, p > q and p >= q both yield 0.

Using const in Pointer Declarations

There are two ways to use the keyword const in declaring a pointer variable. We can declare that the value of the pointer variable is constant, or we can declare that the target data object is constant.

If const immediately precedes the name of the pointer variable, it declares that the value of the pointer variable is constant. Thus

```
int m, n;
int* const p = &m;
```

declare p as a pointer constant with value &m. Consequently p must always point to the same object; attempting to change the value of p is an error:

```
p = &n;   // invalid because p is a constant
```

On the other hand, there is no restriction on changing the value of the object that p points to. Thus

```
*p = 100;
```

is valid and assigns the value 100 to m.

If we place the const before the type of the target data object, then it is that object—and not the pointer variable—that is constant. Thus

```
int m, n;
const int* p = &m;
```

declares p as a pointer to an constant data object of type int. The value of p can be changed as needed; hence

```
p = &n
```

is valid and sets p to point to n. On the other hand, *p is not a *modifiable* lvalue: we cannot use an assignment to *p to change the value of the object pointed to:

```
*p = 100; // invalid because *p is a constant
```

A pointer to constant data can be thought of as a *read-only pointer*; we can use the pointer to read the data that it points to, but the data cannot be changed via the pointer. It is sometimes convenient for member functions of a class to return such a pointer to data stored inside an object; the pointer allows the user to read this private data but not to change it. Unfortunately, the user can circumvent this restriction by changing the type of the pointer with a type cast. Still, returning a pointer to constant data clearly warns users to keep hands off the object's internal data; users who ignore this warning do so at their own risk.

A declaration can impose a constant restriction but not remove one. Thus the following declarations are valid:

```
int n;
int* p = &n;
const int* q = p;
```

The third declaration imposes a restriction of q that does not apply to p; thus the value of n can be changed via p but not via q, because q is a pointer to constant data. On the other hand, the following are not all valid:

```
int n;
const int* p = &n;
int* q = p;   // invalid
```

An initialization cannot remove a constant restriction. Because p has already been declared as a pointer to constant data, its value cannot be used to initialize q, for which there is no constant-data restriction.

The const keyword is often used in function declarations to indicate that the data pointed to by a given argument will not be changed. Thus our functions copy() and sum() could be declared as

```
void copy( int* p, const int* q, int n)
int sum( const int* p, int n )
```

These declarations assure us that copy() will not change array q, the array being copied, and sum() will not change the array whose elements are being summed.

Argument passing always works like initialization. Thus in passing a pointer to a function, we can impose a constant restriction, but we cannot remove one. If a formal argument is a pointer to constant data, the actual argument can be a pointer to either constant or nonconstant data. For example, the first actual argument of sum() and the second actual argument of copy() can have type int* or const int*. The reverse is not true: if the actual argument is a pointer to constant data, it can be passed only to a formal argument that is also a pointer to constant data. Thus the first actual argument of copy() cannot have type const int*, which is a good thing because copy() in fact changes the array pointed to by its first argument.

STRINGS

Strings are stored in memory as arrays of character codes. To indicate where a string ends, the final character of the string is followed by the *null character*, whose code is zero. All string-processing functions assume that every string is terminated by a null character; they will yield incorrect results and possibly crash the program if a terminating null character is missing.

Figure 3-5

The string "dog" *is stored in a four-element array. The first three elements hold the characters* d, o, *and* g; *the final element holds the null character, designated* \0, *which indicates the end of the string.*

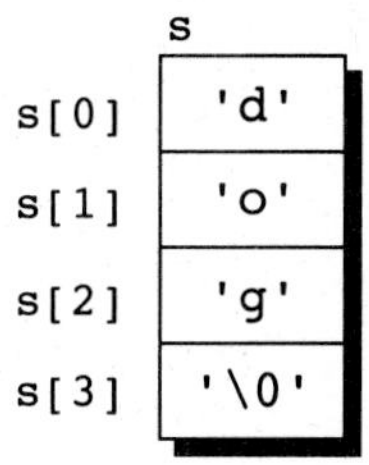
s
s[0]
'd'
s[1]
'o'
s[2]
'g'
s[3]
'\0'

In string literals and character constants, the terminating null character can be represented by the escape sequence \0, which designates the character with integer code zero. We can demonstrate that the null character terminates a string by executing

```
cout << "abcd\0efgh";
```

The computer prints

```
abcd
```

because the first null character encountered is taken to indicate the end of the string.

We can declare an array s to hold strings of up to three characters as follows:

```
char s[ 4 ];
```

The number of array elements must be one more than the number of characters to provide room for the terminating null character. The following declaration initializes s with the string "dog":

```
char s[ 4 ] = "dog";
```

Figure 3-5 illustrates the array s, whose elements have the same values as if we had written

```
char s[ 4 ] = { 'd', 'o', 'g', '\0' };
```

Note the terminating null character, which does not appear in the usual quotation-mark notation, but which we forget about at our peril.

As usual for initialized arrays, we can leave it to the computer to determine the number of array elements:

```
char s[] = "dog";
```

Figure 3-6

A string need not occupy all the elements of an array; here, the string "dog" occupies only the first four elements of array s. The end of the string is indicated by the null character, \0; the elements following the null character contain garbage— arbitrary, meaningless codes.

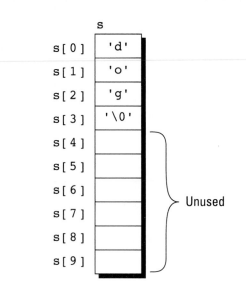

Again, s is given four elements—three for 'd', 'o', and 'g' and one for the terminating null character. Because the null character, and not the size of the array, indicates where a string ends, the array can have more elements than needed for the string. If we declare s by

```
char s[ 10 ] = "dog";
```

then, as shown in Figure 3-6, s has 10 elements, but only the first 4 are used for the string. String-processing functions will ignore the 6 unused elements because the null character following 'g' indicates where the string ends.

We have seen that when an array name such as s is used in an expression, it yields a pointer to the first element of the array. Likewise, when a string literal such as "dog" is used in an expression, it yields a pointer to the first character of the string. Specifically, whenever we use a string literal, the compiler creates a character array to hold the characters of the string; when the string literal is used in an expression, it yields a pointer to the first element of the corresponding array.

We can pass a string argument to a function or operator using either a string literal or the name of a character array. Thus

```
cout << s;
```

and

```
cout << "dog";
```

both cause the computer to print dog. In each case, a pointer to the beginning of the string is passed to the operator. Such a pointer has the type char* or pointer-to-char.

Array names and string literals can also be used to initialize and assign values to pointers. Thus

```
char* p = s;
```

initializes p to point to the first character of s, and

```
char* p = "dog";
```

initializes p to point to the first character of "dog". Because strings are passed to operators and functions as pointers, the statement

```
cout << p;
```

also causes the computer to print "dog".

In short, a string is always designated by a pointer to its first character; the pointer may be represented by an array name, a string literal, or the value of a pointer variable. As with other arrays, we say that a pointer points to a string if it points to the first character of the string. We sometimes use the names of pointer variables to refer to strings to which the variables point; thus we may refer to the strings pointed to by p and q as "string p" and "string q."

FUNCTIONS FOR STRING PROCESSING

The standard library provides a number of string-processing functions, which are declared in the header file string.h. Because these functions are in the standard library, we do not have to define them ourselves. However, looking at some of their definitions will not only familiarize us with the string functions (some of which we will use in Chapter 4) but will also provide some good examples of programming with pointers, arrays, and strings.

The library function

```
char* strcpy( char* p, const char* q );
```

copies string q (that is, the string pointed to by q) into array p (that is, the array pointed to by p); the const in the declaration assures us that the function will not change the string q. The function returns a pointer to the newly created copy.

The array p *must* have enough elements to hold all the characters of string q. The function has no way of determining whether the target array is large enough. If it is not, some characters will be stored in memory locations intended for other purposes, and the program will probably crash.

For example, if we declare s by

```
char* s[ 10 ];
```

then the statement

```
strcpy( s, "canine" );
```

copies the string "canine" into the first seven (not six) elements of s. Note that all that is passed to strcpy() are two pointers: one to the first element of s and one to the first character of "canine".

There are a number of ways to write the definition of strcpy(). The following is a straightforward approach using subscripting:

```
char* strcpy( char* p, const char* q )
{
    for ( int i = 0; q[ i ] != '\0'; i++ )
        p[ i ] = q[ i ];
    p[ i ] = q[ i ];      // copy null character
    return p;
}
```

The for statement has the form we are familiar with, *except* for the control expression, which determines whether repetitions will continue. We are used to something like

```
i < SIZE
```

that allows repetitions to continue as long as the value of i is less than the number of elements to be processed. But we do not know how many characters are in the string to be copied; all we know is that the string is terminated by a null character. Therefore, we use the control expression

```
q[ i ] != '\0'
```

to copy characters until the null character is encountered. The for statement does *not* copy the null character (why?); therefore, a separate assignment statement is needed for this purpose.

Because subscripting does not change the values of p and q, p still points to the array into which string q was copied. Therefore, p points to the copy of string q that the function created, and

```
return p;
```

returns a pointer to this copy.

We can make this code more compact at the expense of making it somewhat harder to read. First, we recall that a control expression is considered *true* if it yields any nonzero value and *false* only if it yields zero. The value of q[i] is zero for the null character and nonzero otherwise. Therefore, the control expression q[i] != '\0' can be replaced by just q[i]:

```
for ( int i = 0; q[ i ]; i++ )
    p[ i ] = q[ i ];
p[ i ] = q[ i ];     // copy null character
```

We can go even further in this direction. The assignment

```
p[ i ] = q[ i ]
```

is itself an expression whose value is the character being copied; that value will be zero when the null character is copied and nonzero otherwise. Thus strcpy() can be coded

```
char* strcpy( char* p, const char* q )
{
    for ( int i = 0; p[ i ] = q[ i ]; i++ )
        ;
    return p;
}
```

In this version, the control expression both copies a character and determines whether the copying should continue. All the work of the for statement is done in the parentheses following for; therefore the controlled statement is the null statement, indicated by an isolated semicolon. This version of the for statement also copies the null character (why?), so no additional assignment statement is required for that purpose.

Despite the preceding discussion, and similar ones later in the chapter, you should not feel compelled to write code in the most compact form possible. Highly compact code can be tricky to write and difficult to read. Studying such code, however, can help you appreciate the possibilities of C++ expressions and statements.

The code for `strcpy()` can also be written using pointer arithmetic. Because the values of the pointers will be changed, we will have to save the initial value of p so that it can be returned as the value of the function:

```
char* strcpy( char* p, const char* q )
{
    char* temp = p;
    while ( *q )
        *p++ = *q++;
    *p = *q;
    return temp;
}
```

The value of *q will be zero only if q points to the null character, so we can use *q as the control expression. We recall that *p++ = *q++ assigns the value of *q to *p and increments both pointers. Again, the control statement does not copy the null character (why?) so an additional assignment statement is needed.

We can make this code more compact by giving another duty to *p++ = *q++, which is already doing double duty (assignment and pointer incrementation). As with any other assignment expression, the value of *p++ = *q++ is the value assigned, which is zero for the null character and nonzero otherwise. Therefore, *p++ = *q++ can also serve as the control expression:

```
char* strcpy( char* p, const char* q )
{
    char* temp = p;
    while ( *p++ = *q++ )
        ;
    return temp;
}
```

In this version, the `while` statement also copies the null character (why?) so that no additional statement is needed for that purpose.

Your compiler may give a warning when it compiles this version of `strcpy()`. Because people frequently write = when they mean ==, many compilers issue a warning if they find an assignment operator where an equality or relational operator is more likely. In this case, however, we are using the assignment operator intentionally, so the warning should be ignored.

The function

```
int strlen( const char* p );
```

returns the number of characters in the string pointed to by p; this count does *not* include the null character. To find the length, we must first find where the string ends, which we do by searching for the null character:

```
int strlen( const char* p )
{
    for ( int i = 0; p[ i ]; i++ )
        ;
    return i;
}
```

The `for` statement sets i to the subscript of the null character (why?). The subscript of an array element is equal to the number of array elements that precede the one designated by the subscript; for example, p[0] is preceded by zero elements, p[1] is preceded by one element, p[2] is preceded by two elements, and so on. Thus the subscript of the null character is the result we are seeking: the number of string characters that precede (and therefore do not include) the null character.

This function can also be coded with pointer arithmetic:

```
int strlen( const char* p )
{
    const char* p_first = p;
    while ( *p )
        p++;
    return p - p_first;
}
```

The `while` statement sets p to point to the terminating null character. Because p - p_first is the number of characters from *p_first (the first character of the string) up to but not including *p (the null character), this difference is the result we are seeking.

If we write the `while` statement as

```
while ( *p++ )
    ;
```

will the function still return the correct result? If not, can we change the `return` statement so that the returned length will be correct?

The function

```
int strcmp( const char* p, const char* q );
```

compares strings for lexicographical order—a generalized alphabetical order in which the order of the characters is the same as the numerical order of their codes. In ASCII, for example, Z follows A in lexicographical order because the value of 'A' (which is the code for A) is 65 and the value of 'Z' is 90. Some of the ordering is less obvious; for example, a follows Z in ASCII because the value of 'a' is 97. And 9 precedes A because the value of '9' is 57.

The function strcmp() returns zero if the two strings are equal, a negative number if the first string precedes the second, and a positive number if the second string precedes the first. If one string equals the initial part of the other, as in "program" and "programmer", the shorter string precedes the longer.

One way to code the function is as follows:

```
int strcmp( const char* p, const char* q )
{
    while ( *p == *q ) {
        if ( *p == '\0' ) return 0;
        p++;
        q++;
    }
    return *p - *q;
}
```

The while statement scans the two strings, comparing corresponding characters, as long as the corresponding characters are equal. The if statement determines if the value of *p is the null character; if it is, then so is the value of *q, because the control expression has verified that the values of *p and *q are equal. When the condition *p == '\0' is true, then, the ends of both strings have been reached and all the corresponding characters in the strings have been found to be equal. Therefore, the return statement exits from the while statement and from the function, returning the value 0 to indicate that the strings are equal.

If the while statement terminates normally, then two corresponding characters have been found to be unequal. The order of the codes for these two characters determines the order of the strings. Therefore, the difference of the codes for the two unequal characters is returned:

```
return *p - *q
```

Verify that this function also yields the correct result when one string equals the initial part of the other.

REFERENCE TYPES

We have seen that passing nonarray arguments by reference is somewhat cumbersome; each actual argument passed by reference must be preceded by a &, which is easily forgotten. In the function definition, arguments passed by reference are accessed via pointers, each of which must be preceded by a * to refer to the argument. Reference types allow us to throw away the &s and *s and pass arguments by reference as easily and naturally as they are passed by value. Reference types are useful only for nonarray arguments; arrays and strings must still be passed using pointers, which are passed by value.

A reference type is designated by a type name followed by an &; for example, `int&` is type reference-to-int, `double&` is type reference-to-`double`, and so on. Reference types are used to declare *references*—new names for objects. A reference is initialized to an lvalue when it is declared, and thereafter it serves as another name for the data object designated by the lvalue. The reference is an alias of any other names the data object might have; because a reference names a data object, it is itself an lvalue.

For example, suppose we declare an integer variable n by

```
int n = 10;
```

and declare the reference r by

```
int& r = n;
```

After this declaration, r is an alias for n; both designate the same data object, which can be referred to by either name. Thus

```
cout << n;
```

and

```
cout << r;
```

both print the value 10. The assignment

```
n = 20;
```

changes the value of both r and n to 20. Likewise, the assignment

```
r = 15;
```

changes the value of both r and n to 15.

Note that initialization and assignment are completely different for references. Initialization establishes the correspondence
between the reference and the data object that it names. Assignment, which is the same for references as for any other lvalue, just
assigns a new value to the designated data object.

We can use pointers and array subscripting to initialized references. Consider the following declarations:

```
int a[ 5 ] = { 10, 20, 30, 40, 50 };
int* p = &a[ 3 ];
```

The pointer p points to a[3], which is element 3 of the five-
element integer array a. Now let's declare and initialize two
references:

```
int& r = a[ 2 ];
int& s = *p;
```

These declarations cause r to refer to a[2] and s to refer to
a[3], which is pointed to by p. Note that s is initialized to the
lvalue *p, *not* to the pointer value p. The values of r and s are 20
and 30, respectively, and assignments to these references will
change the values of elements 2 and 3 of array a.

A reference can be initialized with a value that is *not* an lvalue.
In that case, a data object is created to hold the value, and the
reference is made a name for the data object so created. For
example,

```
int& t = 25;
```

creates an int object with value 25 and name t. The initial
value of t is 25, but that value can be changed with assignment
statements.

References are most commonly used for passing arguments to
functions by reference. For example, we can use references to
define a version of the previously discussed swap( ) function:

```
void swap( int& m, int& n )
{
    int temp = m;
    m = n;
    n = temp;
}
```

As usual, arguments are passed to functions via initialization. Therefore, if we call `swap()` with

```
swap( i, j );
```

the formal arguments of `swap()` are initialized as follows:

```
int& m = i;
int& n = j;
```

Thus m and n become aliases of i and j, respectively; the code for swapping the values of m and n therefore swaps the values of i and j. Comparing this version of `swap()` with our previous one, we see that the &s in the function call and the *s in the function definition have been eliminated.

Returning a value with a `return` statement is also considered to be an initialization. This means that a function can return a reference. For example, let's define a function `rmax()` that returns a reference to whichever of its two arguments has the larger value:

```
int& rmax( int& m, int& n )
{
    if ( m >= n )
        return m;
    else
        return n;
}
```

Because the return type of `rmax()` is int&, the function returns a reference to m or n (rather than the value of m or n, which would be returned if the return type were int). Thus the expression `rmax( i, j )` yields a reference to whichever variable has the larger value. Because `rmax( i, j )` yields a reference, which is an lvalue, this expression can appear on the left side of an assignment operator. For example, the statement

```
rmax( i, j ) = 0;
```

assigns 0 to either i or j, depending on which had the larger value before the statement was executed.

MEMORY MANAGEMENT WITH new AND delete

So far, we have discussed only two options for the lifetime of a data object. A static data object remains in existence throughout the execution of the program. A data object with storage class automatic is created when it is declared and destroyed when it goes out of scope—when the computer leaves the block in which the object was declared. In contrast, the new and delete operators give the programmer complete freedom to create data objects at any time and destroy them when they are no longer needed. The lifetimes of such data objects are unrelated to the block structure of the program. A data object created inside a block with new will remain in existence until it is explicitly destroyed with delete; the data object can thus remain in existence after the computer has left the block and can be manipulated by statements outside the block.

The new operator can be used to create objects of any data type; new is applied to the type of the data object to be created and returns a pointer to the created data object. Thus the expression new int creates an int data object and returns a pointer to the new int object; the returned pointer has type int*. Likewise, new date creates a new instance of class date and returns a pointer of type date*.

The pointers returned by new are normally used to initialize or assign values to pointer variables. Thus

```
int* p = new int;
```

creates a new int data object and sets p to point to it. We could obtain the same result with

```
int* p;
p = new int;
```

In either case, *p refers to the newly created int object. Thus

```
*p = 100;
```

assigns 100 to the new data object, and

```
cout << *p;
```

prints its value.

Likewise, the statement

```
date* p = new date;
```

declares p and sets it to point to a new object of class date. We can use the arrow operator to access the components of the new object:

```
p->day = 24;
p->month = 6;
p->year = 1992;
```

If a class has one constructor and that constructor requires arguments, the required arguments must be supplied when an object is created. Thus

```
account* p = new account( 1000.0, 0.5 );
```

creates an instance of class `account` having a balance of $1000 and a periodic rate of 0.5 percent.

If a class has more than one constructor, each constructor provides an option for initializing class objects. Thus if class `account` defines the three constructors

```
account();
account( double );
account( double, double );
```

then each of the following statements is valid:

```
account* p = new account;
account* p = new account( 1000.0 );
account* p = new account( 1000.0, 0.5 );
```

These three statements would also be valid if the class provided a single constructor with defaults for both arguments:

```
account( double = 0.0, double = 0.5 );
```

To designate derived types such as array and pointer types, we write a declaration for a data object of the desired type, then omit the name of the declared data object and the semicolon at the end of the declaration. For example, we would normally declare an array a of 150 integers by

```
int a[ 150 ];
```

Omitting the array name and the semicolon, we get `int[ 150 ]` as the type of a 150-integer array. Thus

```
int* p = new int[ 150 ];
```

sets p to point to (the first element of) a newly created array of 150 integers; p[0] will refer to the first element of the new array, p[1] to the second element, and so on.

When a data object is no longer needed, we destroy it to make the memory it occupies available for creating new data objects. Normally, we destroy the object pointed to by p with the statement

```
delete p;
```

If the value of p is the null pointer, no action is taken. Otherwise, p *must* point to a data object that was created with new. If p points to a class object for which a destructor is defined, the destructor will be called before the object is destroyed.

A complication arises if the data object to be destroyed is an array. If the elements of the array are class objects for which a destructor is defined, the destructor must be called for each element of the array before the array as a whole can be destroyed. In this case, therefore, the delete operator needs to know the number of elements in the array so it will know how many times it must call the destructor. On the other hand, if the elements of an array are not class objects, or if they are class objects for which no destructor is defined, no destructors need to be called, and so delete does not need to know the number of elements.

The main complication for the programmer is that, during the evolution of C++, three distinct methods for destroying arrays have been introduced into the language. A compiler revision that introduces a new method generally continues to allow existing methods, so most compilers allow more than one method of destroying arrays.

The following discussion takes up the three methods in the order of their appearance in the language. For the sake of examples, assume that p and q each point to a 200-element array. The elements of the array pointed to by p are non-class objects or class objects for which no destructor is defined. The elements of the array pointed to by q are class objects for which a destructor is defined.

Method 1. The number of elements in the array is supplied to delete only if the elements are class objects for which a destructor is defined. Thus the arrays pointed to by p and q are destroyed as follows:

```
delete p;
delete [ 200 ] q;
```

Because q points to an array of class objects for which a destructor is defined, the number of array elements must be supplied to the `delete` operator. The number of elements is enclosed in brackets and appears immediately after the keyword `delete`.

Method 2. The number of elements in the array must always be specified, regardless of whether the elements are class objects or whether a destructor has been defined. Thus the arrays pointed to by p and q are destroyed as follows:

```
delete [ 200 ] p;
delete [ 200 ] q;
```

Programmers objected to this method because it required the programmer to keep track of the number of elements in an array even when the system did not actually require this information to destroy the array.

Method 3. The number of elements in the array is never specified; the system keeps track of this number, relieving the programmer of the need to do so. However, an empty pair of brackets must be placed after the keyword `delete` to notify the `delete` operator that the data object to be destroyed is an array. Thus the arrays pointed to by p and q are destroyed as follows:

```
delete [] p;
delete [] q;
```

Compilers compatible with AT&T Release 2.0 allow Methods 1 and 2. In this book, which is based on Release 2.0, we have used Method 1 to avoid having to keep track of the size of an array unnecessarily. Method 3, introduced in Release 2.1, is (we fervently hope) the final method to be introduced and the one that will eventually replace the other two. Method 3 should be used whenever it is available. In the remainder of this book, we will remind the reader in a footnote when a use of Method 1 should, if possible, be updated to Method 3.

What if the computer runs out of memory, so that the memory area requested by `new` is not available? In that case, `new` returns a null pointer. We could check for the null pointer every time we allocate memory (that's what C programmers do), but such checks would clutter our code, particularly when `new` is used frequently. Fortunately, C++ provides a better method for handling out-of-memory errors. A system variable `_new_handler` can be set to point to a function that will be called whenever an out-of-memory error occurs. Normally, this function will print an error message and terminate the program. The example program discussed later in this chapter illustrates how to declare _new_handler and set it to point to the desired error-handling function.

TYPE-NAME DEFINITIONS

As mentioned earlier, we can designate array, pointer, reference, and function types by writing a declaration for a data object of the desired type, then omitting the name of the data object and the semicolon at the end of the declaration. Types designated in this way are represented by strings of symbols such as int[ ] (int array of unspecified size), double* (pointer-to-double), and long& (reference-to-long). These designations can become complicated or obscure; for example, as we will see later in the chapter, the type of a pointer to a function that takes no arguments and returns no values is void (*)(). We can use the keyword typedef to define meaningful names for such types; such names are referred to as *typedef names*.

A type-name definition has the same form as a variable declaration except that (1) the definition is preceded by typedef and (2) the identifier being declared represents a type name instead of a variable. For example,

```
typedef char* string;
```

defines string as a synonym for char*. Consequently, the declaration

```
string s;
```

is equivalent to

```
char* s;
```

The first declaration, however, emphasizes that s points to the first character of a string rather than to a single isolated character. What's more,

```
string s, t, u;
```

declares s, t, and u as variables of type char*. In contrast, the declaration

```
char* s, t, u;
```

is misleading in that the * applies only to s; thus s is declared as a char* variable and t and u are declared as char variables.

Typedef names are sometimes used to make function and other declarations independent of a particular implementation. For example, in defining the function `strlen()` earlier in the chapter, we (for simplicity) used `int` as the return type. In a particular implementation, however, some other type, such as `unsigned` or `unsigned long`, may be more suitable for representing the lengths of strings. Therefore, if you examine the header file `string.h`, you will probably find `strlen()` declared as follows:*

```
size_t strlen( const char* s );
```

Here, `size_t` is a typedef name for the type that, in a particular implementation, is most appropriate for representing string sizes (and, more generally, for representing the size of any data object). Elsewhere in `string.h` you should find a definition of `size_t`, such as

```
typedef unsigned size_t;
```

or

```
typedef unsigned long size_t;
```

If the C++ implementation is *ported to* (rewritten for) another computer, the definition of `size_t` may need to be changed; but declarations that use `size_t`, such as the declaration of `strlen()`, can remain the same.

EXAMPLE: CLASS `table`

To illustrate the material in this chapter, we will define a class `table` whose instances are lookup tables or directories. Each table entry will consist of two strings: a key, which is what we are looking up, and a value, which is what we are trying to find. For example, if our table represents a telephone directory that lists names and numbers only, the keys will be the names and the values will be the corresponding telephone numbers. A useful property of `table` is that its instances never become full, but increase in size as needed to accommodate new entries. Listing 3-1 gives the header file for class `table`, and Listing 3-2 (p. 143) gives the source file.

* Some C++ implementations use `ssize_t` instead of `size_t` for string sizes.

Listing 3-1

```
// File table.h
// Header file for class table

struct entry {                  // table entry
   char* key;                   // pointer to key string
   char* value;                 // pointer to value string
};

class table {
   entry* tab;                  // pointer to array of entries
   int count;                   // current number of entries
   int size;                    // maximum number of entries

   void grow();                 // enlarge data array
   int search( char* k );       // locate entry with given key
public:
   table( int sz = 4 );         // construct new table
   ~table();                    // dispose of existing table
   void insert( char* k, char* v );   // insert entry
   const char* find( char* k );       // find entry
   void remove( char* k );            // remove entry
};
```

Class Declarations

The header file begins by declaring a class for table entries:

```
struct entry {
   char* key;
   char* value;
};
```

Each entry consists of two strings, one for a key and one for the corresponding value. As usual, a string is represented by a pointer to its first character, so both `key` and `value` have type `char*`.

You may ask why `entry` has been declared as a `struct` rather than as a class with public and private parts and with member functions. The reason is that all we need to do with an entry is to access the values of the instance variables or assign them new values, which are precisely the things we can accomplish with the dot operator. If we made the instance variables private, our member functions would just have to duplicate the capabilities of the dot operator.

We will frequently declare a `struct` that is intended to be used only in declaring and implementing another class. We could indicate the subordinate nature of such a `struct` by placing its declaration inside the declaration of the class it supports. For example, the declaration of `entry` could be nested inside the declaration of `table`:

```
class table {
    struct entry {
        char* key;
        char* value;
    };


    // Remainder of declaration of table
};
```

However, C++ does not nest the scopes of class names: placing the declaration of `entry` inside that of `table` *does not* restrict the use of `entry` to the members of `table`.* In fact, these nested declarations are completely equivalent to the separate ones given in Figure 3-1. For ease of reading, we will give `struct` and `class` declarations separately rather than nesting them.

Each instance of class `table` has three instance variables:

```
entry* tab;
int count;
int size;
```

Table data is stored in an array of entries pointed to by `tab`; because `tab` points to the first element of the array of entries, it has type `entry*`. The individual entries are referred to as `tab[ 0 ]`, `tab[ 1 ]`, and so on. Note that the declaration for `tab` does not allocate storage for the array of entries. The constructor for `table` will have to allocate a data array with `new` and set `tab` to point to that array. The value of `count` is the number of entries currently stored in the table, and `size` holds the current size of the entry array—the maximum number of entries that can be stored without increasing the size of the array.

Class `table` has two private member functions:

---

* Release 2.1 *does* nest the scopes of class names.

```
void grow( );
int search( char* k );
```

Function `grow()` is called to increase the size of the data array so that it can accommodate more entries. Function `search()` returns the subscript of the entry whose key is equal to string k. These functions are for use by other member functions only; they are not intended to be called directly by users of the class. Declaring these functions in the private part of the class gives them access to the member variables but prevents users from calling them via the dot or arrow operator.

Class `table` has five public member functions:

```
table( int sz = 4 );
~table( );
void insert( char* k, char* v );
const char* find( char* k );
void remove( char* k );
```

The constructor `table()` creates a table having a given number of entries. Because the table can increase in size as entries are inserted, it can start off small: the default value for the table size is four entries. The destructor `~table()` must delete the array of entries as well as all the strings pointed to by the `key` and `value` parts of table entries.

We manipulate a table with `insert()`, `find()`, and `remove()`. Function `insert()` inserts a table entry with key k and value v (that is, k and v point to the strings that constitute the key and value). If an entry with key k is already present, the value for that entry is changed to v. Function `find()` returns a pointer to the value corresponding to the key k; if no entry with key k is found, the null pointer is returned. The returned pointer is declared as a pointer to constant data so that the value string — which is part of the data stored by the `table` object — cannot be changed via the pointer. Function `remove()` searches for an entry with key k and, if one is found, removes it from the table.

Class Implementation

The source file for `table` (Listing 3-2) includes the header file `string.h` so that the member functions of `table` can use the string functions `strcpy()` and `strcmp()`.

Listing 3-2

```cpp
// File table.cpp
// Source file for class table

#include <string.h>
#include "table.h"

// Replace data array with one that is twice as large

void table::grow()
{
    int new_size = 2 * size;
    entry* new_tab = new entry[ new_size ]; // allocate array

    for ( int i = 0; i < count; i++ )        // copy data
        new_tab[ i ] = tab[ i ];

    delete tab;                        // delete old array

    tab = new_tab;                     // update instance variables
    size = new_size;
}

// Return subscript of entry having given key
// Return value of count if given key not found

int table::search( char* k )
{
    for ( int i = 0; i < count; i++ )
        if ( strcmp( tab[ i ].key, k ) == 0 )
            break;
    return i;
}

// Allocate data array and initialize instance variables

table::table( int sz )
{
    tab = new entry[ sz ];
    count = 0;
    size = sz;
}
```

(continued)

```
// Deallocate data array and the strings that it points to

table::~table()
{
    for ( int i = 0; i < count; i++ ) {
        delete tab[ i ].key;
        delete tab[ i ].value;
    }
    delete tab;
}

// Insert new entry or update existing one

void table::insert( char* k, char* v )
{
    int i = search( k );

    if ( i == size )          // table full and new entry needed
        grow();

    if ( i == count ) {       // new entry needed
        count++;
        tab[ i ].key = new char[ strlen(k) + 1 ];
        strcpy( tab[ i ].key, k );          // store new key
    }
    else
        delete tab[ i ].value;              // delete old value
    tab[ i ].value = new char[ strlen(v) + 1 ];
    strcpy( tab[ i ].value, v );            // store new value
}

// Return pointer to value corresponding to given key
// If key not found, return null pointer

const char* table::find( char* k )
{
    int i = search( k );
    if ( i < count )
        return tab[ i ].value;
    else
        return 0;   // return null pointer
}
```

```
// Remove item with given key, if present

void table::remove( char* k )
{
    int i = search( k );
    if ( i == count ) return;   // key not found

    delete tab[ i ].key;        // delete key and value
    delete tab[ i ].value;

    for ( int j = i + 1; j < count; i++, j++ ) // close gap
        tab[ i ] = tab[ j ];

    count--;   // decrement entry count
}
```

We begin our discussion of the member functions with the constructor `table()` and the destructor `~table()`. The constructor allocates an array with the requested number of entries, `sz`. It sets `tab` to point to the array of entries, `count` to zero (the newly created table is empty), and `size` to the size of the entry array:

```
tab = new entry[ sz ];
count = 0;
size = sz;
```

When a class object is deleted, the memory for its instance variables is deleted automatically. However, any other data objects that are accessed from the class object via pointers must be deleted explicitly by the destructor. Thus, the destructor for table must delete not only the array pointed to by tab but the strings pointed to by the elements of that array:*

---

* In Release 2.1, the `delete` statements would be written as follows:
```
        delete [] tab[ i ].key;
        delete [] tab[ i ].value;
        delete [] tab;
```
Note that `tab[ i ].key` and `tab[ i ].value` point to strings, which are stored as arrays and so must be destroyed with the array form of the `delete` operator.

```
for ( int i = 0; i < count; i++ ) {
   delete tab[ i ].key;
   delete tab[ i ].value;
}
delete tab;
```

The private function `grow()` doubles the size of the entry array. It first creates an array twice as large as the existing one:

```
int new_size = 2 * size;
entry* new_tab = new entry[ new_size ];
```

Next, the entries from the old array are copied into the new one. Only the elements that contain valid entries (`tab[ 0 ]` through `tab[ count − 1 ]`) are copied:

```
for ( int i = 0; i < count; i++ )
   new_tab[ i ] = tab[ i ];
```

The old array is deleted

```
delete tab;
```

and the instance variables of the `table` object are updated:

```
tab = new_tab;
size = new_size;
```

Note that the value of `count` is not changed: increasing the size of the array does not change the number of valid table entries — the number of array elements that are currently in use.

The function `search()` searches for an entry `tab[ i ]` such that the string pointed to by `tab[ i ].key` is equal to the string pointed to by the argument `k`. If such an entry is found, `search()` returns the subscript of that entry; if no such entry is found, `search()` returns the value of `count`, which is the subscript of the first unused element of the entry array. Note that if the value returned by `search()` is equal to `size`, then we know two things: (1) the search failed, and (2) the entry array is full because `count` equals `size`.

Because our main interest is in the use of classes and not in the study of algorithms, we will generally use the simplest algorithm to accomplish a particular job, even though the simplest algorithm is often the least efficient. For `search()`, therefore, we use the simplest search algorithm, *sequential search* or *linear search*, which starts at the beginning of a table and examines entries one by one until the desired one is found:

```
for ( int i = 0; i < count; i++ )
    if ( strcmp( tab[ i ].key, k ) == 0 )
        break;
return i;
```

If the desired entry is found, the `break` statement causes the computer to exit from the `for` statement with i equal to the subscript of the desired entry, which is the value returned. If the desired entry is not found, the `for` statement terminates normally with i equal to `count`, which is the value returned. The `break` statement could be replaced with `return i` (why?).

The function `insert()` searches the table for an entry with key k; if one is found, the corresponding value is updated to v. If there is no existing entry with key k, a new entry with key k and value v is added to the end of the table.

The function `search()` is called to look for an entry with key k. If the value returned by `search()` is equal to `size`, the search ran off the end of the entry array. Therefore, the following must be true:

- No entry with key k was found, so a new entry has to be created.

- The entry array is full and so must grow to make room for the new entry.

The following code searches for the new key and determines whether the table must grow:

```
int i = search( k );
if ( i == size )
    grow();
```

If i is equal to `count`, a new entry is to be added to the end of the table; `count` is incremented to reflect the new entry and the key part of the new entry is set to point to a copy of the given key string. (Note that i is the subscript of the first unused array element, which will hold the new entry.) If i is not equal to count, then i is the subscript of an existing entry, whose value part is to be updated. In preparation for the update, the string currently pointed to by `tab[ i ].value` is deleted:

```
if ( i == count ) {
    count++;
    tab[ i ].key = new char[ strlen(k) + 1 ];
    strcpy( tab[ i ].key, k );
}
else
    delete tab[ i ].value;
```

The strings pointed to by k and v are generally stored in temporary buffer areas that will be reused after insert() returns; therefore, insert() must make its own permanent copies of any strings that are to be stored in the table. To store a new key, then, insert() sets tab[i].key to point to a new array of strlen(k) + 1 characters (don't forget the + 1). The string pointed to by k is then copied into the new array.

Finally, a new value part is stored in tab[i], which can be an existing entry or a newly created one. Again, insert() must make a permanent copy of the argument string:

```
tab[ i ].value = new char[ strlen(v) + 1 ];
strcpy( tab[ i ].value, v );
```

The function find() looks up a given key and returns a pointer to the corresponding value; if the given key is not found, find() returns the null pointer. The returned pointer has type const char*; it can thus be used to read the characters in the value string, but it cannot be used to change them. (Changing the stored data via a pointer would violate the principle of data hiding, by which the data stored by a table object can be changed only by member functions.)

The code for find() is straightforward:

```
int i = search( k );
if ( i < count )
    return tab[ i ].value;
else
    return 0;
```

The function remove() removes an entry with key k if such an entry is present in the table. If no such entry is found, remove() returns without taking any action:

```
int i = search( k );
if ( i == count ) return;
```

If an entry with the desired key is found, the strings pointed to by that entry are deleted:

```
delete tab[ i ].key;
delete tab[ i ].value;
```

Each entry following the one deleted is moved up by one element to close the gap left by the deleted entry. Note the use of the comma operator to allow the `for` statement to increment two variables:

```
for ( int j = i + 1; j < count; i++, j++ )
    tab[ i ] = tab[ j ];
```

Finally, `count` is decremented to reflect the deletion:

```
count--;
```

EXAMPLE: A PROGRAM USING CLASS `table`

Listing 3-3 shows a program that uses an instance of class `table` to maintain a simple telephone directory. By giving appropriate commands, the user can Insert a new name-number entry or update the number for an existing entry, Find the number corresponding to a given name, Delete an existing entry, or Quit the program.

Function `main()` has the same structure as the dummy command interpreter in Listing 1-8. A `do` statement repeatedly obtains a command letter from the user. For each command, a `switch` statement executes the statements corresponding to the letter that was entered. For the Insert, Find, and Delete commands, the corresponding function `do_insert()`, `do_find()`, or `do_delete()` is called to carry out the command. We will look at the main points of interest in this program, leaving a detailed line-by-line analysis to the reader.

Function Declarations

Near the beginning of the program are declarations for four functions that are defined later in the program:

```
void do_insert( table& dir );
void do_find( table& dir );
void do_delete( table& dir );
void out_of_memory();
```

Each of the do_ functions carries out the corresponding command on a table that is passed to the function via the reference argument dir. The telephone directory that is the subject of the program is declared as a table object near the beginning of main():

```
table directory;
```

To carry out a command, this object is passed to the appropriate function. Thus the statement

```
do_insert( directory );
```

carries out the Insert command on the object directory, the statement

```
do_find( directory );
```

carries out the Find command on the object directory.

Because the argument is passed by reference, the formal argument dir becomes an alias for the actual argument directory: any operation applied to dir is actually carried out on directory. Thus, in do_insert(), the statement

```
dir.insert( name_buf, number_buf );
```

applies the member function insert() to directory. Likewise, in do_delete(), the statement

```
dir.remove( name_buf );
```

applies remove() to directory.

The function out_of_memory() is called if ever new is unable to find enough memory for the object it has been asked to create. The function sends an error message to the standard error stream cerr and terminates the program:

```
void out_of_memory()
{
    cerr << "Out of memory: program terminated\n";
    exit( 1 );
}
```

To terminate the program, we call the library function

```
        void exit( int );
```

which is declared in `stdlib.h`. Its argument is an integer return code that can be used by some programming environments and job-control programs; for example, some program development environments display the return code when the program under development terminates. A zero return code indicates successful termination; a nonzero return code should be used when a program terminates prematurely due to an error.

Listing 3-3

```
// File phone.cpp
// Program to maintain telephone directory

#include <iostream.h>
#include <stdlib.h>
#include "table.h"

void do_insert( table& dir );   // carry out insert command
void do_find( table& dir );     // carry out find command
void do_delete( table& dir );   // carry out delete command
void out_of_memory();           // handle out-of-memory error

extern void ( *_new_handler )();  // pointer to handler for
                                  // out-of-memory error
enum Boolean { FALSE, TRUE };

main()
{
    _new_handler = &out_of_memory; // install error handler

    table directory;            // create object of class table

    Boolean running = TRUE;
    char cmd;

    do {
        cout << "\nCommands: Insert, Find, Delete, Quit\n";
        cout << "Enter first letter of command: ";
        cin >> cmd;                 // read command character
        cin.ignore( 80, '\n' );     // skip rest of line
```
(continued)

```
        switch ( cmd ) {
        case 'i':
        case 'I':
            do_insert( directory );
            break;
        case 'f':
        case 'F':
            do_find( directory );
            break;
        case 'd':
        case 'D':
            do_delete( directory );
            break;
        case 'q':
        case 'Q':
            running = FALSE;
            break;
        default:
            cout << "Invalid command: please try again\n";
            break;
        }
    } while ( running );
 }

void do_insert( table& dir )
{
    char name_buf[ 61 ];
    char number_buf[ 21 ];

    cout << "Name: ";
    cin.getline( name_buf, 61 );

    cout << "Number: ";
    cin.getline( number_buf, 21 );

    dir.insert( name_buf, number_buf );
}

void do_find( table& dir )
{
    char name_buf[ 61 ];
```

```
    cout << "Name: ";
    cin.getline( name_buf, 61 );

    const char* number = dir.find( name_buf );

    if ( number == 0 )        // if number == null pointer
       cout << "Name not in directory\n";
    else
       cout << "Number: " << number << "\n";
}

void do_delete( table& dir )
{
    char name_buf[ 61 ];

    cout << "Name: ";
    cin.getline( name_buf, 61 );

    dir.remove( name_buf );
}

void out_of_memory()
{
    cerr << "Out of memory: program terminated\n";
    exit( 1 );              // terminate program execution
}
```

Declaring and Setting _new_handler

Although we have looked at the declaration and definition of the function `out_of_memory()`, we have yet to see how to arrange for it to be called when an out-of-memory error occurs. For this purpose, the library defines a variable `_new_handler` that we can set to point to a function for handling out-of-memory errors. (Functions, like data objects, can be designated by pointers.) We must declare `_new_handler` in our program (just as we have to declare library functions) and assign to it the address of the error-handling function `out_of_memory()`.

We have to declare `_new_handler` as a pointer to a function that takes no arguments and returns no value. If _new_ `handler` is a pointer to such a function, then `*_new_handler` is an alias for the name of the function. We thus declare `_new_handler` by writing an appropriate function declaration with `*_new_handler` in place of the function name:

```
void ( *_new_handler )();
```

The parentheses around `*_new_handler` are required because the function-call operator, `( )`, has higher precedence than the indirection operator, `*`.

Normally, a variable declaration both *declares* a variable (states its properties) and *defines* it (creates the corresponding data object in memory). Sometimes, however, we want to declare a variable without defining it, because the definition is contained in the library or in another source file. We accomplish this by preceding the declaration with the keyword `extern`:

```
extern void ( *_new_handler )();
```

We cannot use the declaration to specify an initial value for the variable; if we do so, the declaration will become a definition, which is what we are trying to avoid. Therefore, the address of `out_of_memory()` is assigned to `_new_handler` not in the declaration but in the first statement of `main()`:

```
_new_handler = &out_of_memory;
```

The address-of operator, `&`, is optional; a function name is like an array name in that, when it appears in an expression, it is converted automatically to a pointer to the function. Thus, we could just as well have written

```
_new_handler = out_of_memory;
```

A reason for using the optional `&` operator is that it may make the program easier to read, letting us see at a glance that an address is being assigned.

We have seen how to convert a declaration into a type designation by omitting the name of the variable being declared. Thus `_new_handler` has type `void (*)()`, which we can characterize in words as "pointer to a function that takes no argument and returns no value." We could use `typedef` to define a name, `fp`, for this type:

```
typedef void ( *fp )();
```

We could then use the type name `fp` to declare `_new_handler`:

```
extern fp _new_handler;
```

Reading Characters and Strings

The telephone directory program needs to input both characters and strings. Because some of its input needs cannot be met by the extraction operator, >>, the program also uses `ignore()` and `getline()`, which are member functions of `istream`, the class of input streams. The standard input stream `cin` is an instance of `istream`, so `ignore()` and `getline()` can be applied to `cin` with the dot operator.

As in the dummy command interpreters discussed in Chapter 1, we declare a variable `cmd` to hold a one-character command

```
char cmd;
```

and use the extraction operator to input the command character typed by the user:

```
cin >> cmd;
```

When the program requests a command character, the user types the desired character and hits the Return or Enter key; these actions create an input line consisting of the command character followed by a newline character. The extraction operator removes the command character but leaves the newline character in the input stream. This "dangling newline" would not matter if the next input were to be read with >>, because >> skips *whitespace* (spaces, tabs, newlines, and form feeds) before reading the requested input. In this program, however, the next input will be read with `getline()`, which *does not* skip whitespace before reading. We must get rid of the newline following the command character so that it will not interfere with the operation of `getline()`.

There are several ways to get rid of the unwanted newline; the one we will use has the advantage of discarding any unwanted characters that might follow the command character on the same line. The function

```
istream& ignore( int len = 1, int delim = EOF );
```

extracts and discards characters until it encounters the delimiting character, `delim`, which is also extracted and discarded. To assure that this process does not get out of hand, we must specify (via the argument `len`) the maximum number of characters that will be ignored.

The default for the delimiting character `EOF` is a special integer code (usually − 1) that indicates that the end of the file has been reached. To allow for the possibility of `EOF`, character formal arguments are often given type `int`. Actual arguments of type `char` will be automatically promoted to type `int`.

Thus, the statements

```
cin >> cmd;
cin.ignore( 80, '\n' );
```

read a command character and then discard the rest of the input line, including the delimiting newline (however, no more than 80 characters will be discarded). An advantage of using `ignore()` is that the user can type the entire command word, which novice users often prefer to do. The first character of the command word is read into `cmd`, and the remainder of the line is discarded.

The characters of a string are read into a character array that is often referred to as a *buffer*.★ No matter how the characters are read or how the reading process is terminated, the last character to be read is followed by a null character, so that the contents of the buffer will be in the form of a string and can be manipulated by string functions such as `strcpy()`.

When reading a string, we must guard against *buffer overflow* — reading more characters than the buffer array can hold. Any excess characters would be stored in memory locations intended for other purposes, causing the program to malfunction or crash. Failing to protect against buffer overflow not only risks program crashs, it can also provide a security loophole for hostile programs: the infamous Internet Worm used deliberate buffer overflow as one of the several methods that allowed it to gain unauthorized access to thousands of computers.

We can use the extraction operator for reading strings. For example, the statements

```
char buffer[ 81 ];
cin >> setw( 81 ) >> buffer;
```

★ Programmer-defined buffer arrays are not be confused with the buffers that are built into stream objects, such as the buffer in `cout` that is emptied by `endl` and `flush`.

cause the computer to read a string into the character array `buffer`. The manipulator `setw( 81 )`, which specifies the size of the buffer array, is used to prevent buffer overflow. At most 80 characters will be read into `buffer`, thus leaving room for the null character that terminates all strings.

The problem with `>>`, however, is that it only reads one word. After initially skipping whitespace, it reads characters until whitespace is again encountered. For example, if the input line is

```
Now is the time
```

then `>>` will read the string `"Now"` into the buffer. If we invoke `>>` again, it will skip the blank space preceding `is` and read the string `"is"` into the buffer. A third call to `>>` will read `"the"`, and so on.

Frequently we want to read an entire line rather than a single word. For this purpose we can use the member function `get-line()`, which allows us to specify the delimiting character that will terminate reading. The declaration for `getline()` is as follows:

```
istream& getline( char* ptr,
                  int len,
                  char delim = '\n' );
```

The first argument is a pointer to the buffer array, the second is the size of the buffer array, and the third is the delimiting character that terminates reading. The second argument is used to prevent buffer overflow; at most `len – 1` characters will be read, thus leaving room for the terminating null character. In the absence of overflow, `getline()` reads characters into the buffer until the specified delimiting character is encountered. The delimiting character is extracted from the input stream but is not stored in the buffer. If the third argument is omitted, its value defaults to `'\n'`, so `getline()` reads all the way to the end of the current input line.

The telephone directory program uses `getline()` in `do_insert()`, `do_find()`, and `do_delete()`. In `do_insert()`, for example, the following code reads a name into `name_buf` and a telephone number into `number_buf`:

```
char name_buf[ 61 ];
char number_buf[ 21 ];
```

```
cout << "Name: ";
cin.getline( name_buf, 61 );
cout << "Number: ";
cin.getline( number_buf, 21 );
```

Because `getline()` extracts the delimiting character from the input stream, we never have to worry about eliminating a dangling newline after a call to `getline()`.

Using a Pointer to Constant Data

The member function `find` of `table` returns a pointer of type `const char*`. The return pointer must be assigned to a variable of the same type. The statement

```
char* number = dir.find( name_buf );
```

is invalid because assignment will not remove a constant-data restriction. Instead, we must write

```
const char* number = dir.find( name_buf );
```

Thus the pointer `number` cannot be used to change the data stored in the telephone directory. The string argument for the << operator is declared as `const char*`, so that pointers of types `char*` and `const char*` are both acceptable. Thus we can use << to print the telephone number pointed to by `number`:

```
cout << "Number: " << number << "\n";
```

Note that we could not have passed `number` to << if the argument had been declared as `char*` because argument passing cannot remove a constant-data restriction.

EXERCISES

1. The library function

```
char* strchr( const char* s, int c );
```

searches for the first occurrence of character `c` in string `s`. For the purpose of this search, the terminating null character is considered to be part of string `s`. If the search is successful, the function returns a pointer to the character that was found; otherwise, the function returns the null pointer. Write two or more different definitions for `strchr()`.

2. To *concatenate* two strings is to join the end of one to the beginning of the other; for example, the concatenation of `"never"` and `"more"` is `"nevermore"`. The library function

```
char* strcat( char* s1, const char* s2 );
```

concatenates string `s2` to string `s1`; specifically, it copies string `s2` into array `s1` with the first character of the copy replacing the null character that previously terminated string `s1`. The function returns the value of `s1`, which now points to the concatenation of the two strings. Write two or more definitions for `strcat()`.

3. One string is a *substring* of another string if it matches a sequence of adjacent characters in the other string; the terminating null characters of the strings are *not* included in the matching. Thus `"never"` is a substring of `"nevermore"` and `"cat"` is a substring of `"concatenate"`. The library function

```
char* strstr( const char* s1, const char* s2 );
```

searches for the first occurrence of string `s2` as a substring of string `s1`. If the search is successful, the function returns a pointer to the first character of the matching sequence; if the search was unsuccessful, the function returns the null pointer. Thus the call

```
strstr( "concatenate", "ate" )
```

returns a pointer to the first `a` (not the second) of `"concatenate"`, and the call

```
strstr( "concatenate", "eat" )
```

returns the null pointer. Write two or more different definitions of `strstr()`.

4. When a class object stores a sequence of values, we often find it convenient to provide the class with an *iterator*—a set of functions that allows us to step through the stored values one by one. The following functions serve as an iterator for class `table`:

```
void start();
int continue();
void next();
const char* cur_key();
const char* cur_value();
```

One entry of the stored table is singled out as the *current entry*; the functions `cur_key()` and `cur_value()` return pointers to the key and value of the current entry. To implement the iterator, we must provide the class with a *cursor*, an instance variable that designates the current entry; the simplest cursor for `table` is an integer variable that holds the subscript of the current entry. Calling `start()` sets the cursor to the first entry in the table; calling `next()` advances the cursor to the next table entry. The function `continue()` returns 1 (*true*) only if the cursor designates a valid table entry, that is, if it is in the range 0 through `count − 1`; if the cursor does not designate a valid entry, `continue()` returns 0 (*false*), and `cur_key()` and `cur_value()` return the null pointer. Thus, the following code will access all the keys and values in the order in which they are stored in table `t`:

```
for ( start(); continue(); next() ) {
    // access current entry via pointers
    // returned by cur_key() and cur_value()
}
```

Implement an iterator for class `table` and provide the telephone directory program with a command to print out all the names and numbers in the order in which they are stored in the directory.

5. A *set* is a collection of values; the order of the values in the set is irrelevant, and duplicate values are not allowed. Define a class `set` whose class objects are sets of integers. Class `set` has the following member functions:

```
set( int sz = 4 );
~set();
void insert( int v );
int member( int v );
void remove( int v );
```

The constructor creates an empty set that can hold up to `sz` values; as with `table`, a set will grow in size as needed to accommodate additional values. Function `insert()` inserts the value `v` if it does not already belong to the set; `remove()` removes the value `v` if it belongs to the set. Function `member()` returns 1 (*true*) if `v` belongs to the set and returns 0 (*false*) if it does not.

6. Provide class `set` with an iterator that will step through the stored values in some unspecified order (which will, in fact, be the order in which they are stored in memory).

4 *Operators and Friends*

MEMBER FUNCTIONS implement a message-passing approach to object-oriented programming. Whenever a member function is called, one object plays the unique role of message recipient; other values and objects passed as function arguments provide the content of the message. For example, in the message expression

```
acct.deposit( 100 );
```

the formalism makes clear that the object `acct` receives a `deposit` message with content 100.

There is, however, another approach to object-oriented programming, in which class objects are manipulated by functions and operators in much the same way as such basic data objects as integers and floating-point numbers. With this approach, we would make a deposit in `acct` with an ordinary function call, with `acct` as one argument and the amount of the deposit as the other:

```
deposit( acct, 100 );
```

Here, `acct` plays no special role in the formalism; it is just one of the arguments of `deposit()`. If `acct` is passed by reference, then `deposit()` can update `acct`'s instance variables, just as the corresponding member function could. Also, `deposit()` can be overloaded, so if we have several different classes of accounts—checking, savings, money market, and so on—`deposit()` can have a different definition for each kind of account. A single function call can affect the state of more than one object; for example, the statement

```
transfer( acct2, acct1, 100 );
```

could transfer 100 dollars from `acct1` to `acct2`.

This second approach to object-oriented programming is implemented in C++ with *friend* functions. As the name implies, friend functions share most of the privileges of member functions, but they are not as strongly committed to any one class. For example, a function can be a friend of several different classes, but it can be a member of at most one. Constructors, destructors, and virtual functions (discussed in Chapter 6) must be member functions. Aside from these, however, C++ leaves it up to the programmer defining the class to decide which functions will be members and which will be friends.

In most programming languages, operators can have only the definitions that are built into the language. Users can define new functions but they cannot provide new definitions for operators. In contrast, C++ allows users to define operators for class objects. Although there are some restrictions on this capability, it still often enables us to provide compact, intuitive formalisms for manipulating class objects. Like functions, operators can be members or friends to a class. Both kinds of definition are useful: some operators are most naturally defined as members; others are most naturally defined as friends.

OPERATOR OVERLOADING

Every operator has at least one definition built into the language, and many operators are already *overloaded*—defined for operands of more than one type. For example, the + operator can be applied to operands of types `int`, `long`, `float`, `double`, and so on. User-supplied definitions provide additional overloading; that is, they provide additional operand types for which the operator is defined. When an operator is applied, the types of its operands determine which definition will be used. In a user-supplied operator definition, at least one of the operands must be a class object. To avoid confusion with the built-in definitions, C++ does not allow user-supplied operator definitions in which all operands have basic types such as `int`, `long`, and `float`.

We provide a definition for an operator by defining a function whose name is the word `operator` followed by the operator symbol. For example, we provide a definition for the operator + by defining a function `operator+`. Likewise, we provide a definition for the assignment operator by defining a function `operator=`.

The output operator, <<, is a good example of operator overloading. As mentioned in Chapter 1, the built-in definition of << is as an operator for shifting bits within an integral value. However, the header file `iostream.h` declares a class `ostream` of output streams and provides a number of definitions for << where its first operand is an `ostream` object. These definitions allow us to use << to output values of various types, such as `long`, `double`, `char*` (string), and user-defined types. Similar remarks apply to the input operator, >>.

The declaration of << for the output of `int` values has the form:*

```
ostream& operator<< ( ostream& c, int n );
```

The arguments of the function correspond to the operands of the operator. Thus, the operator << takes an output stream as its first operand and the integer to be outputted as its second. The output stream must be passed by reference because its internal state will be modified by the output operation.

The << operator always returns a reference to its first operand, the output stream `c`; this property enables us to use several << operators in succession. Appendix 2 indicates that the << operator groups from left to right; thus an expression such as

```
cout << 100 << "\n";
```

is evaluated as if it had been written

```
(cout << 100) << "\n";
```

Evaluating the expression in parentheses writes 100 to `cout` and returns a reference to `cout`; this reference serves as the first operand for the second << operator. Thus, the second << operator is applied exactly as if we had written

```
cout << "\n";
```

The expression `cout << "\n"` also returns a reference to `cout`, so it could be followed by still another << operator, and so on.

---

* For the sake of this discussion, the declarations of `operator<<` for int and double operands differ from those actually found in `iostream.h`. The declarations in `iostream.h` are for member functions. However, because the argument corresponding to the first operand is omitted when declaring member function, it is clearer to declare these functions as if they were nonmembers or friends.

The declaration of << for the output of `double` values has the following form:

```
ostream& operator<< ( ostream& c, double x );
```

A different definition must be supplied for each declaration. The types of the operands determine which definition will be used. Thus, the statement

```
cout << 100;
```

invokes the code for outputting an `int` value, and

```
cout << 3.5;
```

invokes the code for outputting a `double` value. None of these programmed definitions affect the built-in definition, for which both operands are integers. Thus, `100 << 5` still invokes a bit-shifting operation.

It is quite easy to define an output operator for types of our own invention. For example, suppose we define the class `clock_time` by

```
struct clock_time {
    int hr;
    int min;
    int sec;
}
```

If we declare the `clock_time` variable t by

```
clock_time t = { 11, 45, 20 }
```

we would like the statement

```
cout << t;
```

to print

```
11:45:20
```

We can define such an output operator for `clock_time` objects as follows:

```
ostream& operator<< ( ostream& c, clock_time t )
{
    c << t.hr << ":";
    c << t.min << ":";
    c << t.sec;
    return c;
}
```

Several points are worth noting.

- It may seem strange that the operator << is used in a definition of <<. However, the << operators in the definition output integers and strings; they thus invoke the already existing definitions of << in which the second operand is an integer or a string.

- Because `clock_time` is a `struct`, its member variables are public and can be referred to freely in the operator definition; if the instance variables were private, the operator would have to be declared as a friend of class `clock_time` to give it access to the member variables.

- As already explained, << returns a reference to its first operand so that several << operators can be used in succession.

Users can provide their own definitions for all C++ operators *except* the following:

```
: :
.            ⎫
.*           ⎬  member-access operators
             ⎭
```

`sizeof`   *size operator*

`? :`   *conditional-expression operator*

These excluded operators are very few compared to the large number of operators for which we can supply definitions. Some operators that (perhaps surprisingly) we *can* overload are the function-call operator, ( ), the subscripting operator, [ ], type-cast operators, such as (`int`), the assignment operator, =, and the memory management operators, `new` and `delete`.

Although we can extend the *semantics*, or meaning, of operators by supplying new definitions, we cannot change their *syntax* — the grammatical rules that govern their use. Specifically, we cannot change the following three properties of an operator:

arity	number of operands
precedence	determines how operators are grouped to form subexpressions
associativity	determines whether operators with the same precedence are grouped from left to right or right to left

An overloaded operator can be unary (one operand) or binary

(two operands); the sole trinary (three operand) operator, ?:, cannot be overloaded. The three operators +, −, and * can be used as both unary and binary operators; thus we can supply both unary and binary definitions for each. All other operators are either unary only or binary only, and any definitions for them must take the corresponding number of operands.

We know that the unary operators ++ and −− can be used as both prefix operators (++i, −−i) and postfix operators (i++, i−−), with different built-in definitions for prefix and postfix application. Programmer-defined versions of ++ and −− also can be used as both prefix and postfix operators; however, *there are no provisions for supplying different definitions for prefix and postfix application*. Prefix and postfix application use the same definition and so produce the same results.*

When an `operator` function (such as `operator+`) is not a member function of a class, the number of arguments declared for the function is the same as the number of operands for the corresponding operator. For example, the operator << requires two operands; our definition of `operand<<` is not a member function of any class, so it is likewise declared with two operands:

```
ostream& operator<< ( ostream& c, clock_time t );
```

We recall that a member function is always applied to a particular class object, which precedes the dot operator in expressions such as

```
acct.deposit( 100 );
```

For a member operator, this class object always appears as the first operand. Thus, the number of arguments declared for the `operator` function is *one less than* the number of operands because the first operand is always the class object to which the operator is applied.

For example, suppose we wish to define the operator += as a deposit operator for class `account`, so that

```
acct += 100;
```

will deposit $100 in `acct`. To declare `operator+=` as a public member of account, we insert the following declaration in the public part of class `account`:

```
double operator+= ( double amt );
```

---

* In Release 2.1, different definitions *can* be supplied for prefix and postfix applications of ++ and −−.

Note that only the second argument of `operator+=` is declared explicitly; the first argument will be the class object to which the operator is applied.

We define `operator+=` just like any other member function of `account`:

```
double account::operator+= ( double amt )
{
    balance += amt;   // uses built-in definition of +=
    return amt;
}
```

As with any other member function, the definition of `operator+=` has access to the instance variables (such as `balance`) of the object to which the operator is applied. To make our definition of += behave as much as possible like the built-in definition, we have our definition return the value of the second operand, the amount that is being deposited. Emulating the behavior of built-in definitions as much as possible will aid users of a class in understanding the behavior of overloaded operators.*

FRIEND FUNCTIONS AND OPERATORS

A function or operator definition can be declared as a friend of any number of classes. Such a definition has access to the private parts of all classes that have declared it as a friend. On the other hand, it does not have the unqualified access enjoyed by member functions: it must use qualified names such as `acct1.balance` and `acct2.rate` to refer to the members of classes that have named it as a friend.

For example, let us define a function `transfer()` that transfers a given amount between two accounts. This function is best defined as a friend because it affects two accounts instead of just one. We declare `transfer()` as a friend of `account` by inserting the following declaration in the public part of `account`:

---

* More about ++ and --: In Release 2.0, the member functions `operator++()` and `operator--()` are invoked for both prefix and postfix applications of ++ and --. In Release 2.1, these functions are invoked only for prefix applications. Postfix applications invoke the member functions `operator++( int )` and `operator--( int )`. The `int` argument is a dummy, intended only to distiguish the postfix-application functions from the prefix-application functions. When one of the former is invoked by a postfix application of ++ or --, the value 0 is always passed to the `int` argument.

```
friend double transfer( account& acct1,
                        account& acct2,
                        double amt );
```

Note that the `account` arguments must be passed by reference so that the objects used as actual arguments (and not just copies of them) will be modified. The function tries to transfer the given amount from `acct2` to `acct1` and returns the amount actually transferred:

```
double transfer( account& acct1,
                 account& acct2,
                 double amt )
{
    if ( amt <= acct2.balance ) {
        acct2.balance -= amt;
        acct1.balance += amt;
        return amt;
    }
    else
        return 0;
}
```

Note that, because the function deals with more than one `account` object, qualified names such as `acct1.balance` and `acct2.balance` are essential in referring to instance variables.

Operator definitions are declared as friends in much the same way. For example, let us provide class `account` with an output operator that prints the balance and rate for an account object. We insert the following declaration in the public part of class `account`:

```
friend ostream& operator<< ( ostream& c,
                             account a );
```

The definition of this operator will vary depending on how we wish the account data printed; one possible definition is as follows:

```
ostream& operator<< ( ostream& c, account a )
{
    c << "balance: " << a.balance << "   ";
    c << "rate: " << 100.0 * a.rate;
    return c;
}
```

The rate is multiplied by 100 to convert it to a percentage rate. If the object `acct` is declared by

```
account acct( 666.66, 0.5 );
```

then

```
cout << acct;
```

will print

```
balance: 666.66  rate: 0.5
```

When should a function or operator be declared as a member of a class and when should it be declared as a friend? If a function call changes the internal state of a single class object, if we can think of the function call as sending a message to that object, then the function should be a member of the corresponding class. If the function affects several objects, which may belong to different classes, then it should be a friend of the classes in question.

Membership and friendship can be combined: a member of one class can be a friend of other classes. For example, the arguments of a member function might be class objects belonging to other classes; if the function definition needs access to the instance variables of the arguments, the member function must be declared a friend by the corresponding classes.

We can declare all the member functions of one class to be friends of another class. For example, suppose there is a class `account_manager` whose member functions need access to the instance variables of `account` objects. Inserting the declaration

```
friend class account_manager;
```

into class `account` declares all the member functions of `account_manager` to be friends of `account`.

An operator that has no side effects (does not change its operands) is best declared as a friend. Operators with side effects on their first (or only) operand are best declared as members of the class of the operand in question. If the presence or absence of side effects is the same for the new definitions as for the built-in definitions, then `++` and `--` as well as all the assignment operators (`=`, `+=`, `-=`, and so on) are best declared as members; all other operators are best declared as friends. Of course, if an operator is used in a manner quite different from its built-in definition, these recommendations will not apply.

CLASS vector

Vectors are used to represent quantities that can have both magnitude and direction, such as displacements, velocities, and forces. They are widely used not only in such traditional fields as mathematics and physics but in such computer-oriented fields as computer graphics and robot control. The class `vector` of vectors will serve as the first major example of this chapter.

Mathematically, a vector is just a series of numbers, which are called its *components*. We can display a vector by listing its components in parentheses. For example,

```
(5, 7, 3)
```

represents a vector with three components. The number of components needed varies with the application. As defined here, the class `vector` provides three-component vectors; however, the number of components is determined by constant definitions and so can be changed easily to adapt the class to other applications. The source file must be recompiled if the number of components is changed.

We can define addition, subtraction, and two forms of multiplication for vectors. We add and subtract vectors by adding and subtracting the corresponding components:*

```
(1, 2, 3) + (4, 5, 6) = (5, 7, 9)
(1, 2, 3) - (6, 5, 4) = (-5, -3, -1)
```

We can negate a vector by changing the signs of all its components:

```
-(1, 2, 3) = (-1, -2, -3)
```

Thus both the unary and binary – operators are defined for vectors.

In vector arithmetic, an ordinary number is called a *scalar*. In *scalar multiplication*, we multiply a vector and a scalar by multiplying each component of the vector by the scalar:

```
2 * (1, 2, 3) = (2, 4, 6)
(1, 2, 3) * 3 = (3, 6, 9)
```

Another form of multiplication, called the *scalar product*, multiplies two vectors to get a scalar. The corresponding components

---

* In mathematical examples such as these, = is the mathematical equal sign, not the C++ assignment operator.

of the two vectors are multiplied, and the products are added to yield a scalar result:

```
(1,  2,  3)  *  (4,  5,  6)  =  1*4  +  2*5  +  3*6
                             =  4  +  10  +  18
                             =  32
```

A vector represents a magnitude and a direction; a natural way to obtain a scalar from a vector is to consider only the magnitude and ignore the direction. For example, if a vector represents a displacement, the magnitude represents the distance traveled; if a vector represents a velocity, the magnitude represents the speed. The magnitude of a vector is computed by squaring its components, adding the results, and taking the square root:

```
magnitude (1,  2,  3)  =  sqrt( 1*1  +  2*2  +  3*3 )
                       =  sqrt( 1  +  4  +  9 )
                       =  sqrt( 14 )
                       =  3.74166
```

In defining class **vector**, our aim is to implement these operations in the most intuitive manner possible. For example, we want to be able to use the + sign for vector addition, the – sign for subtraction and negation, and the * sign for both forms of vector multiplication. The operation of computing the magnitude can be implemented in a natural way as a type conversion: if a vector is used where a scalar is expected, the vector will be converted automatically to its scalar magnitude. Class **vector** will also supply a subscripting operator, which enables us to refer to the individual components of a vector.

Listing 4-1 gives the header file for class **vector**, and Listing 4-2 (page 176) gives the source file. Because a header file **vector.h** is already present in some C++ implementations, we will use **vectorc.h** and **vectorc.cpp** to name the header and source file for our class **vector**.

Listing 4-1

```
// File vectorc.h
// Header file for class vector

#include <iostream.h>

const LOWER = 1;                // lower bound for [] operator
const UPPER = 3;                // upper bound for [] operator
const SIZE = UPPER - LOWER + 1; // number of components

class vector {
    double c[ SIZE ];          // array of components
public:
    vector();                  // create null vector
    vector( double* a );       // create vector from array

// Addition, subtraction, and multiplication operators

    friend vector operator+ ( const vector& v,
                              const vector& w );
    friend vector operator- ( const vector& v,
                              const vector& w );
    friend vector operator- ( const vector& v );
    friend vector operator* ( double a, const vector& w );
    friend vector operator* ( const vector& v, double b );
    friend double operator* ( const vector& v,
                              const vector& w );


// Comparison operators

    friend int operator== ( const vector& v,
                            const vector& w );
    friend int operator!= ( const vector& v,
                            const vector& w );

// Operations combined with assignment

    vector& operator+= ( const vector& w );
    vector& operator-= ( const vector& w );
    vector& operator*= ( double b );
```

(continued)

```
    double& operator[] ( int i );     // subscripting
    operator double() const;          // convert to magnitude

// Insertion and extraction operators

    friend istream& operator>> ( istream& ci, vector& v );
    friend ostream& operator<< ( ostream& co,
                                 const vector& v );
};
```

Constant Definitions

The header file begins with a series of constant definitions that determine the number of components in a vector and the way those components are numbered. We can adapt the class to different applications by changing these definitions and then recompiling the source file. LOWER is the subscript of the first component of a vector and UPPER is the subscript of the last component; thus component subscripts run from LOWER through UPPER. The constant SIZE, which is defined in terms of LOWER and UPPER, determines the number of components. The definitions in Listing 4-1 yield three-component vectors with the components numbered from 1 through 3:

```
const LOWER = 1;
const UPPER = 3;
const SIZE = UPPER - LOWER + 1;
```

The Component Array

We choose double as the type of scalars and of the components of vectors. The components of a vector object are held in an array c, which has SIZE elements of type double:

```
double c[ SIZE ];
```

The elements of c are the only instance variables of a vector object.

Note that c is an ordinary C++ array whose subscripts range from 0 through SIZE − 1, as usual; the range of subscripts defined by `LOWER` and `UPPER` is used only when the overloaded subscripting operator is applied to a `vector` object. Although the elements of `c` are the instance variables for a `vector` object, `c` itself is not a vector object but just an ordinary C++ array.

Constructors

Two constructors are declared for class `vector`. The first of these

```
vector();
```

constructs a vector whose components are all 0. Thus

```
vector v;
```

creates a vector `v` and initializes all its components to 0. The second constructor

```
vector( double* a );
```

allows a vector to be initialized from the array pointed to by argument `a`. For example, if we declare array `b` by

```
double b[ SIZE ] = { 10, 20, 30 };
```

then

```
vector v = b;
```

declares `v` as a vector with components 10, 20, and 30. In short, the second constructor allows arrays to be used as vector constants. In declaring such an array, users should employ the constant `SIZE` to assure that the array has the correct number of elements.

Looking at the definitions of the two constructors in Listing 4-2, we see that the first stores zeros in the elements of `c`, and the second copies the elements of the argument array to the corresponding elements of `c`.

Memberwise Initialization and Assignment

Two operators that we do *not* have to define for class `vector` nevertheless deserve mention. A newly declared vector can be initialized with the value of an existing vector, and the value of one vector can be assigned to another vector:

Listing 4-2

```
// File vectorc.cpp
// Source file for class vector

#include <stdlib.h>
#include <math.h>
#include "vectorc.h"

// Constructor:  create null vector

vector::vector()
{
   for ( int i = 0; i < SIZE; i++ )
      c[ i ] = 0.0;
}

// Constructor:  create vector from array

vector::vector( double* a )
{
   for ( int i = 0; i < SIZE; i++ )
      c[ i ] = a[ i ];
}

// Vector addition

vector operator+ ( const vector& v, const vector& w )
{
   vector u;
   for ( int i = 0; i < SIZE; i++ )
      u.c[ i ] = v.c[ i ] + w.c[ i ];
   return u;
}

// Vector subtraction

vector operator- ( const vector& v, const vector& w )
{
   vector u;
   for ( int i = 0; i < SIZE; i++ )
      u.c[ i ] = v.c[ i ] - w.c[ i ];
   return u;
}
```

(continued on page 178)

```
vector v = w;
v = w;
```

If we want to provide our own versions of these operations, we must define the *copy constructor* (which initializes a new class object from an existing one) and the assignment operator, =:

```
vector( const vector& w ); // copy constructor
vector& operator = ( const vector& w ); // assignment
```

In C++, passing an argument or returning a result by value is treated as an initialization; both of these operations invoke the copy constructor to initialize a new copy of the value being passed or returned. Thus, the argument for the copy constructor *must* be passed by reference; passing the argument by value would invoke the copy constructor that we are trying to define. As with all member operators, the first operand of = is the class object to which the operator is applied; only the second operand is declared as an argument. The operand corresponding to argument w supplies the value that is to be copied or assigned; the const keywords guarantee that the value of this operand will not be changed by the copy constructor or the assignment operator.

If these two operators are not defined, then—by default—the corresponding operations are carried out using *memberwise initialization and assignment*: each instance variable of the object to the left of = is initialized with or assigned the value of the corresponding instance variable of the object to the right of =. For example, if u and v are vectors, the assignment

```
u = v;
```

is equivalent to the following (assuming SIZE equals 3):

```
u.c[ 0 ] = v.c[ 0 ];
u.c[ 1 ] = v.c[ 1 ];
u.c[ 2 ] = v.c[ 2 ]
```

If all the data associated with an object is contained within the object itself, as is the case for vectors, the default memberwise initialization and assignment are generally satisfactory. Therefore, class vector does not require the definition of a copy constructor or an = operator. If, however, a class object contains pointers to other objects, then memberwise copying is not generally satisfactory (it copies the pointers but not the objects that they point to). In that case, the copy constructor and assignment operator need to be defined.

```
// Vector negation

vector operator- ( const vector& v )
{
    vector u;
    for ( int i = 0; i < SIZE; i++ )
        u.c[ i ] = -v.c[ i ];
    return u;
}

// Left scalar multiplication

vector operator* ( double a, const vector& w )
{
    vector u;
    for ( int i = 0; i < SIZE; i++ )
        u.c[ i ] = a * w.c[ i ];
    return u;
}

// Right scalar multiplication

vector operator* ( const vector& v, double b )
{
    vector u;
    for ( int i = 0; i < SIZE; i++ )
        u.c[ i ] = v.c[ i ] * b;
    return u;
}

// Scalar product

double operator* ( const vector& v, const vector& w )
{
    double sum = 0.0;
    for ( int i = 0; i < SIZE; i++ )
        sum += v.c[ i ] * w.c[ i ];
    return sum;
}
```

(Listing 4-2 continued on page 180)

Addition, Subtraction, and Multiplication

The operators for addition, subtraction, negation, and scalar multiplication return a vector result:

```
friend vector operator+ ( const vector& v,
                          const vector& w );
friend vector operator- ( const vector& v,
                          const vector& w );
friend vector operator- ( const vector& v );
friend vector operator* ( double a, const vector& w );
friend vector operator* ( const vector& v, double b );
```

The operator for scalar product returns a scalar (`double`) result:

```
friend double operator* ( const vector& v,
                          const vector& w );
```

These operators can be best understood as computing a result from given data, rather than sending a message to a specific object. They are, therefore, declared as friends rather than members of class `vector`.

The vector operands are all passed by reference for the sake of efficiency; passing them by value would require a new copy to be made of each operand every time an operator is invoked. The `const` keywords preclude the possibility that the operators will change the values of the operands, something that is otherwise possible when operands are passed by reference. The operators that return vector results must return them by value, even though returning them by reference would be more efficient. The reason is that each of the corresponding definitions declares a local vector u to hold the result of the operation. But local objects are destroyed when a function returns; it is thus meaningless to return a reference to a local object.

The definitions of all these operators are similar; therefore we will look in detail only at the definition of the addition operator:

```
vector u;
for ( int i = 0; i < SIZE; i++ )
    u.c[ i ] = v.c[ i ] + w.c[ i ];
return u;
```

Vector u is declared to hold the sum of the two given vectors and its value is returned as the result of the operation. Because `operator+` is a friend rather than a member of class `vector`,

```
// Test for equality

int operator== ( const vector& v, const vector& w )
{
    for ( int i = 0; i < SIZE; i++ )
       if ( v.c[ i ] != w.c[ i ] ) return 0;
    return 1;
}

// Test for inequality

int operator!= ( const vector& v, const vector& w )
{
    for ( int i = 0; i < SIZE; i++ )
       if ( v.c[ i ] != w.c[ i ] ) return 1;
    return 0;
}

// Addition and assignment

vector& vector::operator+= ( const vector& w )
{
    for ( int i = 0; i < SIZE; i++ )
       c[ i ] += w.c[ i ];
    return *this;
}

// Subtraction and assignment

vector& vector::operator-= ( const vector& w )
{
    for ( int i = 0; i < SIZE; i++ )
       c[ i ] -= w.c[ i ];
    return *this;
}

// Right scalar multiplication and assignment

vector& vector::operator*= ( double b )
{
    for ( int i = 0; i < SIZE; i++ )
       c[ i ] *= b;
    return *this;
}
```

(Listing 4-2 continued on page 182)

we must use qualified names to refer to the instance variables of vectors u, v, and w. The `for` statement sets each instance variable `u.c[ i ]` of u to the sum of the corresponding instance variables `v.c[ i ]` of v and `w.c[ i ]` of w.

Equality Operators

Two vectors are equal if and only if their corresponding components are equal. To allow the user to test for equality of vectors, we provide definitions for the equality operators `==` and `!=`:

```
friend int operator== ( const vector& v,
                        const vector& w );
friend int operator!= ( const vector& v,
                        const vector& w );
```

The `==` operator returns 0 (*false*) if its two operands are equal and 1 (*true*) if they are not; the `!=` operator returns the opposite result in each case. As usual, the vector operands are passed by reference for the sake of efficiency. The definition of `==` is straightforward:

```
for ( int i = 0; i < SIZE; i++ )
    if ( v.c[ i ] != w.c[ i ] ) return 0;
return 1;
```

The definition for `!=` is identical except that the 0 and 1 in the `return` statements are interchanged.

Assignment Operators

As already mentioned, we do not define the basic assignment operator, `=`, but accept instead the default of memberwise assignment. However, we can define three operators that combine assignment with an operation:

```
vector& operator+= ( const vector& w );
vector& operator-= ( const vector& w );
vector& operator*= ( double b );
```

These operators can be used as follows:

```
v += w;    // add w to v
v -= w;    // subtract w from v
v *= 2;    // multiply v by 2
```

```
// Subscripting

double& vector::operator[] ( int i )
{
    if ( i < LOWER || i > UPPER ) {
        cout << "Subscript out of range\n";
        exit( 1 );
    }
    return c[ i - LOWER ];
}

// Type conversion from vector to double
// Yields magnitude of vector

vector::operator double() const
{
    double sum = 0.0;
    for ( int i = 0; i < SIZE; i++ )
        sum += c[ i ] * c[ i ];
    return sqrt( sum );
}

// Vector input

istream& operator>> ( istream& ci, vector& v )
{
    for ( int i = 0; i < SIZE; i++ )
        ci >> v.c[ i ];
    return ci;
}

// Vector output

ostream& operator<< ( ostream& co, const vector& v )
{
    co << "(" << v.c[ 0 ];
    for ( int i = 1; i < SIZE; i++ )
        co << ", " << v.c[ i ];
    co << ")";
    return co;
}
```

Note that the other two forms of multiplication (2 * v and v * w) cannot be combined with assignment because the type of the result is different from that of the first operand. Because each of the assignment operators changes the value of its first operand, we can think of an assignment operator as sending a message to its first operand. Hence we declare assignment operators as members rather than friends.

As discussed earlier, the first operand of a member operator is the object to which the operator is applied. For example, the statement

```
v += w;
```

is equivalent to the function call

```
v.operator+= ( w );
```

Thus the first operand is not declared as an argument for the `operator` function. Note that the `const` keywords in the declarations guarantee that the value of the *second* operand will not be changed by the assignment; the value of the *first* operand is, of course, generally changed.

In defining the operator function, we use unqualified names to refer to the instance variables of the first operand, but we must use qualified names to refer to the instance variables of the second operand, if it is a class object. Thus, in the code for `operator+=`, `c` refers to the component array for the first operand and `w.c` refers to the component array for the second operand:

```
for ( int i = 0; i < SIZE; i++ )
    c[ i ] += w.c[ i ];
return *this;
```

The predefined variable `this` is a pointer to the object to which a member function or operator is applied; thus for an operator, `this` always points to the first operand. An assignment operator always returns the result of the assignment—the value that was assigned to the first operand. Because *this is an alias for the first operand, the statement

```
return *this;
```

returns the desired result. Note from the declarations of the assignment operators that they return their results by reference. Because the first operand is *not* a local object, a meaningful reference to it can be returned, so we can use this more efficient method to return the result of an assignment.

Subscripting Operator

We provide access to the individual components of a vector by overloading the subscripting operator, [ ]:

```
double& operator[] ( int i )
```

We define `operator[]` as a member function. The operator [ ] is applied to the vector being subscripted; the argument `i` is the subscript. Thus

```
v[ 2 ]
```

has the same effect as the function call

```
v.operator[] ( 2 )
```

In either case, the expression returns a reference to a component of the vector, that is, a reference to an element of the component array `c`. The reference is an lvalue that can be used both to get the value of a component and to assign it a new value. The numbering of components is determined by the constants LOWER and UPPER: `v[ LOWER ]` is the first component of vector `v`, and `v[ UPPER ]` is the last component.

The code for `operator[]` is as follows:

```
if ( i < LOWER || i > UPPER ) {
    cerr << "Subscript out of range\n";
    exit( 1 );
}
return c[ i - LOWER ];
```

If the subscript is out of range, then an error message is printed and the program is terminated. Otherwise, a reference to `c[ i - LOWER ]` is returned. The expression `i - LOWER` converts the subscript from the range specified for `operator[]` (LOWER through UPPER) to the range required by `c` (0 through SIZE - 1).

Because the element of `c` is returned by reference, assigning a value to `v[ k ]` has the effect of assigning that value to `v.c[ k - LOWER ]`.

Conversion to a Scalar Magnitude

We have previously seen how a constructor with a single argument defines a conversion from another type to the type defined by a class. For example, the constructor

```
vector( double* a );
```

converts the array `a` to a vector. This conversion will be applied implicitly where appropriate. For example, if `u` and `v` are vectors and `b` is an array-of-`double`, then expressions such as

```
u + b
v - b
u + b + v
```

are valid. In each case, array `b` will be converted to a vector before being added to or subtracted from another vector.

Constructors only convert objects of other types to the type of a class object. We can, however, define type-conversion operators that will convert a class object to other types. For example, the operator `double()` converts a class object to type `double`, the operator `int()` converts a class object to type `int`, and so on.

We will use the operator `double()` to convert a vector to the corresponding scalar magnitude. To some readers this use of type conversion may seem arbitrary. However, we can think of a vector as having a magnitude and a direction; in converting it to a scalar, we retain the magnitude (which can be represented by a scalar) and discard the direction (which cannot be represented by a scalar). This is analogous to converting a floating-point number to an integer, where we retain the integer part of the floating-point number (which can be represented by an integer) and discard the fractional part (which cannot be represented by an integer).

The operator `double()` is declared as follows:

```
operator double() const;
```

Because `double()` starts with a letter, there is a space between `operator` and `double()`. The operator is declared as a class member; its single operand is the object to which the operator is applied. No return type is specified in the declaration because the return type can only be `double`, the type the operand is being converted to. The `const` specifies that the member function `operator double()` is a constant function—it does not change the value of the object to which it is applied and so it can be applied to constant objects.

The operator `double()` is defined as follows:

```
vector::operator double() const
{
    double sum = 0.0;
    for ( int i = 0; i < SIZE; i++ )
        sum += c[ i ] * c[ i ];
    return sqrt( sum );
}
```

Recall that we compute the magnitude of a vector by summing the squares of its components and taking the square root of the sum. The library square-root function `sqrt()` is declared in header file `math.h`.

The operator `double()` can be used in either functional or type-cast notation. Thus both

```
double( v )
```

and

```
(double) v
```

yield the magnitude of `v`. The conversion will be applied implicitly where appropriate. Thus if `v` is a vector and `x` a variable of type `double`, then

```
x = v;
```

will assign the magnitude of `v` to `x`.

Input and Output

We provide for input and output of vectors by overloading the operators `>>` and `<<` via the following declarations:

```
friend istream& operator>> ( istream& ci, vector& v );
friend ostream& operator<< ( ostream& co,
                             const vector& v );
```

Note that the vector operand for `>>` *must* be passed by reference because `>>` changes the value of the operand. The vector operand for `<<` could be passed by either value or reference; we use reference only for the sake of efficiency, and we use `const` to guarantee that the operator does not change the value of the operand.

The operator `>>` reads `SIZE` values from stream `c` and stores them in the elements of `v.c`:

```
for ( int i = 0; i < SIZE; i++ )
    ci >> v.c[ i ];
return ci;
```

The parenthesis-and-comma notation is not used for input; the input consists of just the required component values separated by whitespace.

The definition of << is slightly more complicated than that of >> because << does use parenthesis-and-comma notation:

```
co << "(" << v.c[ 0 ];
for ( int i = 1; i < SIZE; i++ )
    co << ", " << v.c[ i ];
co << ")";
return co;
```

Demonstration Program

Programs that actually use vectors tend to be complex and understanding their operation calls for application-specific knowledge that is beyond the scope of this book. Therefore we will be content with a simple demonstration program that illustrates the operators defined for class vector. Listing 4-3 shows the example program and Listing 4-4 (p. 190) shows the output that results when the program is run.

The program and its output are largely self-explanatory, so only a few comments are needed. The constant SIZE, declared in vectorc.h, is used in the declarations of a and b to assure that each array has the correct number of components. In main(), the first three statements declare vectors u, v, and w; u and v are initialized from a and b, and all the components of w are initialized to zero.

The next group of statements prompts the user to enter the components of a vector and reads the vector into w. Then come four groups of statements that print the values of u, v, and w and the values of various expressions formed using them. The next-to-last group of statements uses the assignment operators to modify the values of u, v, and w, and the last group of statements prints the modified values. For ease of reading, the lines of output in Listing 4-4 are grouped in the same way as the corresponding statements in Listing 4-3.

Listing 4-3

```
// File testvc.cpp
// Demonstration program for class vector

#include <iostream.h>
#include "vectorc.h"

double a[ SIZE ] = { 1, 2, 3 };
double b[ SIZE ] = { 4, 5, 6 };

main()
{
    vector u = a;
    vector v = b;
    vector w;

    cout << "Enter components for vector w: ";
    cin >> w;
    cout << "\n";

    cout << "u = " << u << "\n";
    cout << "v = " << v << "\n";
    cout << "w = " << w << "\n\n";

    cout << "u + v = " << u + v << "\n";
    cout << "u - v = " << u - v << "\n";
    cout << "-u = " << -u << "\n";
    cout << "2 * u = " << 2 * u << "\n";
    cout << "u * 3 = " << u * 3 << "\n";
    cout << "u * v = " << u * v << "\n\n";

    cout << "(u == v) = " << (u == v) << "\n";
    cout << "(u != v) = " << (u != v) << "\n\n";

    cout << "magnitude u = " << double( u ) << "\n";
    cout << "w[ 2 ] = " << w[ 2 ] << "\n\n";

    u += w;
    v -= w;
    w *= 5;
```

```
        cout << "After\n    u += w;\n    v -= w;\n    w *= 5;\n\n";
        cout << "u = " << u << "\n";
        cout << "v = " << v << "\n";
        cout << "w = " << w << "\n";
    }
```

DEFENDING AGAINST MULTIPLE INCLUSIONS

Listings 4-1 and 4-3 illustrate a problem that occurs frequently. The header file `vectorc.h` includes the header file `iostream.h`, which it must do to gain access to the declarations of `istream` and `ostream`. Because `iostream.h` is already included in `vectorc.h`, we do not include it again in `vector.cpp`, which includes `vectorc.h`. On the other hand, we cannot expect a user of class `vector` to worry about what is or is not included in `vectorc.h`. Therefore, the program in Listing 4-3 includes both `iostream.h` and `vectorc.h`; `iostream.h` is thus included twice, once directly and once via `vectorc.h`. If nothing is done to defend against this multiple inclusion, all the declarations and definitions in `iostream.h` will occur twice, which is not allowed.

Fortunately, a defense against this problem is built into `iostream.h`. If we examine this file with a text editor, we will find that it has the following form:

```
#ifndef IOSTREAMH
#define IOSTREAMH

// remainder of iostream.h

#endif
```

As with `#include`, the statements beginning with `#` are preprocessor directives. The preprocessor directive

```
#define IOSTREAMH
```

defines the identifier `IOSTREAMH` for the preprocessor. If `iostream.h` has already been included, `IOSTREAMH` will already be defined; if `iostream.h` has not yet been included, `IOSTREAMH` will not be defined. The preprocessor directive

```
#ifndef IOSTREAMH
```

Listing 4-4

```
Enter components for vector w: 1 3 5

u = (1, 2, 3)
v = (4, 5, 6)
w = (1, 3, 5)

u + v = (5, 7, 9)
u - v = (-3, -3, -3)
-u = (-1, -2, -3)
2 * u = (2, 4, 6)
u * 3 = (3, 6, 9)
u * v = 32

(u == v) = 0
(u != v) = 1

magnitude u = 3.74166
w[ 2 ] = 3

After
    u += w;
    v -= w;
    w *= 5;

u = (2, 5, 8)
v = (3, 2, 1)
w = (5, 15, 25)
```

checks whether IOSTREAMH has already been defined. If it has not been, then the #ifndef and #endif have no effect. The #define directive is processed (defining IOSTREAMH) and the remainder of iostream.h is included. If, however, IOSTREAMH has already been defined (indicating that ios-tream.h has already been included), everything from the #ifndef directive through the #endif directive is deleted by the preprocessor. Thus the declarations and definitions of ios-tream.h are not erroneously included a second time.

You can provide this defense against multiple inclusion for

your own header files. For example, `vectorc.h` could have the following form:

```
#ifndef VECTOR_H
#define VECTOR_H

// remainder of vectorc.h

#endif
```

To avoid cluttering the listings, these preprocessor statements will not appear in most example header files. On the other hand, they are recommended for any header file that is to be used by programmers other than the one who wrote it.

CLASS `string`

As we saw in Chapter 3, C and C++ implement strings via character arrays, pointers, and the `str...` functions in `string.h`. This implementation has some drawbacks:

- Instead of storing the length of a string in memory, the end of the string is indicated with a null character. The advantage to this approach is that there is no limit on the length of a string. A disadvantage, however, is that `strlen()` is inefficient—it must scan through an entire string in order to determine its length. Tests for equality are also needlessly inefficient; if string lengths could be determined quickly, an equality test could return *false* immediately when applied to strings of unequal length.

- There are no operators for manipulating strings; all built-in string operations are invoked via sometimes cumbersome calls to `str...` functions.

- The user must handle all memory management explicitly. Whenever a string is to be stored, the user must determine the number of characters in it and use `new` to allocate the required amount of memory.

In C, we are pretty much stuck with these limitations. In C++, however, we can do something about them—we can create our own class of string objects with properties much more to our liking than those of the built-in representation for strings.

String Representation

Having complained about the built-in representation for strings, we must now figure out how to do better. To begin with, we will let one of the instance variables of a string object hold the length of the string. Thus the length of a string can be returned by a very efficient inline function, and strings of different lengths can be recognized instantly as unequal.

Because strings vary greatly in size, efficiency demands that the character arrays that hold them also vary in size. We therefore use `new` to allocate an array of the correct size for each string object and use an instance variable to point to the array. Thus, as shown in Figure 4-1, a string object will have two instance variables:

```
int len;
char* p;
```

The `int` variable `len` gives the length of the string; the `char*` variable `p` points to the array that holds the characters of the string.

Copying and Reference Counts

There are two situations in which a string object `s` will be created from another string object `t`: initialization

```
string s = t;
```

and assignment

```
s = t
```

If we do not define a copy constructor for initialization and an assignment operator for assignment, these two operations will be carried out by memberwise initialization and assignment — the instance variables of `s` will be given the same values as the corresponding instance variables of `t`.

When all the data for an object is stored in the object itself, as was the case for vectors, memberwise initialization and assignment are usually satisfactory. But when objects contain pointers to memory areas allocated with `new`, as string objects do, memberwise initialization and assignment cause problems. For exam-

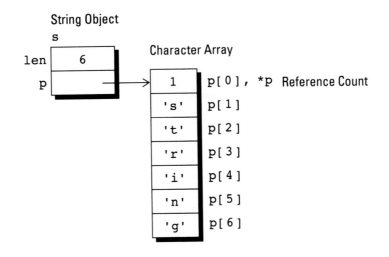

String Object

s

len	6
p	→

Character Array

1	p[0], *p Reference Count
's'	p[1]
't'	p[2]
'r'	p[3]
'i'	p[4]
'n'	p[5]
'g'	p[6]

Figure 4-1

A string object has two instance variables: len, *which gives the number of characters in the string, and* p, *which points to the array that holds the characters of the string. The first element of the character array contains the reference count, whose significance is illustrated in Figure 4-2. The reference count can be referred to as* *p *or* p[0]; *the characters are referred to as* p[1] *through* p[len].

ple, after either the initialization or the assignment just shown, s.p will have the same value as t.p, and both will point to the same character array. Thus changing a character of s also will change the corresponding character of t, and vice versa. Even worse, if either s or t is deleted along with its character array, then the other string object will also lose its character array.

One solution to this problem is to define the copy constructor and assignment operator so that a new copy of the string array is made whenever a class object is copied. Thus every string object will have its own private string array, and the problems just mentioned cannot occur. Unfortunately, this solution is inefficient because initialization and assignment operations can occur very frequently. For example, an initialization takes place (the copy constructor is called) whenever an object is passed to a function or returned from a function by value. Also, some programs make extensive use of assignment to rearrange an array of strings — to sort the strings into lexicographical order, for example. If every initialization and assignment causes a new copy of the character

Figure 4-2

The first element of the character array is the reference count, which gives the number of string objects that have pointers to the array in question. By using the reference count to determine if an object's character array is shared with other objects, we can avoid inadvertently modifying or deleting a shared array.

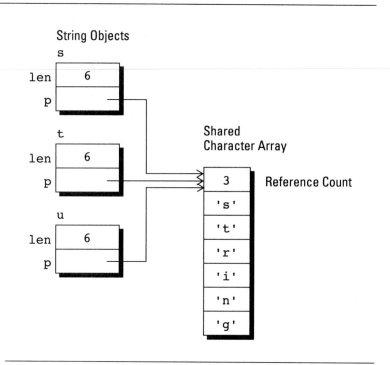

data to be made, many programs will spend much of their time allocating character arrays and copying characters into them.

Thus, to avoid inefficient initialization and assignment, we would like to let different string objects share the same character array. But the sharing must be managed carefully to prevent the problems mentioned earlier. To aid us with this management, we store in the first element of each character array a *reference count*, which gives the number of string objects referring to the character array. Every time a new string object is set to refer to the array, the reference count is incremented. Every time a string object ceases to refer to the array, the reference count is decremented. A character array is deleted when (and only when) its reference count goes to zero. When the content of a character array is to be modified, the reference count will tell us if the array is being shared with another string object. If it is, then a new, unshared copy must be made for the string object whose array is to be modified.

Figure 4-2 shows three string objects, **s**, **t**, and **u**, all sharing the same character array. The first element of the array holds the reference count; the remaining elements hold the characters of the string. The character array can be accessed via the instance variable p of any of the three string objects. The element containing the reference count can be referred to as *p or p[0]; elements p[1] through p[len] hold the characters.

We must cope with one final problem. The values allowed for type char typically range up to only 127 or 255, depending on the implementation; because a reference count is stored in an element of a character array, its value cannot exceed the maximum value for type char. Usually, this figure will not even be approached; most reference counts will be small. But we can imagine situations that would give rise to large reference counts; for example, one string object might be used to assign values to all the elements of a large array of string objects. To deal with these exceptional situations, the copy constructor and the assignment operator must check whether the reference count of a character array has reached the maximum allowable value. If it has, then no additional string objects can refer to that array; instead, a new copy of the array must be made for the string object that is the subject of the current initialization or assignment.

Listings 4-5 and 4-6 give, respectively, the header and source files for class string. Because there already exists a header file string.h (containing the declarations of the built-in string functions), we will use stringc.h and stringc.cpp as the names for the header and source files of our string class.

Referring to Listing 4-5, the header file includes iostream.h to provide the declarations of classes istream and ostream. It defines the constant RC_MAX as the maximum value allowed for a reference count:

```
const RC_MAX = 127;
```

As already indicated, two instance variables are declared for a string object; len holds the length of the string and p points to the character array:

```
int len;
char* p;
```

Listing 4-5

```
// File stringc.h
// Header file for class string

#include <iostream.h>

const RC_MAX = 127;

class string {
    int len;
    char* p;
public:
    string() { len = 0; p = 0; }   // create null string
    string( const char* a );       // create string from array
    string( const string& t );     // copy constructor
    ~string();                     // destructor

// Concatenation operator

    friend string operator+ ( const string& s,
                              const string& t );

// Equality and comparison operators (only two implemented)

    friend int operator== ( const string& s,
                            const string& t );
    friend int operator<= ( const string& s,
                            const string& t );

// Functions for substring position, string length, and
// (for demonstration only) number of references to array

    friend int pos( const string& s,
                    const string& t, int i = 1 );
    friend int length( const string& s ) { return s.len; }
    friend int refs( const string& s )
       { return s.p == 0 ? 0 : *s.p; }

// Assignment operators
```

```
    string& operator= ( const string& t );
    string& operator+= ( const string& t );

// Subscripting and substring operators

    char& operator[] ( int i );
    string operator() ( int i, int n ) const;

// Insertion and extraction operators

    friend istream& operator>> ( istream& ci, string& t );
    friend ostream& operator<< ( ostream& co,
                                  const string& t );

};
```

Construction, Destruction, and Assignment

Class `string` declares three constructors and a destructor:

```
string() { len = 0; p = 0; }
string( const char* a );
string( const string& t );
~string();
```

The constructor with no arguments is an inline function that creates a *null string* — a string with no characters — by setting `len` to 0 and p to the null pointer. Thus the declarations

```
string s, t, u;
```

initialize s, t, and u to the null string. Most other operators and functions must treat the null string as a special case; a null string is signaled by either a zero value for `len` or a null value for p.

The constructor `string( const char* a )` provides a type conversion from ordinary C++ strings to objects of type `string`. Array a contains a C++ string: a sequence of characters terminated by a null character. Frequently array a will be a string literal, such as `"computer"`; this constructor allows us to use the familiar quotation-mark notation to designate string objects. Also, array a may be a buffer array into which a C++ string has been read by an input operation.

Listing 4-6

```cpp
// File stringc.cpp
// Source file for class string

#include <iostream.h>
#include <iomanip.h>
#include <stdlib.h>
#include <string.h>
#include "stringc.h"

// Constructor:  create string from array

string::string( const char* a )
{
   len = strlen( a );
   if ( len == 0 )
      p = 0;
   else {
      p = new char[ 1 + len ];
      *p = 1;
      memcpy( p + 1, a, len );
   }
}


// Copy constructor

string::string( const string& t )
{
   len = t.len;
   if ( t.p == 0 )
      p = 0;
   else if ( *t.p != RC_MAX ) {
      (*t.p)++;
      p = t.p;
   }
   else {
      p = new char[ 1 + len ];
      *p = 1;
      memcpy( p + 1, t.p + 1, len );
   }
}
```

(continued on page 200)

The code for `string( const char* a )` is as follows:

```
len = strlen( a );
if ( len == 0 )
    p = 0;
else {
    p = new char[ 1 + len ];
    *p = 1;
    memcpy( p + 1, a, len );
}
```

Because `a` is a C++ string, we can use `strlen()` to compute its length, which is assigned to instance variable `len` of the string object under construction. If `len` is 0, then the given string is a null string, and instance variable `p` is set to the null pointer. Otherwise, `p` is set to point to a new array of `1 + len` characters (the `1` is for the reference count). The reference count of the new array is set to 1 (`*p = 1`), and the library function `memcpy()` is called to copy the characters of `a` into array `p` beginning at element 1 (because element 0 holds the reference count).

The function `memcpy()` which is declared in `string.h`, works like `strcpy()` except that it does not expect a string to be terminated by a null character. Because it does not recognize a terminating character, we must specify in a third argument the number of characters to be copied. Thus

```
memcpy( p + 1, a, len );
```

copies `len` characters from the array pointed to by `a` to the array pointed to by `p + 1`. Note that if we had used `strcpy()` here the terminating null character of string `a` would have been copied, which we do not want because our string objects do not use terminating null characters.

The constructor `string( const string& t )` is the copy constructor that initializes a new string object from an existing string object `t`. The code for the copy constructor must deal with two string objects: the new object being initialized and the object `t`. The instance variables of the new object are referred to by their unqualified names `len` and `p`. The instance variables of object `t` are referred to by the qualified names `t.len` and `t.p`:

```
// Destructor

string::~string()
{
    if ( p != 0 && --*p == 0 ) delete p;
}

// String concatenation

string operator+ ( const string& s, const string& t )
{
    if ( s.len == 0 )
        return t;
    else if ( t.len == 0 )
        return s;
    else {
        string u;
        u.len = s.len + t.len;
        u.p = new char[ 1 + s.len + t.len ];
        *u.p = 1;
        memcpy( u.p + 1, s.p + 1, s.len );
        memcpy( u.p + 1 + s.len, t.p + 1, t.len );
        return u;
    }
}

// Test for equality

int operator== ( const string& s, const string& t )
{
    if ( s.len != t.len )
        return 0;
    else
        return memcmp( s.p + 1, t.p + 1, s.len ) == 0;
}

// Test for lexicographical order
```

(Listing 4-6 continued on page 202)

```
len = t.len;
if ( t.p == 0 )
    p = 0;
else if ( *t.p != RC_MAX ) {
    (*t.p)++;
    p = t.p;
}
else {
    p = new char[ 1 + len ];
    *p = 1;
    memcpy( p + 1, t.p + 1, len );
}
```

The length `len` of the new string object is set to the length `t.len` of the existing string object. For setting the instance variable p of the new object we have three cases. If `t.p` is the null pointer (the existing object is the null string) then p is likewise set to the null pointer. If the reference count `*t.p` of the existing object is not equal to the maximum value, then the new object can share the same character array as the existing one. We increment the reference count of the existing character array and set p to point to the existing array:

```
(*t.p)++;
p = t.p;
```

Note that the parentheses are required because postfix ++ has higher precedence than *. If the parentheses were absent, the grouping `*(t.p++)` would be assumed, and the pointer `t.p` would be incremented instead of the reference count `*t.p`.

The final case arises when the reference count of the existing character array has the maximum value possible. In that case, no more references to the existing array are allowed, so a new character array must be created for the new object:

```
p = new char[ 1 + len ];
*p = 1;
memcpy( p + 1, t.p + 1, len );
```

The reference count of the new character array is set to 1 (`*p = 1`) because only one object—the newly created one—refers to the new array. Because both the old and new arrays have reference counts, character copying begins at element 1 of both arrays.

The task of the destructor is to decrement the reference count of the character array pointed to by the object that is about to be

```
int operator<= ( const string& s, const string& t )
{
    int m = ( s.len <= t.len ) ? s.len : t.len;
    int c = memcmp( s.p + 1, t.p + 1, m );
    if ( c != 0 )
        return c < 0;
    else
        return s.len <= t.len;
}


// Search string for first occurrence of given substring

int pos( const string& s, const string& t, int i )
{
    if ( i < 1 || i > s.len ) return 0;
    int imax = s.len - t.len + 1;
    for ( ; i <= imax; i++ )
        if ( memcmp( s.p + i, t.p + 1, t.len ) == 0 ) return i;
    return 0;
}


// Assignment

string& string::operator= ( const string& t )
{
    len = t.len;
    if ( t.p == 0 )
        p = 0;
    else if ( *t.p != RC_MAX ) {
        (*t.p)++;
        if ( p != 0 && --*p == 0 ) delete p;
        p = t.p;
    }
    else {
        if ( p != 0 && --*p == 0 ) delete p;
        p = new char[ 1 + len ];
        *p = 1;
        memcpy( p + 1, t.p + 1, len );
    }
    return *this;
}
```

(Listing 4-6 continued on page 204)

destroyed. If the decremented reference count is zero, the character array is deleted:

```
if ( p != 0 && --*p == 0 ) delete p;
```

We must first check whether the string object being deleted is the null string, which does not have a character array. If `p != 0` yields 0 (*false*), `&&` returns *false* without evaluating its right operand; this property of `&&` is frequently used where evaluating the right operand is invalid if the pointer tested by the left operand is null.

If `p` is not the null pointer, the expression

```
--*p
```

is used to decrement the reference count and return the decremented value. Note that in this case, right-to-left associativity causes `*` and `--` to be applied in the correct order to decrement `*p`, so that no parentheses are needed.

The character array is deleted with `delete p` only if both the operands of `&&` yield *true*—that is, `p` is not the null pointer and the decremented reference count `--*p` is equal to 0.★

In general, before making an existing, non-null string object point to a new character array, we must decrement the reference count of the array to which the object currently points; if the decremented reference count is 0, the current array must be deleted. Therefore, before assigning a new value to instance variable `p` of an existing object, we must execute the same `if` statement used in the destructor. When we encounter this `if` statement in other function definitions we will refer to it as the "destructor `if` statement."

A case in point is the simple assignment operator, `operator=`, which is very similar to the copy constructor. The main difference is that the copy constructor is creating a new object, whereas `operator=` assigns a new value to an existing object that already has a value. Therefore, before changing the value of `p` for the existing object, the `if` statement used in the destructor must be executed. Thus the code for the case where array `t.p` can be shared becomes

```
(*t.p)++;
if ( p != 0 && --*p == 0 ) delete p;
p = t.p;
```

★ For Release 2.1, each occurrence of `delete p` should be replaced by `delete [ ] p` because `p` points to an array.

```
// Concatenation and assignment

string& string::operator+= ( const string& t )
{
    if ( len == 0 )
        *this = t;
    else if ( t.len != 0 ) {
        int new_len = len + t.len;
        char* new_p = new char[ 1 + new_len ];
        *new_p = 1;
        memcpy( new_p + 1, p + 1, len );
        memcpy( new_p + 1 + len, t.p + 1, t.len );
        len = new_len;
        if ( p != 0 && --*p == 0 ) delete p;
        p = new_p;
    }
    return *this;
}

// Subscripting

char& string::operator[] ( int i )
{
  if ( i < 1 || i > len ) {
      cerr << "Subscript out of range\n";
      exit( 1 );
  }

  if ( *p > 1 ) {
      char* q = new char[ 1 + len ];
      *q = 1;
      memcpy( q + 1, p + 1, len );
      --*p;
      p = q;
  }
  return p[ i ];
}
```

(Listing 4-6 continued on page 206)

Likewise, the code for the case where a new array must be created becomes

```
if ( p != 0 && --*p == 0 ) delete p;
p = new char[ 1 + len ];
*p = 1;
memcpy( p + 1, t.p + 1, len );
```

We must be careful in writing the code for the case where array t.p is shared; if we reverse the order of the first two statements, the assignment t = t may not work properly.* If array t.p has a reference count of 1, the array will be deleted before being reassigned to t. The best way to avoid this kind of problem is to always execute the destructor if statement (the if statement that appears in the definition of the destructor function) at the last possible moment, just before assigning a new value to p.

Another difference between operator= and the copy constructor is that operator= returns the assigned value, which it does by returning a reference to the object that was the target of the assignment. This object is pointed to by the predefined pointer this, so the statement

```
return *this;
```

returns the desired result.

Concatenation

The concatenation operator

```
friend string operator+ ( const string& s,
                          const string& t );
```

returns a string consisting of the characters of string s followed by the characters of string t. Use of the addition operator, +, for concatenation is intuitively justified because the word *add* can be used to mean "attach" or "combine with," as when we add a room to a house or add books to a library. Also, one widely used existing language, BASIC, uses + for concatenation.

If either s or t is the null string, operator+ just returns the other operand. Otherwise, it declares a string u and provides it

---

* Although a programmer is unlikely to write this redundant assignment statement, the assignment in question might still occur inadvertently via different pointers or references to t.

```
// Extract and return specified substring

string string::operator() ( int i, int n ) const
{
    if ( i < 1 || i > len ) {
        cerr << "Substring position out of range\n";
        exit( 1 );
    }
    if ( n < 0 ) {
        cerr << "Negative substring length\n";
        exit( 1 );
    }
    if ( n == 0 ) return string();   // return null string
    if ( n > len - i + 1 ) n = len - i + 1;

    string sub;
    sub.len = n;
    sub.p = new char[ 1 + n ];
    *sub.p = 1;
    memcpy( sub.p + 1, p + i, n );
    return sub;
}

// String input

istream& operator>> (istream& ci, string& t )
{
    char buffer[ 256 ];

    cin >> setw( 256 ) >> buffer;
    t = string( buffer );
    return ci;
}

// String output

ostream& operator<< ( ostream& co, const string& t )
{
    for ( int i = 1; i <= t.len; i++ )
        co << t.p[ i ];
    return co;
}
```

with a character array large enough to hold the result of the concatenation:

```
string u;
u.len = s.len + t.len;
u.p = new char[ 1 + s.len + t.len ];
*u.p = 1;
```

The characters of first s and then t are copied into the character array of u:

```
memcpy( u.p + 1, s.p + 1, s.len );
memcpy( u.p + 1 + s.len, t.p + 1, t.len );
```

String u is returned as the result of the concatenation:

```
return u;
```

The += operator

```
string& operator+= ( const string& t );
```

modifies its first operand by concatenating string t onto the existing value of the first operand. As usual, operator+= is implemented as a member function; the first operand of += is the object to which the operator is applied.

If the first operand is the null string, then string t can be simply assigned to the first operand:

```
*this = t;
```

If string t is null, then no change is made in the first operand; thus this case "falls through" the main if statement in the function definition. If neither of these special cases holds, then operator+ creates a character array large enough to hold the concatenation:

```
int new_len = len + t.len;
char* new_p = new char[ 1 + new_len ];
*new_p = 1;
```

It then copies the characters of the two existing strings into the new array:

```
memcpy( new_p + 1, p + 1, len );
memcpy( new_p + 1 + len, t.p + 1, t.len );
```

Finally, it updates the instance variables of the first operand. Before assigning a new value to p, the now-familiar destructor `if` statement must be executed to adjust the reference count of, and perhaps delete, the character array currently pointed to by **p**:

```
len = new_len;
if ( p != 0 && --*p == 0 ) delete p;
p = new_p;
```

As usual, the += operator returns the result of the assignment:

```
return *this;
```

Comparisons

We can compare strings with ==, !=, <, <=, >, and >=; the relational operators compare for lexicographical order. For simplicity, we define only == and <=:

```
friend int operator== ( const string& s,
                        const string& t );
friend int operator<= ( const string& s,
                        const string& t );
```

The definitions for the remaining operators can be obtained from the definitions of == and <= by appropriately modifying the `return` statements.

Because our strings are not terminated by null characters, we must use a `mem...` function rather than a `str...` function for comparisons. The function `memcmp()` works like `strcmp()` except that we must supply a third argument giving the length of the strings to be compared. This means that `memcmp()` cannot compare strings of unequal lengths, so we have to supply additional code to make sure that strings with different lengths are compared properly.

The definition of `operator==` begins by comparing the lengths of the two strings; if the lengths are not equal, the strings cannot possibly be equal, so 0 can be returned. Otherwise, `memcmp()` is called to compare two strings of equal length; the two strings are equal if `memcmp()` returns 0:

```
if ( s.len != t.len )
   return 0;
else
   return memcmp( s.p + 1, t.p + 1, s.len ) == 0;
```

Note that == returns its result very quickly if the strings have different lengths. When a large number of equality tests are made, as when searching a list, most of the strings compared will have different lengths. Thus, on the average, == is much more efficient that `strcmp()`, which must scan all the way to the end of the shorter string before it can determine that two strings are not equal. We could make `operator==` even more efficient by defining it as a inline function.

The definition of `operator<=` begins by setting m to the length of the shorter of the two operand strings and c to the result of comparing the shorter string with the first m characters of the longer one:

```
int m = ( s.len <= t.len ) ? s.len : t.len;
int c = memcmp( s.p + 1, t.p + 1, m );
```

If the value returned by `memcmp()` is not 0, then that value determines the result of the comparison: the first string precedes the second if `memcmp()` has returned a negative value. If `memcmp()` returned 0, then one string is equal to the first m characters of the other; in that case, the lengths of the string determines which string precedes which:

```
if ( c != 0 )
    return c < 0;
else
    return s.len <= t.len;
```

Function pos()

The function

```
friend int pos( const string& s,
                const string& t,
                int i = 1 );
```

searches s for the first occurrence of substring t. The search begins at character p[i] of s; if no starting point is specified, the value of i defaults to 1. If the search is successful, `pos()` returns the subscript of the first character of the matching substring; if the search fails, `pos()` returns 0. Thus `pos( "concatenate", "ate" )` returns 5, `pos( "concatenate", "ate", 6 )` returns 9, and `pos( "concatenate", "eat" )` returns 0.

The definition of `pos()` begins by checking to see if i is in the range 1 through `s.len`; if it is not, the function returns 0 (alternatively, it could give an error message):

```
        if ( i < 1 || i > s.len ) return 0;
```

Starting with the given value of i, the characters of t must be compared with characters p[i] through p[i + t.len − 1] for successive values of i. The maximum value of i is imax:

```
    int imax = s.len - t.len + 1;
```

When i has this value, the characters of t are compared with the last t.len characters of s. The following code conducts the search:

```
for ( ; i <= imax; i++ )
    if ( memcmp( s.p + i, t.p + 1, t.len ) == 0 )
        return i;
return 0;
```

Note that i already has its starting value when the search begins, so the initialization part of the for statement is empty.

Function length( )

The inline function

```
friend int length( const string& s )
    { return s.len; }
```

returns the length of a string. Note that length() is much more efficient than strlen(), which must search for the end of a string before computing its length. Also note that a friend function, like a member function, can be made inline by including the function definition in the class definition.

Function refs( )

The inline function

```
friend int refs( const string& s )
    { return s.p == 0 ? 0 : *s.p; }
```

returns the reference count *s.p for the character array of s; if s is the null string, refs() returns 0. Function refs() is a debugging and demonstration function; it does not provide users of class string with any useful information, and its definition can be deleted after the reference-counting mechanism has been debugged.

We can use `refs()` to demonstrate reference counting and check that it is working properly. For example, after

```
string s, t, u;
s = t = u = "reference";
```

s, t, and u share the same character array; thus `refs( s )`, `refs( t )`, and `refs( u )` should all yield 3. If we then execute

```
u = "count";
```

`refs( s )` and `refs( t )` should yield 2 and `refs( u )` should yield 1.

Subscripting

Subscripting allows us to access individual characters within a string. As with vectors, we declare `operator[ ]` as a member function:

```
char& operator[] ( int i );
```

Because element 0 of the character array holds the reference count, subscripts of characters range from 1 through `len`. The operator returns a reference to the designated element of the character array; the reference can be used to access the value of the element or to assign the element a new value.

The operator gives an error message if the subscript is out of range:

```
if ( i < 1 || i > len ) {
    cerr << "Subscript out of range\n";
    exit( 1 );
}
```

Attempting to subscript a null string will always cause an error (why?).

The reference returned by `operator[ ]` allows an array element to be modified. However, we do not want to modify an array that is shared by more than one object, because doing so would change the value of all objects sharing the array. Thus if the object being subscripted shares its character array with other objects—the reference count for the character array is greater than one—the object must be given its own private copy of the character array before the requested reference is returned:

```
if ( *p > 1 ) {
    char* q = new char[ 1 + len ];
    *q = 1;
    memcpy( q + 1, p + 1, len );
    --*p;
    p = q;
}
```

When it comes time to assign a new value to **p**, we already know that **p** is not the null pointer and that the array it points to has a reference count greater than 1 (why?). Therefore, in place of the now familiar destructor **if** statement, we need only use

```
--*p;
```

to update the reference count of the existing character array. How can we be sure that this array does not need to be deleted?

Regardless of whether it is necessary to create a new copy of the character array, the reference to the requested element is returned with

```
return p[ i ];
```

Substring Extraction

We can specify a substring of a given string by its position (the subscript of its first character) and its length. In the string "concatenate", for example, the substring with position 4 and length 3 is "cat"; the substring with position 5 and length 3 is "ate". The substring "ate" occurs again at position 9.

We would like to use a notation similar to subscripting to designate a given substring. We cannot use the subscript operator for this purpose, not only because it is already being used for subscripting, but because we need two arguments—position and length—to specify a substring and the subscript operator allows only one argument inside the brackets. We can solve both problems by overloading the function-call operator, ( ), which allows any number of arguments between the parentheses. If **s** is a string object, then **s(i, n)** will yield the substring with position i and length n. For example, if the value of **s** is "concatenate", the value of **s(4, 3)** is "cat" and the value of **s(5, 3)** and **s(9, 3)** is "ate".

We overload the function-call operator by declaring and defining the function **operator( )**:

```
string operator() ( int i, int n );
```

Be careful not to confuse `operator()` with type conversion operators such as `operator int()` and `operator double()`.

If the position is out of range or the requested length is negative, `operator()` gives an error message:

```
if ( i < 1 || i > len ) {
    cerr << "Substring position out of range\n";
    exit( 1 );
}
if ( n < 0 ) {
    cerr << "Negative substring length\n";
    exit( 1 );
}
```

If the requested length is 0, `return string();` is executed to return the null string; if the requested length is too large—if the substring would extend beyond the end of the string from which it is being extracted—the length is reduced to the largest valid value:

```
if ( n == 0 ) return string();
if ( n > len - i + 1 ) n = len - i + 1;
```

After all argument checking and adjustment has been done, the specified substring is created and returned:

```
string sub;
sub.len = n;
sub.p = new char[ 1 + n ];
*sub.p = 1;
memcpy( sub.p + 1, p + i, n );
return sub;
```

Input and Output

As usual, we overload `>>` and `<<` to provide input and output for values of class `string`:

```
friend istream& operator>> ( istream& ci, string& t );
friend ostream& operator<< ( ostream& co,
                             const string& t );
```

The function `operator>>` uses an existing definition of `>>` to read one word of input into a buffer array, `buffer`. The content of the buffer is then converted to a string object and assigned to reference argument `t`:

```
char buffer[ 256 ];

cin >> setw( 256 ) >> buffer;
t = string( buffer );
return ci;
```

To guard against buffer overflow, we use the manipulator `setw( 256 )`, which specifies that the next `>>` operation will read at most 255 characters. These characters, together with a terminating null character, are guaranteed to fit into the 256-character array buffer. The parameterized manipulator `setw()` is declared in the header file `iomanip.h`, which must be included whenever `setw()` is to be used.

Because the relevant existing definition of `<<` outputs only null-terminated strings, our definition of `operator<<` must output a string character by character:

```
for ( int i = 1; i <= t.len; i++ )
    co << t.p[ i ];
return co;
```

Demonstration Program

As was the case with vectors, a realistic string-processing program would be too long and complicated to include here, so we will be content with a simple demonstration program to illustrate the properties of class `string`. Listing 4-7 shows the demonstration program and Listing 4-8 (p. 217) shows the output produced when the program is run. The two listings, taken together, are largely self-explanatory, so that just a few comments about them will suffice.

The first group of statements in `main()` declare string objects `s`, `t`, and `u`, which are initialized from quoted strings. Also declared as string objects are `v`, `w`, `x`, `y`, `z`, which are all initialized to the null string. The next group of statements inputs a value for `v`, and the group after that outputs the current values of `s`, `t`, `u`, and `v`.

Next comes a test of reference counting. After the assignments

```
        v = w = s;
        x = y = z = t;
```

there are three references to the character array of **s** and four references to the character array of **t**. The assignment

```
        v = x;
```

causes **v** to refer to the character array of **x** (and hence to that of **t**) rather than to the character array of **s**; therefore, after this assignment there are two references to the character array of **s** and five references to the character array of **t**

The rest of the program demonstrates the operators +, +=, ==, and <=, the functions `length()` and `pos()`, substring extraction with the overloaded function-call operator, and subscripting.

Listing 4-7

```
// File testst.cpp
// Demonstration program for class string

#include <iostream.h>
#include "stringc.h"

main()
{
    string s = "concatenate";
    string t = "get";
    string u = "her";
    string v, w, x, y, z;

    cout << "Enter a word: ";
    cin >> v;
    cout << "\n";

    cout << "s = " << s << "\n";
    cout << "t = " << t << "\n";
    cout << "u = " << u << "\n";
    cout << "v = " << v << "\n\n";

    v = w = s;
    x = y = z = t;
```

(continued)

```cpp
    cout << "After\n   v = w = s;\n   x = y = z = t;\n\n";
    cout << "refs( s ) = " << refs( s ) << "\n";
    cout << "refs( t ) = " << refs( t ) << "\n";
    cout << "refs( u ) = " << refs( u ) << "\n\n";

    v = x;

    cout << "After\n   v = x;\n\n";
    cout << "refs( s ) = " << refs( s ) << "\n";
    cout << "refs( t ) = " << refs( t ) << "\n\n";

    cout << "\"to\" + t + u = " << "to" + t + u << "\n\n";

    w = string();   // assign null string
    w += "get";
    w += "a";
    w += "way";

    cout << "After\n   w = string();\n   w += \"get\";\n"
         << "   w += \"a\";\n   w += \"way\";\n\n";
    cout << "w = " << w << "\n\n";

    cout << "(t == u) = " << (t == u) << "\n";
    cout << "(t == t) = " << (t == t) << "\n";
    cout << "(t <= u) = " << (t <= u) << "\n";
    cout << "(u <= t) = " << (u <= t) << "\n";
    cout << "(t <= w) = " << (t <= w) << "\n";
    cout << "(w <= t) = " << (w <= t) << "\n";
    cout << "(t <= t) = " << (t <= t) << "\n\n";

    cout << "length( s ) = " << length( s ) << "\n";
    cout << "pos( s, \"ate\" ) = " << pos( s, "ate") << "\n";
    cout << "pos( s, \"ate\", 6 ) = "
         << pos( s, "ate", 6) << "\n";
    cout << "s( 4, 3 ) = " << s( 4, 3 ) << "\n";
    cout << "s[ 6 ] = " << s[ 6 ] << "\n";
}
```

Listing 4-8

```
Enter a word: polymorphism

s = concatenate
t = get
u = her
v = polymorphism

After
  v = w = s;
  x = y = z = t;

refs( s ) = 3
refs( t ) = 4
refs( u ) = 1

After
  v = x;

refs( s ) = 2
refs( t ) = 5

"to" + t + u = together

After
  w = string();
  w += "get";
  w += "a";
  w += "way";

w = getaway

(t == u) = 0
(t == t) = 1
(t <= u) = 1
(u <= t) = 0
(t <= w) = 1
(w <= t) = 0
(t <= t) = 1
```

(continued)

```
length( s ) = 11
pos( s, "ate" ) = 5
pos( s, "ate", 6 ) = 9
s( 4, 3 ) = cat
s[ 6 ] = t
```

EXERCISES

1. Define a class `clock_time` whose objects store a time in hours, minutes, and seconds; use the 24-hour system to avoid having to otherwise distinguish between A.M. and P.M. Equip class `clock_time` with the constructor

   `clock_time( int h = 12, int m = 0, int s = 0 )`

   along with the following operators: +, −, +=, −=, ++, <<, and >>. Operators + and − add and subtract times as follows: imagine a clock set to the time of the first operand, then turn it forward or backward by the number of hours, minutes, and seconds given in the second operand. Operator ++ represents a clock tick: the expression ++t advances the reading of `clock_time` object t by one second and returns the new time. Operator >> reads three integers and interprets them as hours, minutes, and seconds; operator << prints a time in the form `12:55:30`.

2. A set of integers, all in the range `MIN` through `MAX`, can be represented by a character array c of size `MAX − MIN + 1`; element `c[ i − MIN ]` is 1 if i belongs to the set and 0 if it does not. Define a class `set` that represents sets of integers in this way; `MAX` and `MIN` will be defined as constants and apply to all objects of class `set`. Provide class `set` with constructors `set()` (no arguments), which creates an empty set, and `set( int n )`, which creates a "singleton" set containing only the integer n. Equip `set` with operators +, − (unary and binary), *, +=, −=, *=, ==, !=, <, >, <=, >=, and <<. Operator + yields the *union* of two sets, which contains those elements that belong to either or both sets. Binary − yields the *difference* of two sets, which contains those elements

that belong to the first set but not to the second. Unary − yields the *complement* of a set, which contains those elements (in the specified range) that do not belong to the given set. Operator * yields the *intersection* of two sets, which contains those elements that belong to both sets. Two sets are equal if they have the same elements. Set comparisons are based on the *subset* relation <=: one set is a subset of a second if every element of the first set also belongs to the second. Operator << prints a set in the usual mathematical notation: the set containing 3, 5, and 7 is printed as {3, 5, 7}. Although we can provide functions `insert()`, `remove()`, and `member()` for inserting an integer, removing an integer, and testing whether an integer belongs to the set, these functions are not really necessary (why?).

3. Equip the class `set` defined in Exercise 2 with an iterator that allows the user to step through the elements of a set.

4. In Exercise 2, the range of values that can be stored in a set is fixed by the constants `MIN` and `MAX`. Define a class `set` in which these limits can vary from set to set. The constructor `set( int min, int max )` constructs an empty set whose elements can range from `min` through `max`. The range for the result of a union operation must encompass the ranges of both operands: thus

```
set( 1, 10 ) + set ( 20, 30 )
```

yields a set whose elements can range from 1 through 30. For the difference operator, the range for the result is the same as that of the first operand; for the intersection operator, the range of the result is the overlap of the ranges of the two operands. Eliminate the complement operation, which is no longer very useful (why?). If you use the most obvious implementation technique, you will need to provide a copy constructor and a simple assignment operator. You also may wish to consider using reference counts to prevent unnecessary copying of data arrays.

5. Define a class `rational`, each of whose objects stores a rational number (proper or improper fraction) represented by a `long` numerator and a `long` denominator. Provide operators for addition, subtraction, multiplica-

tion, division, comparison, input, and output of rational numbers. The stored fractions should be reduced to lowest terms to minimize the size of the numerator and denominator. To reduce a fraction to lowest terms, we need to find the *greatest common divisor* of the numerator and denominator—the largest number that will divide evenly into both. The following function returns the greatest common divisor of its arguments:

```cpp
long gcd( long m, long n)
{
    if ( m < 0 ) m = -m;
    if ( n < 0 ) n = -n;
    while ( n != 0 ) {
        long r = m % n;
        m = n;
        n = r;
    }
    return m;
}
```

5 *Inheritance: Derived Classes*

*I*NHERITANCE ALLOWS a new class to be defined by extending or modifying one or more existing classes; the new class is called a *derived class* and the existing classes are its *base classes*. A derived class can itself serve as a base class for other derived classes, enabling us to build hierarchies of classes related by inheritance. Inheritance allows us to avoid reinventing the wheel: instead of having to define every class from scratch, we can use existing classes as foundations on which to build new classes.

We speak of *single inheritance* when a derived class has only one base class and of *multiple inheritance* when a derived class has several base classes. Multiple inheritance allows us to combine the properties of existing classes; for example, we can think of the class of clock radios as inheriting its clock properties from the class of clocks and its radio properties from the class of radios. Although multiple inheritance is introduced and illustrated in this chapter, most of our work will be with single inheritance, which is the most widely used form.

EXAMPLE: BANK ACCOUNTS

For our first example of inheritance, we will return to our first example of a class, a bank account. Now, however, we will consider several kinds of accounts. Class `account` defines a generic account that can be opened with a given balance, will accept deposits, and will return its current balance. Class `sav_acct`

Figure 5-1

Class hierarchy for classes
account, sav_acct,
chk_acct, *and* time_acct.
*Each arrow connects a base class
to a derived class; the direction of
the arrow is the direction of
inheritance. Note that (1)*
account *serves as a base class
for both* sav_acct *and*
chk_acct, *and (2)*
sav_acct *is both a derived
class of* account *and the base
class of* time_acct.

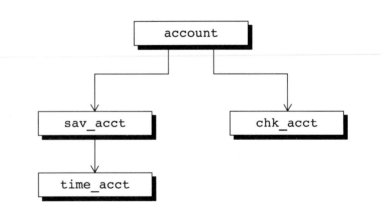

defines a traditional savings account (no checking privileges) that provides compound interest and withdrawal privileges. Class chk_acct defines a traditional checking account (no interest) that allows check cashing and imposes a per-check charge if the balance falls below a given limit. Class time_acct defines a simplified form of time-deposit account that allows only accumulated interest to be withdrawn.

These four classes of accounts can be arranged in a *class hierarchy* as shown in Figure 5-1. At the top of the hierarchy is account, from which the other three classes are derived either directly or indirectly. Class account is not useful by itself (it provides no means of computing interest or withdrawing funds), but is intended only as a starting point for deriving more specialized (and more useful) account classes. Both sav_acct and chk_acct are extensions of account and so are derived directly from it. Class time_acct defines a modified form of savings account and so is derived from sav_acct.

Class account *and the Keyword* protected

When a derived class is declared, the declarations for both the derived class and the base class must be included in the source file. The simplest way to assure that this will be done is to declare the base and derived classes in the same header file; this principle is followed in accounts.h (Listing 5-1), which contains the declarations of all the account classes. The source file accounts.cpp (Listing 5-2) defines the non-inline functions for all the account classes.

Another approach would be to declare each class in a separate header file, but to place in the header file of each derived class an #include directive that includes the header file of the base class. If this approach is followed, the method discussed in Chapter 4 for defending against multiple inclusions must be used; otherwise, it is likely that the header file of the base class would be included more than once.

The declaration for class account is as follows:

```
class account {
protected:
    double balance;
public:
    account( double bal = 0.0 ) { balance = bal; }
    void deposit( double amt ) { balance += amt; }
    double get_balance() const { return balance; }
};
```

As usual, private members of a base class are accessible only to member and friend functions of the base class; in particular, private members of a base class are *not* accessible to member and friend functions of a derived class. Frequently, however, the member and friend functions of a derived class need to manipulate instance variables declared in the base class, yet we do not want to make these instance variables generally accessible by declaring them public. Protected members, declared using the keyword protected,

Listing 5-1

```
// File accounts.h
// Header file for account classes

class account {
protected:
    double balance;   // current balance
public:
    account( double bal = 0.0 ) { balance = bal; }
    void deposit( double amt ) { balance += amt; }
    double get_balance() const { return balance; }
};
```

(continued)

```
class sav_acct : public account {
protected:
   double rate;   // decimal periodic interest rate
public:
   sav_acct( double bal = 0.0, double pct = 0.5 );
   double compound();      // compute and deposit interest
   double withdraw( double amt );    // attempt withdrawal
};

class chk_acct : public account {
protected:
   double limit;      // lower limit for free checking
   double charge;     // per-check charge for low balance
public:
   chk_acct( double bal = 0.0,
             double lim = 500.0,
             double chg = 0.50 );
   double cash_chk( double amt );   // cash check
};

class time_acct : public sav_acct {
protected:
   double funds_avail;   // amount available for withdrawal
public:
   time_acct( double bal = 0.0,
              double pct = 0.5   );
   double compound();                    // redefinition
   double withdraw( double amt );    // redefinition
   double get_avail() const { return funds_avail; }
};
```

provide the solution to this problem. Protected members are accessible to the member and friend functions of the base class and of any derived classes. Unlike public members, however, they are *not* accessible to functions that are not members or friends of the base class or of a derived class. In class account, balance is declared as a protected member so that it will be accessible to the member functions of classes derived from account.

The remainder of the declaration for account is straightforward. The constructor account() opens an account with a given starting balance; deposit() increases the balance by a given amount; and get_balance() returns the current balance.

Listing 5-2

```
// File accounts.cpp
// Source file for account classes

#include "accounts.h"

// FUNCTIONS FOR sav_acct

// Constructor

sav_acct::sav_acct( double bal,
                    double pct ) : account( bal )
{
    rate = pct / 100.0;
}

// Compute and deposit interest for one period

double sav_acct::compound()
{
    double interest = rate * balance;
    balance += interest;
    return interest;
}

// Attempt withdrawal; return amount actually withdrawn

double sav_acct::withdraw( double amt )
{
    if ( amt <= balance ) {
        balance -= amt;
        return amt;
    }
    else
        return 0.0;
}

// FUNCTIONS FOR chk_acct

// Constructor
```

(continued)

```
chk_acct::chk_acct( double bal,
                    double lim,
                    double chg ) : account( bal )
{
    limit = lim;
    charge = chg;
}

// Attempt to cash check; impose per-check charge if
// necessary; return amount by which account is debited

double chk_acct::cash_chk( double amt )
{
    if ( (balance < limit) && (amt + charge <= balance) )
    {
        balance -= amt + charge;
        return amt + charge;
    }
    else if ( (balance >= limit) && (amt <= balance) ) {
        balance -= amt;
        return amt;
    }
    else
        return 0.0;
}

// FUNCTIONS FOR time_acct

// Constructor

time_acct::time_acct( double bal,
                      double pct ) : sav_acct( bal, pct )
{
    funds_avail = 0.0;
}

// Redefine inherited function to
// keep track of available funds

double time_acct::compound()
{
    double interest = sav_acct::compound();
    funds_avail += interest;
    return interest;
```

```
}
// Redefine inherited function to allow only available
// funds to be withdrawn

double time_acct::withdraw( double amt )
{
    if ( amt <= funds_avail ) {
        funds_avail -= amt;
        balance -= amt;
        return amt;
    }
        else
            return 0.0;
}
```

Class sav_acct, *Public Base Classes, and Constructors*

The derived class for savings accounts is declared as follows:

```
class sav_acct : public account {
protected:
    double rate;
public:
    sav_acct( double bal = 0.0, double pct = 0.5 );
    double compound();
    double withdraw( double amt );
};
```

In declaring a class, we specify inheritance by following the class name by a colon and a list of base classes; for single inheritance, this list will name only one base class. We specify each base class to be private or public by preceding its name in the base-class list with the appropriate keyword.*

If a base class is public, the public members of the base class are also public members of the derived class. Thus users of the derived class can refer to public members defined in the base class. If the base class is private, however, the public members of the base class become private members of the derived class. They

---

*If neither private nor public is specified, private is assumed by default. The preferred style, however, is to specify one or the other.

	Base Class	Derived Class (public base class)	Derived Class (private base class)
Table 5-1 *Accessibility in Derived Classes*	private	inaccessible	inaccessible
	protected	protected	private
	public	public	private

can be accessed by member and friend functions of the derived class, but they are not accessible to users of the derived class.

Generally, we use a public base class if we want the public member functions of the base class to also be available to users of the derived class. We use a private base class if we need to provide a different set of functions for users of the derived class and so want to block access to the functions defined in the base class. In class `sav_acct`, we designate class `account` as a public base class so that the public member functions `deposit()` and `get_balance()`, defined for `account`, will also be available to users of `sav_acct`.

More generally, the accessibility of members inherited by a derived class depends on their accessibility in the base class and on whether the base class is private or public. Table 5-1 covers all possible cases: Protected and public members of a public base class are inherited as, respectively, protected and public members of the derived class. Protected and public members of a private base class are inherited as private members of the derived class.

Note that a member inherited from a public base class has the same protected or public status in the derived class that it had in the base class. If all base classes in a hierarchy are public, then a class member declared as protected or public will retain that status in any class that inherits it; this is true regardless of whether the member is inherited directly from the class that defined it or indirectly from another class that also inherited it.

An object of class `sav_acct` has two instance variables: `balance`, which is inherited from `account`; and `rate`, which is declared in `sav_acct`. Both `rate` and `balance` are protected members of `sav_acct`: `rate` because it is declared as protected in `sav_acct`, and `balance` because it is a protected member of a public base class (row 2, column 2 of Table 5-1). Thus an instance of `sav_acct` has the same structure as if the class had been declared (without using inheritance) by

```
class sav_acct {
protected:
    double balance;
    double rate;
public:
    //...
};
```

Because `balance` and `rate` are protected members of `sav_acct`, they are accessible to the member and friend functions of any class derived from `sav_acct`.

Because an instance of a derived class contains instance variables from both the base class and the derived class, the constructors for both the base and derived class must be called to initialize the instance. In the constructor for the derived class, the function heading can be followed by a colon and an *initialization list* that contains calls to constructors for base classes.* For example, the constructor `sav_acct()` initializes `rate` itself, but to initialize `balance` it calls the constructor `account()` and passes to it the argument `bal`:

```
sav_acct::sav_acct( double bal,
                    double pct ) : account( bal )
{
    rate = pct / 100.0;
}
```

A base-class constructor that takes no arguments need not appear in the initialization list; if no constructor is listed for a particular base class, the constructor for that base class is called with no arguments. The base-class constructors are called *before* the constructor for the derived class is executed. Thus, in the example, the call `account( bal )` takes place before `rate` is assigned its initial value. Destructors, by the way, are called in the reverse order: the destructors for the base classes are called *after* the destructor for the derived class has been executed.

In earlier versions of C++, which did not provide multiple inheritance, a derived class could have only one base class. The name of the base-class constructor was redundant and was thus omitted from the initialization list. In earlier versions of C++, the definition of `sav_acct()` would be written

---

* The initialization list is also used to call constructors to initialize member variables that are themselves class objects.

```
sav_acct::sav_acct( double bal,
                            double pct ) : ( bal )
{
    rate = pct / 100.0;
}
```

For compatibility with earlier versions, Release 2.0 will accept this style when a derived class has only one base class. But the preferred style is to include the constructor name even when there is only one base class.

The function `compound()` computes, deposits, and returns the interest for the current period. The function `withdraw()` withdraws an amount `amt`, provided this amount does not overdraw the account; `withdraw()` returns the amount actually withdrawn. The definitions of these functions are straightforward and similar to the corresponding functions discussed in Chapter 2.

Because `account` is a public base class of `sav_acct`, the inherited functions `deposit()` and `get_balance()` are available for manipulating objects of class `sav_acct`. Thus, if `acct` is an object of type `sav_acct`, the following operations are all valid:

```
acct.deposit( 500 );
cout << acct.get_balance() << "\n";
cout << acct.compound() << "\n";
cout << acct.withdraw( 100 ) << "\n";
```

Class chk_acct

The derived class for traditional checking accounts is declared as follows:

```
class chk_acct : public account {
protected:
    double limit;
    double charge;
public:
    chk_acct( double bal = 0.0,
                    double lim = 500.0,
                    double chg = 0.50    );
    double cash_chk( double amt );
};
```

Like `sav_acct`, `chk_acct` specifies `account` as a public base class; thus `chk_acct` inherits from `account` the protected instance variable `balance` and the public member functions `deposit()` and `get_balance()`. Class `chk_acct` declares two more protected instance variables: `limit`, which is the smallest balance for which free checking is provided; and `charge`, the per-check charge that is applied when `balance` is less than `limit`. We declare `limit` and `charge` as protected only for uniformity and to allow other classes to be derived from `chk_acct`; class derivation aside, `chk_acct` would have the same properties if `limit` and `charge` were declared private.

Because `chk_acct` inherits `balance` from `account`, an object of class `chk_acct` has three instance variables, just as if `chk_acct` had been declared (without using inheritance) by

```
class chk_acct {
protected:
    double balance;
    double limit;
    double charge;
public:
    //...
};
```

The constructor `chk_acct()` takes three arguments (for which defaults are provided): the starting balance, the free-checking limit, and the per-check charge. The initialization list calls the constructor `account` with argument `bal`:

```
chk_acct::chk_acct( double bal,
                    double lim,
                    double chg  ) : account( bal )
{
    limit = lim;
    charge = chg;
}
```

The function `cash_chk()` cashes a check for a given amount; it is similar to the function `withdraw()` for `sav_acct`, except that it applies the per-check charge if the balance is below the free-checking limit. Class `chk_acct` also inherits functions `deposit()` and `get_balance()` from `account`; therefore, the three functions `deposit()`, `get_balance()`, and `cash_chk()` can all be applied to objects of class `chk_acct`.

Class `time_acct` and Redefining Inherited Functions

Class `time_acct` illustrates another important principle of inheritance: functions inherited from a base class can be redefined in the derived class; we sometimes say that the definition in the derived class *overrides* the definition inherited from the base class. For every such function the designer of the derived class can choose to either accept the definition inherited from the base class or provide a new definition for the derived class. What's more, the code for the new definition can invoke the inherited function, which is often convenient when we need to extend the inherited function — carry out the actions of the inherited function together with additional actions that are relevant only to the derived class.

Class `time_acct` defines a simplified version of a time-deposit account. In an actual time-deposit account, a deposit cannot be withdrawn until a given time has elapsed; accumulated interest, however, can be withdrawn at any time. For simplicity, we omit the mechanism that determines when each deposit becomes available for withdrawal. Thus in our simplified version, deposits never become available for withdrawal (until, presumably, the account is closed); only accumulated interest can be withdrawn.

Like a savings account, a time-deposit account has a balance and an interest rate, and it provides for compounding interest and for withdrawals. Thus, we define `time_acct` as a derived class of `sav_acct`. However, `time_acct` requires another instance variable, `funds_avail`, which specifies what part of the balance is available for withdrawal. Also, the inherited functions `compound()` and `withdraw()` have to be redefined: `compound()` to update `funds_avail` and `withdraw()` to make withdrawals only from available funds. An additional function, `get_avail()`, is provided to return the value of `funds_avail`. Thus we declare `time_acct` as follows:

```
class time_acct : public sav_acct {
protected:
    double funds_avail;
public:
    time_acct( double bal = 0.0,
               double pct = 0.5  );
    double compound();
    double withdraw( double amt );
    double get_avail() const
       { return funds_avail; }
};
```

Thus objects of class `time_acct` have three instance variables: `balance` and `rate` inherited from `sav_acct` (which inherited `balance` from `account`) and `funds_avail` declared in `time_acct`. Five functions can be applied to objects of class `time_acct`: `deposit()` and `get_balance()`, which are inherited from `sav_acct` (which inherited them from `account`); `compound()` and `withdraw()`, which, although inherited from `sav_acct`, are redefined in `time_acct`; and `get_avail()`, which is defined in `time_acct`. The version of `compound()` inherited from `sav_acct` is used in defining the version for `time_acct`.

The constructor `time_acct()` initializes `funds_avail` to 0 and passes its arguments to the constructor for `sav_acct`:

```
time_acct::time_acct( double bal,
                      double pct  )
                    : sav_acct( bal, pct )
{
    funds_avail = 0.0;
}
```

The function `sav_acct::compound()`, inherited from `sav_acct`, computes the interest for one period, adds the interest to `balance`, and returns the interest as the value of the function. The redefined function `time_acct::compound()` must do these things and also add the interest to `funds_avail`. Therefore, the definition for `time_acct::compound()` calls `sav_acct::compound()` and uses the value returned to update `funds_avail`:

```
double time_acct::compound()
{
    double interest = sav_acct::compound();
    funds_avail += interest;
    return interest;
}
```

It is extremely important that we use the qualified name `sav_acct::compound` in the function definition. If we use only `compound`, `time_acct::compound` will be assumed, and the function will be defined in terms of itself. Although self-definition (called *recursion*) can be a powerful programming technique, an unintended recursion will probably cause the program to crash when the function is called.

DEQUES, QUEUES, AND STACKS

In our preceding examples, all the public functions of the base class are also public functions of a derived class, either with the original definitions inherited from the base class or with new definitions for the derived class. Therefore the base classes are public so that the public functions of the base class will be public functions of the derived class. Sometimes, however, we want to give the derived class a completely different set of functions that do not merely redefine functions inherited from the base class. In that case, we use a private base class so that the inherited functions are not available to users of the base class. The inherited functions are still available to members and friends of the derived class, however, and can be used in defining the new set of public functions.

As an example, we consider *limited-access sequences*—sequences of values such that values can be inserted or removed only at the left and right ends of the sequence. The most general limited-access sequence is the *double-ended queue* or *deque* (pronounced *deck*), which allows both insertions and removals at both the left and right ends. Two special cases of the deque, the *queue* and the *stack*, are very widely used. A queue, which behaves like a waiting line, allows only insertions at one end ("the rear of the line") and only removals at the other end ("the front of the line"). A stack, which behaves like a stack of plates or coins, allows both insertions and removals at only one end ("the top of the stack").

Assuming that our sequences consist of integers, we need the following four functions to manipulate a deque:

```
void insert_left( int item );
void insert_right( int item );
int remove_left();
int remove_right();
```

Functions `insert_left()` and `insert_right()` insert the integer `item` at the corresponding end of the deque; `remove_left()` and `remove_right()` return an integer removed from the corresponding end of the deque.

For a queue, we need only two of these functions. For example, if we consider the rear of the queue to be to the left and its front to be to the right, we can use `insert_left()` and `remove_right()`. Alternatively, if we think of the queue as moving from right to left, we can use `insert_right()` and `remove_left()`. Because a queue has only one insert function and one remove function, it is customary to name them simply insert() and remove(). For a queue, then, we need to define insert() and remove() either in terms of insert_left() and remove_right() or in terms of insert_ right() and remove_left().

A stack allows insertions and removals at only one end; we can use either insert_left() and remove_left() or insert_right() and remove_right() for this purpose. In naming the functions for manipulating a stack, we think of the stack as being held by a spring-operated mechanism such as a coin holder or the mechanism that holds a stack of plates so that the top plate is always level with the counter. We think of the stack as being "pushed down" when an item is placed on top of it and "popped up" when an item is removed. Thus a stack is usually manipulated with functions push() and pop(), which we need to define either in terms of insert_left() and remove_left() or in terms of insert_right() and remove_ right().

Listing 5-3 shows the header file that contains the declarations of classes deque, queue, and stack; class deque is declared as follows:*

```
class deque {
    int* seq;
    int size;
    int left;
    int right;

    void underflow();
    void overflow();
public:
    deque( int sz = 10 );
    ~deque() { delete seq; }
    void insert_left( int item );
    void insert_right( int item );
    int remove_left();
    int remove_right();
};
```

Instance variable seq points to the array that holds the sequence; the remaining instance variables will be discussed presently, when we consider the implementation of class deque. The private functions underflow() and overflow() are used to

---

* For Release 2.1, delete seq should be delete [ ] seq.

Listing 5-3

```
// File limacc.h
// Header file for classes deque, queue, and stack

class deque {
    int* seq;    // pointer to data array
    int size;    // number of items in deque
    int left;    // subscript of element before left-most item
    int right;   // subscript of right-most item

    void underflow();   // signal underflow
    void overflow();    // signal overflow
public:
    deque( int sz = 10 );               // constructor
    ~deque() { delete seq; }            // destructor
    void insert_left( int item );   // insert item at left
    void insert_right( int item );  // insert item at right
    int remove_left();                  // remove item from left
    int remove_right();                 // remove item from right
};

class queue : private deque {
public:
    queue( int sz = 10 ) : deque( sz ) {}
    void insert( int item )                 // insert at rear
        { deque::insert_left( item ); }
    int remove()                            // remove from front
        { return deque::remove_right(); }
};

class stack : private deque {
public:
    stack( int sz = 10 ) : deque( sz ) {}
    void push( int item )                   // insert at top
        { deque::insert_right( item ); }
    int pop()                               // remove from top
        { return deque::remove_right(); }
};
```

Figure 5-2

Classes queue *and* stack *are both derived from class* deque.

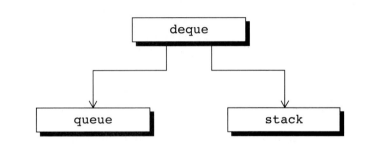

print error messages when the user attempts to remove an item from an empty deque or insert an item when array seq is full. Because these declarations are private rather than protected, they will not be available to derived classes; derived classes will be able to manipulate the member variables of **deque** only via the public functions of the class.

The constructor creates a deque that can hold up to **sz** items; the destructor deletes the array pointed to by **seq**. The functions insert_left(), insert_right(), remove_left(), and remove_right() insert and remove items as previously described.

The classes queue and stack are derived from class **deque** as indicated in Figure 5-2. Class queue is declared as follows:

```
class queue : private deque {
public:
  queue( int sz = 10 ) : deque( sz ) {}
  void insert( int item )
     { deque::insert_left( item ); }
  int remove()
     { return deque::remove_right(); }
};
```

Because **deque** is a private base class, its functions will not be publicly available for **queue**; like other private functions, however, they can be used by the definitions of the public functions of **queue**. Class **queue** inherits all its instance variables from **deque**; it does not declare any additional instance variables of its own. It cannot access the inherited instance variables directly, but must manipulate them via the functions inherited from **deque**.

The constructor for **queue** passes its argument to the constructor for **deque**; as indicated by the empty braces, the constructor for `queue` takes no action on its own. The destructor for `deque` is called whenever an object of class `queue` is destroyed; `queue` does not require a separate destructor of its own.

Assuming that items are inserted at the left end of a queue and removed from the right end, we define `insert()` by the statement

```
deque::insert_left( item );
```

and `remove()` by the statement

```
return deque::remove_right();
```

The qualified names `deque::insert_left` and `deque::remove_right` are required to refer to the corresponding members of `deque`.

We declare class `stack` as follows:

```
class stack : private deque {
public:
   stack( int sz = 10 ) : deque( sz ) {}
   void push( int item )
      { deque::insert_right( item ); }
   int pop()
      { return deque::remove_right(); }
};
```

As with `queue`, the constructor for `stack` merely passes its argument to the constructor for `deque` and takes no action on its own. We choose the right end of a deque to represent the top of a stack, so `push()` is defined by the statement

```
deque::insert_right( item );
```

and `pop()` is defined by the statement

```
return deque::remove_right();
```

Implementation of Class deque

Listing 5-4 shows the source file for class `deque`. The corresponding header file declares classes `stack`, `queue`, and `deque`; however, the member functions of `stack` and `queue` are defined in the header file using inline definitions, so Listing 5-4 need only define the member functions of `deque`.

Listing 5-4

```
// File limacc.cpp
// Source file for class deque

#include <stdlib.h>
#include <iostream.h>
#include "limacc.h"

// Warn of attempt to remove item from empty deque

void deque::underflow()
{
   cerr << "\nUnderflow error\n";
   exit( 1 );
}

// Warn of attempt to exceed capacity of data array

void deque::overflow()
{
   cerr << "\nOverflow error\n";
   exit( 1 );
}

// Construct deque with maximum capacity of sz items

deque::deque( int sz )
{
   seq = new int[ sz + 1 ];
   size = sz;
   left = right = 0;
}

// Insert item at left end of deque

void deque::insert_left( int item )
{
   seq[ left ] = item;
   if ( left > 0 ) left--; else left = size;
   if ( left == right ) overflow();
}
```

(continued)

```
// Insert item at right end of deque

void deque::insert_right( int item )
{
    if ( right < size ) right++; else right = 0;
    if ( left == right ) overflow();
    seq[ right ] = item;
}


// Remove and return item from left end of deque

int deque::remove_left()
{
    if ( left == right ) underflow();
    if ( left < size ) left++; else left = 0;
    return seq[ left ];
}


// Remove and return item from right end of deque

int deque::remove_right()
{
    if ( left == right ) underflow();
    int item = seq[ right ];
    if ( right > 0 ) right--; else right = size;
    return item;
}
```

We store a deque in an array using a representation widely discussed in computer-science texts. Figure 5-3a illustrates the significance of the instance variables seq, left, right, and size. Array seq holds the elements of the deque; size is the maximum number of items that can be stored in the deque. In the representation we will use, one element of array seq is always unused; therefore, array seq must contain size + 1 elements, and the subscripts for elements of seq run from 0 through size.

In Figure 5-3, the arrows indicate the array elements designated by particular subscripts; left designates the element immediately preceding the left-most element of the deque, and right designates the right-most element of the deque. The element seq[left] can never validly contain an item of the

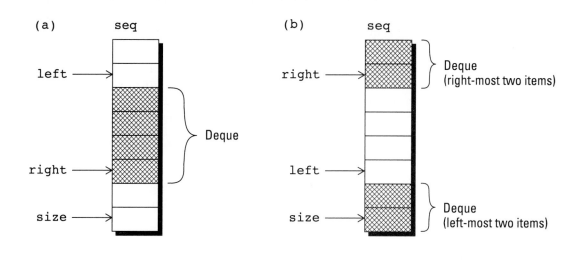

Figure 5-3

The items of a deque are stored in the array seq, *which contains* size + 1 *elements;* size *is the subscript of the last element. The part of the array used by the deque is designated by* left *and* right: left *is the subscript of the unused array element preceding the left-most item of the deque, and* right *is the subscript of the right-most item of the deque. As shown in part b, the deque can wrap around from the end of the array to the beginning.*

deque; if an item is stored in seq[left], it is an indication of *overflow*—we have attempted to store more than size items in the deque. The requirement that seq[left] remain unused is why array seq must contain size + 1 elements.

The unsymmetrical usage of left and right may seem strange, but it allows us to use the condition left == right to detect two special situations. If this condition is true before an operation is attempted, it represents an empty deque—one that contains no items. Attempting to remove an item from an empty deque causes an *underflow* error, because the empty deque contains no items to remove. Therefore, a remove operation must check the condition left == right *before* the operation is attempted. On the other hand, if the condition in question holds after an item has been inserted, it indicates that the item was stored in seq[left], which is an indication of overflow. Therefore, an insert operation must check the condition left == right *after* performing the operation to see if the insertion caused an overflow error.

The block of elements representing the deque can be anywhere within array seq. In fact, as illustrated in Figure 5-3b, the deque can wrap around from the end of the array to the beginning. Array seq behaves as if it has been bent into a ring, with element seq[0] joined to element seq[size]. Whenever we increment or decrement left or right, we must take the possibility of wraparound into consideration. For example, the following code must be used to increment right:

```
if ( right < size ) right++; else right = 0;
```

If right designates the last element of the array, seq[size], incrementing right will cause it to designate the first element, seq[0]. To decrement right, we must use

```
if ( right > 0 ) right--; else right = size;
```

If right designates the first element of the array, seq[0], decrementing right will cause it to designate the last element of the array, seq[size]. The same considerations apply to left.

With the aid of these remarks on the representation, we should have no trouble following the code in Listing 5-4. The functions underflow( ) and overflow( ) print error messages for the corresponding situations and terminate program execution. The constructor deque( ) creates an empty deque able to hold sz items:

```
seq = new int[ sz + 1 ];
size = sz;
left = right = 0;
```

As already mentioned, the array must contain one element more than the maximum number of items to be stored. We could have set left and right to any valid subscript of seq; as long as left and right have the same value, they will represent an empty deque.

The functions for inserting and removing elements are similar, so we need look at only one in detail. The function insert_left( ) is coded as follows:

```
seq[ left ] = item;
if ( left > 0 ) left--; else left = size;
if ( left == right ) overflow();
```

The function stores the value of item in the unused array element seq[left], then decrements the value of left. The decrementation must, of course, take the possibility of wrap-around into account. Finally, the function must check for overflow: if the condition `left == right` is *true*, it means that the insertion has caused the left and right ends of the deque to collide, leaving no room for the unused element that must always separate the two.

LINKED LISTS

Linked data structures are formed by letting some objects contain pointers to other objects; the pointers link the separate objects into a single data structure. The objects so linked are often called nodes; *node* comes from a Greek word meaning *knot*, as in the knots that hold a net together. A linked data structure often involves two classes: one for the entire structure and one for the nodes.

The simplest linked structure is the *linked list*, which is illustrated in Figure 5-4. Each node except the last contains a pointer to the next node on the list. The last node contains the null pointer, which is represented in diagrams by a diagonal line through a pointer variable. A pointer variable `head` points to the first node of the list.

Inheritance allows us to create general purpose list and node classes that can, in turn, be used to define linked-list classes for a variety of node objects. We define a class `node` whose objects have a single instance variable, which contains a pointer to the next node on a linked list. Thus objects of class `node` contain pointers only; they do not contain the data that we actually want to store on the list. However, any class derived from `node` will inherit the next-node pointer and can contain additional instance variables to hold useful information. We will build linked lists from objects whose classes are derived from class `node`.

Figure 5-4

Each object on a linked list has an instance variable that points to the next object on the list. For the last object on the list, this instance variable contains the null pointer, which is indicated in diagrams by a diagonal line. A pointer variable head *points to the first object of the list.*

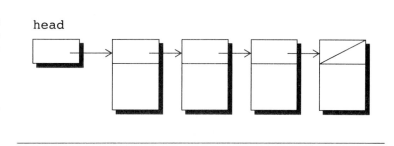

Likewise, we define a class `list` whose objects represent linked lists of `node` objects. Just as the items on a list will belong to a class derived from `node`, so the list itself will belong to a corresponding class derived from `list`.

In this chapter we will consider only *homogeneous lists*, in which all the objects on a list belong to the same class. In Chapter 6 we will consider *heterogeneous lists*, in which a single list can contain objects of several different classes.

Classes `list` *and* `node`

Listing 5-5 shows the header file for classes `node` and `list`, and Listing 5-6 (p. 247) shows the corresponding source file. As promised, class `node` contains only a single instance variable, `next`, which points to the next node on the list.

The member functions of class `list` need access to member variable `next` of class `node`. There are several ways this access could be provided. We could define `node` as a `struct` rather than a class, therefore making `next` accessible to any and all. Or we could equip `node` with public member functions for setting and returning the value of `next`, which would again make `next` generally accessible. What we do instead is to declare class `list` to be a friend of class `node`; this makes all the member functions of `list` friends of `node` (remember that a function can be both a member of one class and a friend of another). Thus `next` is accessible to the member functions of `list` but not to the member functions of any other class or to functions that are not members of a class.

An object of class `list` represents a linked list of `node` objects. The list in question is, of course, made up of the various node objects that are joined by the links; what a `list` object provides are some pointers for accessing the list and some functions for manipulating it.

The most important instance variable of a `list` object is `head`, which points to the first node of the corresponding linked list. We wish to provide a linked list with a cursor that can be used to scan through the list. Because following links can take us only forward in the list, not backward, it is convenient to have pointers to both the node we are working with and the one that precedes it in the list. Therefore, our cursor consists of two pointers: `cur` points to the current node — the node designated by the cursor — and `prev` points to the node that precedes it.

Listing 5-5

```
// File list.h
// Header file for linked-list classes node and list

enum Boolean { FALSE, TRUE };   // truth values

class node {
   friend class list;   // grant access to next
   node* next;          // pointer to next node
};

class list {
   node* head;        // pointer to first node of list
                      // cursor (designates current node):
   node* prev;        //     pointer to node preceding current
   node* cur;         //     pointer to current node
public:
   list() { head = prev = cur = 0; }
   void insert( node* p ); // insert new node before current
   node* remove();          // delete current node
   node* first()            // make first node current node
      { prev = 0; cur = head; return cur; }
   node* next();                // advance cursor to next node
   Boolean empty()              // return TRUE for empty list
      { return Boolean( head == 0 ); }
};
```

The cursor can designate any node of the list or it can designate a position just past the last node of the list; the latter position is convenient for appending new nodes to the end of a list. When the cursor designates the first node, `prev` holds the null pointer (because no node precedes the first one) and `cur` points to the first node on the list. When the cursor is positioned beyond the end of the list, `prev` points to the last node on the list and `cur` holds the null pointer (because no node follows the last one). When the list is empty, `head`, `prev`, and `cur` all hold the null pointer.

The constructor `list()` creates an empty list by setting `head`, `prev`, and `cur` to the null pointer. The function `insert()` inserts the node pointed to by `p` immediately *before* the node designated by the cursor. If the cursor is positioned beyond the end of the list, or the list is empty, the new node is appended to the end of the list. The function `remove()` removes from the list the node designated by the cursor and returns a pointer to the node removed. If the cursor is positioned beyond the end of the list, or the list is empty, `remove()` takes no action and returns the null pointer.

Functions `first()` and `next()` constitute an iterator for stepping through the elements of a list: `first()` positions the cursor at and returns a pointer to the first node; `next()` moves the cursor to and returns a pointer to the next node on the list. If the list is empty, `first()` returns the null pointer; `next()` returns the null pointer if it moves the cursor beyond the end of the list. If the cursor is already beyond the end of the list when `next()` is called, it returns the null pointer and takes no action.

Function `empty()` returns TRUE if the list is empty and FALSE otherwise; it determines whether the list is empty by checking whether `head` contains the null pointer.

Because several functions are defined inline in the header file, the source file need only define `insert()`, `remove()`, and `next()`.

Now let's turn to Listing 5-6 and look at the code for `insert()`, `remove()`, and `next()` — the three functions that are not defined inline. Because manipulation of linked lists can be tricky, we will need the full notational capabilities of C++ to describe the manipulations in a concise, straightforward manner. Bear in mind, then, that `*prev`, `*p`, and `*cur` are the objects respectively pointed to by `prev`, `p`, and `cur`. Likewise, `prev>next`, `p->next`, and `cur->next` are the respective next pointers for objects `*prev`, `*p`, and `*cur`.

In general, `insert()` inserts object `*p` between objects `*prev` and `*cur`. If, however, `prev` holds the null pointer, then `*p` is inserted at the beginning of the list, where it is immediately followed by object `*cur`.

Therefore, if `prev` holds the null pointer, `head` is set to `p` (making `*p` the first object on the list); otherwise, `prev->next` is set to `p` (making the new object follow object `*prev`):

```
if ( prev == 0 )
    head = p;
else
    prev->next = p;
```

Listing 5-6

```
// File list.cpp
// Source file for class list

#include "list.h"

// Insert node *p immediately before current node

void list::insert( node* p )
{
   if ( prev == 0 )
      head = p;
   else
      prev->next = p;
   p->next = cur;
   prev = p;
}

// Delete current node and return pointer to deleted node

node* list::remove()
{
   if ( cur == 0 ) return 0;
   if ( prev == 0 )
      head = cur->next;
   else
      prev->next = cur->next;
   node* p = cur;
   cur = cur->next;
   return p;
}

// Advance cursor to the next node in list

node* list::next()
{
   if ( cur == 0 ) return 0;
   prev = cur;
   cur = cur->next;
   return cur;
}
```

In either case, object *p is to be followed by object *cur, so p->next is set to cur:

```
p->next = cur;
```

Finally, object *cur is now preceded by object *p rather than object *prev, so the value of prev must be updated accordingly:

```
prev = p;
```

Note that the preceding code also works when cur holds the null pointer. In that case, p->next is set to the null pointer, indicating that object *p was appended to the end of the list.

If the cursor is beyond the end of the list, remove() returns the null pointer and takes no further action:

```
if ( cur == 0 ) return 0;
```

Otherwise, the object *cur is to be removed. The links must be adjusted so as to bypass object *cur: the link that now points to *cur must be set to point to the object following *cur, the object now pointed to by cur->next.

If prev is null, then *cur is the first object on the list and so head must be set to cur->next. If prev is not null, prev->next now points to object *cur and so must be set to cur->next:

```
if ( prev == 0 )
    head = cur->next;
else
    prev->next = cur->next;
```

Because we need to return a pointer to the object *cur that was removed, we save the value of cur in p. Like other pointers to *cur, the value of cur must be updated to cur->next (thus the object that followed *cur becomes the new current node). Finally, the value of p is returned as the pointer to the object that was removed:

```
node* p = cur;
cur = cur->next;
return p;
```

If the cursor is positioned beyond the end of the list, next() returns the null pointer and takes no action. Otherwise, it moves both prev and cur forward in the list by one node and returns a pointer to the new current node:

```
      if ( cur == 0 ) return 0;
      prev = cur;
      cur = cur->next;
      return cur;
```

Defining Derived Classes

By themselves, the classes list and node are useless, because each node stores only a pointer to the next node — there is no provision for storing useful information on our lists. Once list and node have been defined, however, it is easy to define derived classes of list and node in which useful information can be stored. The program in Listing 5-7 illustrates how to define and use such derived classes.

We begin by defining a derived class of node; node can be designated as either a private or public base class. The derived class will inherit the next pointer from node, so objects of the derived class can be placed on linked lists. Beyond this, we can give the derived class whatever member variables are needed to store the desired information and whatever member and friend functions are needed to manipulate that information.

To keep things simple, the program in Listing 5-7 defines a derived class inode that stores a single integer value. The derived class defines one member function and one friend: the member is a constructor that creates an object holding a given integer value; the friend overloads the output operator so that the integer stored in an inode object can be printed:

```
class inode : private node {
   int value;
public:
   inode( int i ) { value = i; }
   friend ostream& operator<< ( ostream& c, inode& n )
      { return c << n.value; }
};
```

Note that each inode object has two instance variables: next, which was inherited from node, and value, which was declared in inode.

We now have to define a derived class of list for manipulating lists of inodes. Fortunately, this is very easy to do because all that is required are some type conversions. The functions of

Listing 5-7

```
// File testl.cpp
// Defines and tests classes inode and ilist

#include <iostream.h>
#include "list.h"

// Class of integer nodes, each of which stores one integer

class inode : private node {
    int value;              // value to be stored
public:
    inode( int i ) { value = i; }
    friend ostream& operator<< ( ostream& c, inode& n )
        { return c << n.value; }        // output value of inode
};

// Class whose objects represent lists of integer nodes

class ilist : private list {
public:
    ilist() {}
    void insert( inode* p ) { list::insert( (node*)p ); }
    inode* remove() { return (inode*)list::remove(); }
    inode* first() { return (inode*)list::first(); }
    inode* next() { return (inode*)list::next(); }
    Boolean empty() { return list::empty(); }
};

// Test program for classes inode and ilist

main()
{
    ilist il;
    inode* p;

    // Build linked list

    for ( int i = 1; i <= 10; i++ )
        il.insert( new inode( 10 * i ) );
```

```
// Print contents of list

for ( p = il.first(); p != 0; p = il.next() )
    cout << *p << " ";
cout << "\n";

// Remove third through fifth elements, print elements
// removed, and print resulting list

il.first(); il.next(); il.next();
cout << *il.remove() << "\n";
cout << *il.remove() << "\n";
cout << *il.remove() << "\n";

for ( p = il.first(); p != 0; p = il.next() )
    cout << *p << " ";
cout << "\n";

// Insert two new elements before fifth element
// and print resulting list

il.first(); il.next(); il.next(); il.next(); il.next();
il.insert( new inode ( 1000 ) );
il.insert( new inode( 2000 ) );

for ( p = il.first(); p != 0; p = il.next() )
    cout << *p << " ";
cout << "\n";
}
```

list deal with pointers to node objects, that is, with pointers of type node*. Pointers to inodes, however, have type inode*. Therefore, any pointer to an inode must be converted to type node* before being passed to a function of list, and any pointer returned by a function of list must be converted back to type inode*.*

* There is an implicit conversion from *pointer-to-derived-class* to *pointer-to-base-class*, so the conversion from inode* to node* will take place automatically if an inode* pointer is used where a node* pointer is expected. This implicit conversion is discussed further in Chapter 6; for now, however, we will indicate all pointer conversions explicitly with type casts.

These conversions cause the functions of list to handle inodes as if they were nodes. This is possible because an inode object is just a node object expanded to include an additional instance variable. The functions of list will work only with the part of the object that was defined in node and will ignore any additional instance variables defined in a derived class.

Class ilist, whose objects represent lists of inodes, is defined with list as a private base class. Thus the public functions of list become private functions of ilist. Each public function of ilist is defined directly in terms of the corresponding function inherited from list:

```
class ilist : private list {
public:
    ilist() {}
    void insert( inode* p ) { list::insert( (node*)p ); }
    inode* remove() { return (inode*)list::remove(); }
    inode* first() { return (inode*)list::first(); }
    inode* next() { return (inode*)list::next(); }
    Boolean empty() { return list::empty(); }
};
```

The argument of ilist::insert() is converted to type node* before being passed to list::insert(). The pointers returned by list::remove(), list::first(), and list::next() are converted to type inode* before being returned by, respectively, ilist::remove(), ilist::first(), and ilist::next(). The dummy constructor ilist() is needed to get the constructor list invoked when an ilist object is created.

Using ilist and inode

The rest of Listing 5-7 is a demonstration program illustrating the use of ilist and inode. We begin by declaring an ilist il and an inode pointer p:

```
    ilist il;
    inode* p;
```

Next, we create inodes with values 10, 20, 30, . . . 100 and use insert() to insert them into the ilist il:

```
for ( int i = 1; i <= 10; i++ )
    il.insert( new inode( 10 * i ) );
```

To see that these inodes have been inserted properly, we use the iterator functions `first()` and `next()` along with the overloaded output operator `<<` to print the integers stored on the list:

```
for ( p = il.first(); p != 0; p = il.next() )
    cout << *p << " ";
cout << "\n";
```

The printout is

    10 20 30 40 50 60 70 80 90 100

To illustrate `remove()`, we use the iterator functions to position the cursor on the third element of the list; we then execute `remove()` three times to remove the third through the fifth elements of the list. The calls to `remove()` are placed in output statements so that the value of each removed element will be printed:

```
il.first(); il.next(); il.next();
cout << *il.remove() << "\n";
cout << *il.remove() << "\n";
cout << *il.remove() << "\n";
```

The printout is

    30
    40
    50

The same output code as discussed previously is used again to print the integer values of the inodes remaining on `il`:

    10 20 60 70 80 90 100

Finally, the iterator functions are used to position the cursor on the fifth element of the list—the one with integer value 80—and `insert()` is used to insert elements with values 1000 and 2000 before the element with value 80.

```
il.first(); il.next(); il.next(); il.next();
il.next();
il.insert( new inode ( 1000 ) );
il.insert( new inode( 2000 ) );
```

The output code is used still another time to print the final result of all the preceding manipulations:

```
10 20 60 70 1000 2000 80 90 100
```

EXTENDING AN EXISTING CLASS

As an example of using inheritance to extend an existing class, we will see how to provide an iterator for class `table`, defined in Chapter 3. We will define a derived class `itable` that provides functions for stepping through the stored table entries.

Listing 5-8 show the header file for both `table` and `itable`. Only one change has been made in the declaration of `table`: the derived class needs access to the instance variables `tab` and `count`, so these variables—originally private—have been redeclared as protected:

```
class table {
protected:
    entry* tab;
    int count;
private:
    int size;
    void grow();
    int search( char* k );
public:
    //...
};
```

Thinking more generally, rather than merely in terms of this particular example, we might also put the declaration of `search()` in the protected section, because a derived class might reasonably want to use this function to search a table. On the other hand, `size` and `grow` should definitely remain private: we don't want a derived class tampering with `table`'s memory management. The source file for `table` does not need to be changed.

The derived class `itable` names `table` as a public base class so that `itable` can offer all the public functions defined in `table`. In addition to the functions inherited from `table`, `itable` must provide the iterator functions: `first()`, which sets the cursor to the first table entry; `cont()`, which checks whether the cursor has passed the last table entry; `next()`, which advances the cursor to the next table entry; and

Listing 5-8

```
// File table.h
// Header file for class table

struct entry {                    // table entry
    char* key;                    // pointer to key string
    char* value;                  // pointer to value string
};

class table {
protected:
    entry* tab;                   // pointer to array of entries
    int count;                    // current number of entries
private:
    int size;                     // maximum number of entries
    void grow();                  // enlarge data array
    int search( char* k );        // locate entry with given key
public:
    table( int sz = 4 );          // construct new table
    ~table();                     // dispose of existing table
    void insert( char* k, char* v );  // insert entry
    const char* find( char* k );      // find entry
    void remove( char* k );           // remove entry
};

class itable : public table {
    int i;                             // cursor
public:
    itable( int sz = 4 ) : table( sz ) { i = 0; }
    void first() { i = 0; }   // cursor to beginning of table
    int cont()                // cursor past end of table?
        { return ( i < count ); }
    void next() { i++; }       // advance cursor to next entry
    const char* cur_key()      // return key of current entry
        { if ( 0 <= i && i < count )
            return tab[ i ].key;
          else return 0; }
    const char* cur_value()  // return value of current entry
        { if ( 0 <= i && i < count )
            return tab[ i ].value;
          else return 0; }
};
```

cur_key() and cur_value(), which return pointers to the key and value of the table entry currently designated by the cursor. For example, we could use these functions to print a list of all the keys and values stored by an itable object t:

```
for ( t.first(); t.cont(); t.next() ) {
    cout << t.cur_key() << "\n";
    cout << t.cur_value() << "\n\n";
}
```

In addition to the functions mentioned, itable also defines the cursor—an instance variable i that serves as the subscript of the current table entry, the entry whose key and value can be accessed via cur_key() and cur_value().

The constructor itable passes its argument to the constructor for table; the only action it takes on its own is to initialize the cursor i to 0, to help prevent disaster if someone should use one of the other functions without having first called first():

```
itable( int sz = 4 ) : table( sz ) { i = 0; }
```

The functions first(), cont(), and next() manipulate the cursor i as one would normally manipulate the control variable in a for statement. Thus first() sets i to 0, cont() checks whether i is less than count, and next() increments i:

```
void first() { i = 0; }
int cont() { return ( i < count ); }
void next() { i++; }
```

The functions cur_key() and cur_value() return pointers to the key and value of table entry tab[i]. Both functions check the value of i for validity; if i is outside the range 0 through count – 1, both functions return the null pointer:

```
const char* cur_key()
    { if ( 0 <= i && i < count )
        return tab[ i ].key;
      else return 0; }
const char* cur_value()
    { if ( 0 <= i && i < count )
        return tab[ i ].value;
      else return 0; }
```

The functions return pointers to constant data so that the stored table entries cannot be changed via the pointers (unless the user circumvents the constant-data restriction).

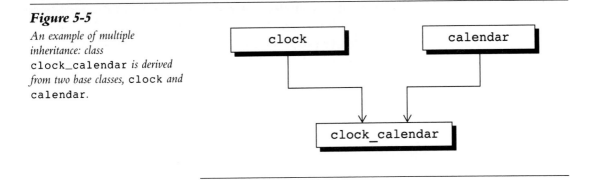

Figure 5-5

An example of multiple inheritance: class clock_calendar *is derived from two base classes,* clock *and* calendar.

MULTIPLE INHERITANCE

Multiple inheritance allows us to take the combined features of several existing classes as a starting point for defining a new class. For example, let's define a class clock, whose objects store a time, and a class calendar, whose objects store a date. We will then use multiple inheritance to derive a class clock_calendar, whose objects store both a time and a date. Figure 5-5 shows the *class network** for these three classes.

We define class clock as follows:

```
class clock {
protected:
    int hr;
    int min;
    int sec;
    int is_pm;
public:
    clock( int h, int s, int m, int pm );
    void set_clock( int h, int s, int m, int pm );
    void read_clock( int& h, int& s, int& m, int& pm );
    void advance();
};
```

Instance variables hr, min, and sec hold the time in hours, minutes, and seconds; instance variable is_pm is 0 for A.M. and 1 for P.M. The constructor clock() creates a new clock and sets it to a given time; set_clock() sets an existing clock to a given time, read_clock() returns the current time via its reference parameters, and advance() advances the time by one

* In a class hierarchy, every derived class has a single base class. For multiple inheritance, therefore, we speak of a "class network" rather than a "class hierarchy."

second. The definitions of these member functions are left as exercises for the reader.

Class `calendar` is similar to `clock`:

```
class calendar {
protected:
    int mo;
    int day;
    int yr;
public:
    calendar( int m, int d, int y );
    void set_calendar( int m, int d, int y );
    void read_calendar( int& m, int& d, int& y );
    void advance();
};
```

Instance variables `mo`, `day`, and `yr` hold a date. The constructor `calendar()` creates a calendar and sets it to a given date; `set_calendar()` sets an existing calendar to a given date, `read_calendar()` returns the current date via its reference parameters, and `advance()` advances the date by one day. Again, the definitions of the member functions are left as exercises; note that the definition of `calendar::advance()` will be considerably more complicated than that of `clock::advance()` (why?).

We are now ready to define `clock_calendar`:

```
class clock_calendar : public clock, public calendar {
public:
    clock_calendar( int mt, int d, int y,
                    int h, int mn, int s, int pm );
    void advance();
};
```

Following the class name and the colon is a list of all the base classes from which the class is derived. Each base class can be specified individually as `public` or `private`; because we want `clock_calendar` to offer the functions inherited from `clock` and `calendar`, we declare them both as public base classes.

To initialize a `clock_calendar` object, the constructor `clock_calendar()` needs to invoke the constructors of both `clock` and `calendar`. As with single inheritance, this is done by placing calls to the `clock()` and `calendar()` on `clock_calendar()`'s initialization list. Thus, we define `clock_calendar()` as follows:

```
clock_calendar::clock_calendar
    ( int mt, int d, int y,
      int h, int mn, int s, int pm )
    : calendar( mt, d, y ), clock( h, mn, s, pm )
{ }
```

Unfortunately, the length of the argument list makes this definition somewhat hard to read. Note, however, that the qualified function name is followed by the argument list, then by an initialization list that calls both `calendar()` and `clock()`. All the work of the constructor is accomplished by the calls in the initialization list: the block that defines the body of the function is empty.

The member functions `set_clock()`, `read_clock()`, `set_calendar()`, and `read_calendar()` are all inherited by `clock_calendar` and all work in exactly the same way for `clock_calendar` objects as they do for `clock` or `calendar` objects. All three classes declare a function `advance()`; the version of `advance()` declared in `clock_calendar` overrides those inherited from `clock()` and `calendar()`. However, the inherited functions `clock::advance()` and `calendar::advance()` can be used in the definition of `clock_calendar::advance()`:

```
void clock_calendar::advance()
{
    int was_pm = is_pm;
    clock::advance();
    if ( was_pm && !is_pm )
        calendar::advance();
};
```

The function calls `clock::advance()` to advance the clock; if advancing the clock changes P.M. to A.M., then `calendar::advance()` is called to advance the calendar.

Let's look for a moment at what the situation would be if the inherited versions of `advance()` were *not* overridden by a declaration for `advance()` in `clock_calendar`. In that case, if cc is a `clock_calendar` object, the statement

```
cc.advance();
```

is ambiguous (and hence invalid) because `advance` could refer to either `clock::advance()` or `calendar::advance()`, both of which would be inherited as public members of `clock_calendar`. Thus we must write either

```
cc.clock::advance();
```

to advance the clock part of cc or

```
cc.calendar::advance();
```

to advance the calendar part.

It is generally undesirable to require users to employ such complex qualified names. The best solution is what we have in fact done: provide clock_calendar with an advance() function that overrides the inherited advance() functions and whose definition calls them as needed for advancing a clock_calendar object. Because clock::advance() and calendar::advance() are overridden by clock_calendar::advance(), the statement

```
cc.advance();
```

is valid and invokes clock_calendar::advance().

Virtual Base Classes

Consider the not uncommon situation illustrated in Figure 5-6. The class grandparent serves as a public base class for the derived classes parent_1, parent_2, and so on. Via multiple inheritance, the classes parent_1, parent_2, and so on, serve as public base classes for the derived class child. We refer to parent_1, parent_2, and so on as *intermediate base classes* because each provides an avenue of inheritance between the derived class child and the base class grandparent.

However, this configuration of classes can give rise to the following problem. Each intermediate base class inherits the public and protected members of grandparent, which are in turn inherited by child. Because child inherits from each intermediate base class, it ends up with many duplicate sets of the members inherited from grandparent. For example, suppose that grandparent defines both a variable data and a function clear() that clears the value of data to zero. From parent_1, child will inherit a variable parent_1::data and a function parent_1::clear() to clear it to zero; from parent_2, child will inherit a variable parent_2::data and a function parent_2::clear() to clear it to zero; and so on.

To avoid this duplication of inherited members, the intermediate base classes parent_1, parent_2, and so on must each specify grandparent to be a *virtual base class*. Only one set of members will be inherited from a virtual base class, regardless of

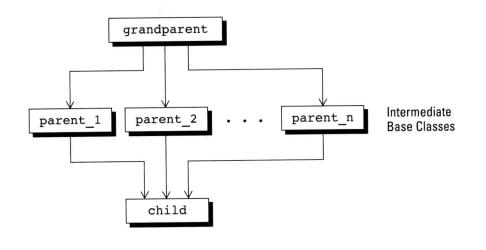

Figure 5-6

The protected and public members of `grandparent` *are inherited by each of the intermediate base classes* `parent_1, parent_2,` *and so on;* `child` *inherits a different set of these members from each intermediate base class. This duplication of members inherited from* `grandparent` *can be avoided by making* `grandparent` *a virtual base class.*

how many inheritance paths exist between the virtual base class and a derived class.

For a specific example, consider the class network of Figure 5-7. Class `counter` stores a count and defines a function for setting the count to a given value. From `counter` we derive the class `incr_c` of incrementable counters (which provides a function for incrementing the count) and the class `disp_c` of displayable counters (which provides a function for displaying the count). Finally, we derive from both `incr_c` and `disp_c` the class `incr_disp_c` of incrementable, displayable counters. To assure that members of `counter` are inherited only once by `incr_disp_c`, the intermediate base classes `incr_c` and `disp_c` must specify `counter` as a virtual base class.

We define class `counter` as follows:

```
class counter {
protected:
    int count;
public:
    counter( int c = 0 ) { count = c; }
    void reset( int c = 0 ) { count = c; }
}
```

Figure 5-7

Class incr_disp_c inherits from counter via the two intermediate base classes incr_c and disp_c. Class counter must be a virtual base class so that only one (and not two) sets of its public and protected members will be inherited by incr_disp_c.

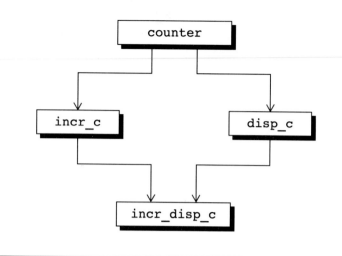

If a virtual base class defines any constructors, it must provide a default constructor that either (1) has zero arguments or (2) provides defaults for all its arguments. The single constructor defined for counter meets the requirements for the default constructor because it provides a default for its single argument. The default constructor will be called with no arguments *if* no constructor for the class is called explicitly from an initialization list.

We now derive the two intermediate base classes, each of which names counter as a public virtual base class by preceding its name in the base-class list with the keywords public and virtual. Class incr_c defines incrementable counters—counters whose count can be incremented with the function increment():

```
class incr_c : virtual public counter {
public:
    incr_c() : counter( 100 ) {}
    void increment() { count++; }
};
```

To illustrate a point, each of our derived classes will initialize the count to a different value. For example, the constructor incr_c() invokes the constructor counter() with argument 100, so an incrementable counter is always created with a starting count of 100.

Likewise, we declare the class disp_c of displayable counters, whose counts can be displayed with a call to the function show():

```
class disp_c : virtual public counter {
public:
    disp_c() : counter( 200 ) {}
    void show()
        { cout << "Count: " << count << endl; }
};
```

The constructor `disp_c()` invokes the constructor `counter()` with an argument of 200, so a displayable counter is always created with a starting count of 200.

Finally, we define the class `incr_disp_c` of incrementable, displayable counters:

```
class incr_disp_c : public incr_c, public disp_c {
public:
    incr_disp_c() : counter( 300 ) {}
};
```

If `counter` were not a virtual base class, the definition of `incr_disp_c()` would not be valid. In the absence of virtual base classes, a class can only call constructors for its own immediate base classes—the ones that appear in its base-class list. It cannot go over their heads and call constructors for their base classes. If `counter` were not a virtual base class, `incr_disp_c()` would be limited to calling the constructors of the intermediate base classes `incr_c` and `disp_c`.

```
incr_disp_c() : incr_c(), disp_c() {}
```

However, it is easy to see the problem with using this definition with a virtual base class: `incr_c()` calls `counter( 100 )` and `disp_c()` calls `counter( 200 )`; to what value, then, will an incrementable, displayable counter be initialized? To avoid such conflicts, different rules govern the calling of constructors for virtual base classes. *A constructor for a virtual base class must be called from the derived class that is actually creating an object; calls from intermediate base classes are ignored.* Thus if we actually used the above alternate definition for `incr_disp_c()`, the calls to `counter()` in `incr_c()` and `disp_c()` would be ignored, and the default constructor would be used (`counter()` would be called with no arguments). On the other hand, the definition that is actually used

```
incr_disp_c() : counter( 300 ) {}
```

calls `counter()` directly to initialize to 300 the count of an incrementable, displayable counter.

There is one additional restriction on virtual base classes. In our discussion of linked lists, we dealt with a derived class `inode` and its base class `node`; we used type casts to convert pointers from type `inode*` to type `node*` and from type `node*` to type `inode*`. For a virtual base class, the second conversion is invalid: we cannot convert a pointer to base-class objects into a pointer to derived-class objects. The opposite pointer conversion, from derived-class to base-class, is still allowed, however. Fortunately, the allowed conversion turns out to be the most important one; in Chapter 6 we will see that derived-class to base-class pointer conversions play a crucial role in polymorphism and heterogeneous lists.

EXERCISES

1. Define a derived class of `sav_acct` that places a limit on the number of withdrawals that can be made each period —that is, between calls to `compound()`. The withdrawal limit should be set when a class object is created; after the limit is reached, `withdraw` returns 0 and has no other effect.

2. Some calculators provide their stack with a `rotate_up` operation, which transfers the topmost item to the bottom, and a `rotate_down` operation, which transfers the bottommost item to the top. Define a derived class of `deque` that provides `rotate_up()` and `rotate_down()` as well as `push()` and `pop()`. Why must this class be derived from `deque` and not from `stack`?

3. Define a derived class of `vector` (defined in Chapter 4) that allows vectors to be compared for lexicographical order with the operators <, <=, >, and >=. To compare two vectors, scan them in order of increasing subscripts, comparing corresponding components. If all corresponding components are equal, the vectors are equal; otherwise, the numerical order of the first pair of unequal components determines the order of the vectors.

4. Define a derived class of `table` (or `itable`) that allows (pointers to) strings to be used as subscripts; the subscript expression returns a pointer to the corresponding value. If the key value is not found in the table, the null pointer

should be returned. Specifically, your derived class should provide the operator

```
const char* operator[] ( char* s );
```

If table t contains the key-value pairs

```
Jack    555-7891
Jill    555-3245
```

then

```
cout << t[ "Jack" ] << "\n";
```

should print Jack's phone number and

```
cout << t[ "Jill" ] << "\n";
```

should print Jill's. *Hint:* modify `table` as indicated in this chapter except make `search()` protected rather than private.

5. Define a version of class `table` that uses a linked list, rather than an array, to store the keys and values.

6. Extend the bank-account hierarchy (Figure 5-1, Listings 5-1 and 5-2) by defining the class `int_chk_acct` of interest checking accounts, which combine the properties of savings and checking accounts. Use multiple inheritance to derive `int_chk_acct` from `sav_acct` and `chk_ acct`. Class `account` must be made a virtual base class (why?). The declaration of `account` can be left unchanged, but the declarations of `sav_acct`, `chk_ acct`, and `time_acct` must be modified slightly. *Hint:* remember that the initialization of a base class by derived classes is handled differently for virtual and nonvirtual base classes.

6

Polymorphism: Virtual Functions

*P*OLYMORPHISM REFERS to the situation in which objects belonging to different classes can respond to the same message, usually in different ways. For example, suppose we have classes box, triangle, and circle, whose objects represent the corresponding geometrical figures. The objects of these classes might all understand a message show(), which causes an object to draw the corresponding figure on the screen. However, the response to a show message—the particular figure that is drawn—will clearly be different for box objects, triangle objects, and circle objects.

An essential feature of polymorphism is that we be able to send messages without knowing the class of the recipient object. For example, we might have a list of objects representing all the figures that are to appear on the screen. To display the figures, we can send a show() message to every object on the list, without having to worry about which objects represent boxes, which represent circles, and so on. A list containing objects from different classes is called a *heterogeneous list*; polymorphism greatly simplifies manipulating the objects in a heterogeneous list.

In C++, polymorphism is implemented via *virtual functions*. Although virtual functions are slightly less efficient (in both memory requirements and execution time) than nonvirtual functions, their power and flexibility often recommend their use.

POINTERS, REFERENCES, AND VIRTUAL FUNCTIONS

An essential requirement of polymorphism is the ability to refer to objects without regard to their classes. We cannot use ordinary (nonpointer, nonreference) variables for this purpose. Every such variable is associated with a memory area that is just large enough to hold objects of one class, the class declared for the variable. Objects of different classes will generally have different sizes and so cannot be assured of fitting in the allocated memory space. Pointers and references, on the other hand, refer to objects by their addresses. The memory space required for an address is the same regardless of the size of the corresponding object, so a single pointer variable or reference can refer to objects belonging to different classes.

Heterogeneous Lists

Consider the following two classes:

```
class parent {
protected:
    int j, k;
public:
    //...
};
class child : public parent {
    int m, n;
public:
    //...
};
```

Objects of class `parent` have two instance variables, `j` and `k`. Objects of class `child` have four instance variables: `j` and `k` inherited from `parent` and `m` and `n` declared in `child`.

The type of an object, pointer, or reference will be implicitly converted from a derived class to a *public* base class. Thus if we declare

```
parent prnt, prnt1;
child chld, chld1;
```

then the assignment

```
prnt = chld;
```

is allowed. Unfortunately, this assignment is not useful for polymorphism because `prnt` has room for only two instance variables, j and k. With memberwise assignment, the preceding statement is equivalent to

```
prnt.j = chld.j;
prnt.k = chld.k;
```

The value of chld is converted to type parent by discarding the instance variables m and n. What we need is some way of referring to objects of different classes without actually changing the objects referred to.

We have better luck with pointers and references. The following declarations are also valid:

```
parent* pp = &chld;
parent& rr = chld;
```

Pointers and references refer to objects via their addresses, which have the same size regardless of the class to which an object belongs. Thus pp and rr can both refer to the complete chld object; no information is lost when chld is referred to via pp and rr.

We will focus on pointers, which generally are more useful than references for manipulating objects. (References are better suited to the more specialized tasks of argument passing and value return.) Although pp is declared with type parent*, it can point to objects of both parent and child. Thus the assignments

```
pp = &prnt1;
```

and

```
pp = &chld1;
```

are both valid.

Now consider an array list of pointers to parent objects:

```
parent* list[ 4 ];
```

Each element of list has type parent* and so, like pp, can point to either a parent object or a child object. Thus the following assignments are valid:

```
list[ 0 ] = &prnt;
list[ 1 ] = &chld;
list[ 2 ] = &prnt1;
list[ 3 ] = &chld1;
```

The array list implements a heterogeneous list in that it contains pointers to objects of two different classes, parent and child.

Virtual Functions

To use heterogeneous lists effectively, we need functions that can be applied to any object on the list without regard to its class. Such functions will generally have different definitions for different classes. We want the appropriate definition to be used whenever a function is applied to an object, even though the class of the object was not known at compile time. In C++ these capabilities are provided by virtual functions.

Let's give class `parent` two member functions, one virtual and one not:

```
class parent {
protected:
    int j, k;
public:
    virtual void vf() { cout << "vf: parent\n"; }
    void nvf() { cout << "nvf: parent\n"; }
};
```

The keyword `virtual` declares `vf()` to be a virtual function; in the absence of this keyword, `nvf()` is just an ordinary, non-virtual function. Each function prints its name and the class in which it is defined. Now let's redefine each function in the derived class `child`:

```
class child : public parent {
    int m, n;
public:
    void vf() { cout << "vf: child\n"; }
    void nvf() { cout << "nvf: child\n"; }
};
```

Note that the keyword `virtual` is used only in the base class; functions that override a virtual function are always virtual and do not have to be explicitly declared so.

When `vf()` and `nvf()` are applied to objects referred to directly—that is, not via pointers or references—the results are as we might expect. Applying `vf()` and `nvf()` to the `parent` object `prnt` causes the definitions in class `parent` to be used, and applying them to the `child` object `chld` causes the definitions in class `child` to be used. Thus

```
prnt.vf();
prnt.nvf();
```

print

```
vf: parent
nvf: parent
```

and the statements

```
chld.vf();
chld.nvf();
```

print

```
vf: child
nvf: child
```

To see the difference between virtual and nonvirtual functions, consider the case in which the objects are referenced via a pointer. As before, let pp have type parent*; if pp points to an object of class parent, then the definition for the parent class will be used for both functions. Thus the statements

```
pp = &prnt;
pp->vf();
pp->nvf();
```

print

```
vf: parent
nvf: parent
```

If pp points to an object of class child, the virtual function will use the definition for class child, whereas the nonvirtual function will use the definition for class parent. Thus

```
pp = &chld;
pp->vf();
pp->nvf();
```

produce the printout

```
vf: child
nvf: parent
```

For a nonvirtual function, then, *the declaration of the pointer variable* determines which function definition will be used. Because pp is declared with type parent*, the definition in parent will always be used for a nonvirtual function. For a virtual function, however, *the class of the object pointed to* determines which function definition will be used. If pp points to a parent object, the definition in `parent` will be used; if `pp` points to a `child` object, the definition in `child` will be used.

The reason for this difference is that the names of virtual and nonvirtual functions are *bound*—associated with definitions—at different times. The names of nonvirtual functions are bound at compile time (*early binding*); the compiler does not know what kind of object a pointer variable will eventually point to, so it must rely on the information in the declaration of the pointer variable. The names of virtual functions, however, are bound at run time, specifically, at the time of each function call (*late binding*). The binding is thus determined by the class of the object pointed to by the pointer variable at the time of the function call.

Let's apply `vf()` to the objects on the heterogeneous list implemented by `list`:

```
for ( int i = 0; i < 4; i++ )
    list[ i ]->vf();
```

For each element of `list`, the class of the object pointed to determines which definition for `vf()` will be used. Parent and child objects alternate on the list, so we get the following printout:

```
vf: parent
vf: child
vf: parent
vf: child
```

If we performed the same experiment with `nvf()`, `nvf: parent` would be printed four times (why?).

A function that overrides a virtual function must have the same argument list and return type as the virtual function—the types, number, and order of the arguments, as well as the return type, must be the same for the corresponding function definitions in the base and derived classes. Thus in

```
class base {
public:
    virtual void f( int );
};
class derived : public base {
public:
    void f( int );
};
```

`derived::f` overrides `base::f` because both functions have the same argument list and return type. Because `derived::f` overrides a virtual function, it is itself virtual, even though it is not explicitly declared as such.

It is permissible for a derived class to define a function with the same name as an inherited virtual function but with a different argument list:

```
class base {
public:
    virtual void f( int );
};
class derived : public base {
public:
    void f( double );
};
```

In this case, however, the derived-class function is *not* virtual and does *not* override the inherited virtual function. Thus `derived::f` is overloaded with two definitions: the virtual function inherited from `base` and the nonvirtual function defined in `derived`. As usual with overloaded functions, the types of the arguments in a function call determine which definition should be used. If `d` is an object of class `derived`, then `d.f( 3 )` calls the inherited virtual function, while `d.f( 3.0 )` calls the nonvirtual function defined in the derived class.

It is illegal for a derived-class function to have the same name and argument list as an inherited virtual function but a different return type:

```
class base {
public:
    virtual int f( int );
};
class derived : public base {
public:
    double f( int );   // error
};
```

If such were allowed, it would be impossible to determine whether a function call such as `d.f( 3 )` should invoke the inherited virtual function or the nonvirtual function declared in the derived class.

Constructors cannot be virtual. A virtual constructor would be useless because a constructor is always called to create an object of a specified class; the specified class determines which definition should be used. Virtual *destructors* are allowed, however. When the destructor of a base class is declared virtual, then destructors in derived classes override the base-class destructor, even though destructor functions for different classes have different names. When an object referred to by a pointer or reference is destroyed, the class of the object determines which definition of the virtual destructor will be called.

EXAMPLE: BREEDS OF DOGS

Consider the class hierarchy in Figure 6-1, which classifies dogs according to their breeds. Listing 6-1 contains definitions for each class in the hierarchy as well as a short program for demonstrating virtual functions.

The base class, dog, defines a virtual function print_breed() for printing the breed of a dog. Because the breed is not defined for the base class, the base-class definition prints the message Breed not defined:

```
class dog {
public:
    virtual void print_breed()
        { cout << "Breed not defined\n"; }
};
```

The base-class definition is overridden in each derived class with a definition that prints the corresponding breed. For example, class schnauzer defines print_breed() to print Schnauzer:

```
class schnauzer : public dog {
public:
    void print_breed() { cout << "Schnauzer\n"; }
};
```

and class miniature_schnauzer defines print_breed() to print Miniature Schnauzer:

```
class miniature_schnauzer : public schnauzer {
    void print_breed()
        { cout << "Miniature Schnauzer\n"; }
};
```

Note that print_breed() is declared virtual only in the base class; any function in the entire hierarchy that overrides print_breed() will also be virtual.

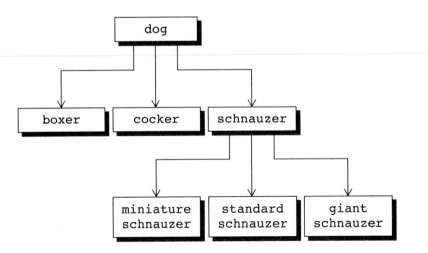

Figure 6-1

The class hierarchy for the breeds of dogs example.

Listing 6-1

```cpp
// File dogs.cpp
// Class definitions and program for
// demonstrating virtual functions

#include <iostream.h>

// Topmost class of hierarchy

class dog {
public:
   virtual void print_breed()
       { cout << "Breed not defined\n"; }
};

// Classes derived from class dog

class boxer : public dog {
public:
   void print_breed() { cout << "Boxer\n"; }
};
```

```
class cocker : public dog {
public:
    void print_breed() { cout << "Cocker Spaniel\n"; }
};

class schnauzer : public dog {
public:
    void print_breed() { cout << "Schnauzer\n"; }
};

// Classes derived from class schnauzer

class miniature_schnauzer : public schnauzer {
    void print_breed() { cout << "Miniature Schnauzer\n"; }
};

class standard_schnauzer : public schnauzer {
public:
    void print_breed() { cout << "Standard Schnauzer\n"; }
};

class giant_schnauzer : public schnauzer {
    void print_breed() { cout << "Giant Schnauzer\n"; }
};

// Program to demonstrate virtual functions

main()
{
    // Create objects for classes in dogs hierarchy

    dog d;
    boxer b;
    cocker c;
    schnauzer s;
    miniature_schnauzer ms;
    standard_schnauzer ss;
    giant_schnauzer gs;

    // dp can point to an object of class dog or to an
    // object of any class derived from dog
```

(continued)

```
dog* dp;

// Set dp to point to class objects from dogs hierarchy
// Invoke virtual function print_breed() for each object

dp = &d; dp->print_breed();
dp = &b; dp->print_breed();
dp = &c; dp->print_breed();
dp = &s; dp->print_breed();
dp = &ms; dp->print_breed();
dp = &ss; dp->print_breed();
dp = &gs; dp->print_breed();

cout << "\n";

// A reference of type dog& can refer to object of any
// class in dogs hierarchy

dog& rd = d;
dog& rs = s;
dog& rm = ms;

// Calling virtual function via reference

rd.print_breed();
rs.print_breed();
rm.print_breed();
}
```

Now let's turn to the function main(), which contains a short program for demonstrating virtual functions. We first declare a class object for each class in the hierarchy:

```
dog d;
boxer b;
cocker c;
schnauzer s;
miniature_schnauzer ms;
standard_schnauzer ss;
giant_schnauzer gs;
```

Next, we declare dp to point to objects of the base class:

```
dog* dp;
```

In fact, however, dp can point to class objects of any class in the hierarchy. What's more, if we apply print_breed() to an object pointed to by dp, then the correct definition of print_breed() will be used. Thus the statements

```
dp = &d; dp->print_breed();
dp = &b; dp->print_breed();
dp = &c; dp->print_breed();
dp = &s; dp->print_breed();
dp = &ms; dp->print_breed();
dp = &ss; dp->print_breed();
dp = &gs; dp->print_breed();
```

produce this printout:

```
Breed not defined
Boxer
Cocker
Schnauzer
Miniature Schnauzer
Standard Schnauzer
Giant Schnauzer
```

The same principle applies to references:

```
dog& rd = d;
dog& rs = s;
dog& rm = ms;
```

Although rd, rs, and rm all have type dog&, the class of the object referred to determines which definition to use for a virtual function. Thus

```
rd.print_breed();
rs.print_breed();
rm.print_breed();
```

produce the printout

```
Breed not defined
Schnauzer
Miniature Schnauzer
```

ABSTRACT BASE CLASSES AND PURE VIRTUAL FUNCTIONS

A class that is used only for deriving other classes, and not for creating class objects, is called an *abstract base class*. It is often impossible to provide useful definitions for the functions declared in an abstract base class; any definitions provided are dummy definitions that are intended to be overridden in the derived classes. For virtual functions only, it is possible to declare a function without providing any definition. Such *pure virtual functions* can occur only in abstract base classes: a class that declares pure virtual functions cannot be used to declare class objects. In a class derived from an abstract base class, each pure virtual function must be either defined or redeclared as a pure virtual function. In the latter case, the derived class will also be an abstract base class.

We can use the hierarchy in Figure 6-1 as an example. Suppose that we need to create class objects only for classes such as `boxer` and `cocker`, which refer to a specific breed of dog. Because no objects of class `dog` will be created, `dog` is an abstract base class. Yet class `dog` still plays several important roles. It occupies a central position in the class hierarchy; without class `dog`, the hierarchy would disintegrate. Even though there are no objects of class `dog`, we can still use pointers of type `dog*` and references of type `dog&` to refer to objects of other classes in the hierarchy. Most important of all, `dog` gives us a place to declare the virtual function `print_breed()`, which is then redefined in each of the other classes in the hierarchy.

What kinds of definitions, if any, should be provided for virtual functions in abstract base classes? When such definitions are provided, they serve as defaults: if a derived class does not redefine a function, the definition in the base class will be used. Frequently a "do-nothing" definition is used as the default:

```
virtual void print_breed() {}
```

If `print_breed()` is called for a derived class that does not redefine the function, the do-nothing definition in the abstract base class will be used and no action will be taken. However, functions that take no action are not helpful when we are debugging the program; we thus might have the default definition print an error message:

```
virtual void print_breed()
    { cerr << "print_breed() called for a class "
        << "for which it was not redefined\n"; }
```

Beginning with release 2.0, C++ provides an even better alternative. A pure virtual function is declared but not defined in the abstract base class; the compiler requires each derived class to either define the function or redeclare it as a pure virtual function. A pure virtual `print_breed()` is declared in class `dog` as follows:

```
virtual void print_breed() = 0;
```

The = 0 after the function heading designates the virtual function as pure; no definition of `dog::print_breed()` need be or can be provided. Because a class that declares a pure virtual function is perforce an abstract base class, the use of pure virtual functions is a good way of making clear which base classes are abstract.

Each class derived from `dog` must either define `print_breed()` or redeclare it as a pure virtual function (thereby making the derived class an abstract base class). For classes `boxer` and `cocker`, the only thing that makes sense is to define `print_breed()` (an abstract base class without any derived classes serves no useful purpose); the redefinitions already present in Listing 6-1 will also serve as definitions for a pure virtual function.

For class `schnauzer` we have two reasonable choices. One is to leave the class as it is in Listing 6-1, in which case it will define `print_breed()` to print `Schnauzer`. The other choice is to redeclare the virtual function `print_breed()` as pure:

```
void print_breed() = 0;
```

This declaration makes `schnauzer` an abstract base class: we cannot declare objects of class `schnauzer`. The responsibility for defining `print_breed()` is passed on to the derived classes `miniature_schnauzer`, `standard_schnauzer`, and `giant_schnauzer`. Note that if the function is defined in class `schnauzer`, that definition can, as usual, be overridden in the classes derived from `schnauzer`.

Suppose that `print_breed()` is indeed declared as a pure virtual function in class `dog`, and that it is defined (rather than redeclared as pure virtual) in each derived class. The only restriction this imposes is that objects of class `dog` cannot be created or (of course) used. Thus the only lines that have to be removed from the demonstration program are those that create or refer to an object of class `dog`; the invalid lines are

```
dog d;
dp = &d; dp->print_breed();
dog& rd = d;
rd.print_breed();
```

The remainder of the program works exactly the same as with the original declaration of class dog.

EXAMPLE: GRAPHICS FIGURES

Objects are frequently used to represent displayed items such as menus, icons, windows, and graphics figures. Figure 6-2 shows a simple class hierarchy that includes three kinds of figure (box, solid block, and triangle) as well as a label field for displaying captions or instructions to the user.

There is no standard graphics library for C or C++; when graphics functions are available, their definitions vary widely from one implementation to another. Rather than use an implementation-dependent set of graphics functions, we will confine ourselves to "typewriter art," produced with printed characters on a text display. We can produce such graphics via the standard output channel cout, provided we have some way of positioning the cursor on the screen. Listing 6-2 is the header file for the classes in Figure 6-2, and Listing 6-3 (page 286) is the corresponding source file.

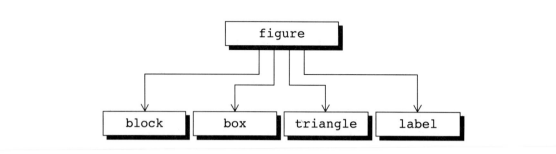

Figure 6-2

The class hierarchy for the figures example.

Listing 6-2

```
// File figures.h
// Header file for figures classes

#include <iostream.h>
#include <string.h>

// Utility functions using ANSI escape sequences to clear
// the screen and position the cursor

inline void clear_screen() { cout << "\xlb[2J"; }

inline void set_cur_pos( int r, int c )
   { cout << "\xlb[" << r << ";" << c << "H"; }

// Topmost class in figures hierarchy

class figure {
protected:
   int row;      // row of anchor point
   int col;      // column of anchor point
public:
   figure( int r, int c ) { row = r; col = c; }
   virtual ~figure() {}                 // virtual destructor
   virtual void show() = 0;             // draw figure
   virtual void hide() = 0;             // erase figure
   void move_by( int dr, int dc )       // move figure
      { hide(); row += dr; col += dc; show(); }
};

// Classes derived from class figure

class block : public figure {
   int height;      // height of block
   int width;       // width of block
public:
   block( int r, int c, int h, int w ) : figure( r, c )
      { height = h; width = w; }
   void show();
   void hide();
};
```

(continued)

```
class box : public figure {
    int height;      // height of box
    int width;       // width of box
public:
    box( int r, int c, int h, int w ) : figure( r, c )
        { height = h; width = w ; }
    void show();
    void hide();
};

class triangle : public figure {
    int height;       // height of triangle
public:
    triangle( int r, int c, int h ) : figure( r, c )
        { height = h; }
    void show();
    void hide();
};
class label : public figure {
    char* text;       // pointer to text of label
public:
    label( int r, int c, char* t ) : figure( r, c )
        { text = new char[ strlen( t ) + 1 ];
          strcpy( text, t ); }
    ~label() { delete text; }   // redefine virtual destructor
    void show();
    void hide();
};
```

Using ANSI Escape Sequences

A text display typically is divided into 24 or 25 rows (one for each line of text) and 80 columns (one for each character on a line). To draw on the screen, we need a function that positions the cursor at the intersection of a given row and column; a function to clear the screen is also useful. Some implementations may already provide library functions for these operations. If not, we can define our own using *ANSI escape sequences*, which are recognized by many terminals, communications programs, and display drivers.

ANSI escape sequences are distinct from C++ escape sequences, although the two serve the same general purpose—allowing special coding to be inserted in a text stream. An ANSI escape sequence begins with the control character ESC (escape), followed by a left bracket. The ESC character, in turn, must be represented by a C++ escape sequence. There is no C++ escape sequence specifically defined for ESC; however, we can use the general purpose sequence \x*hhh,* where *hhh* represents one or more hexadecimal digits giving an ASCII character code. The hexadecimal code for ESC is 1b, so \x1b represents ESC and the string "\x1b["—ESC followed by a left bracket—signals the beginning of an ANSI escape sequence.

Two inline functions, clear_screen() and set_cur_pos(), are defined at the beginning of Listing 6-2. Function clear_screen() clears the screen by outputting \x1b[followed by the command code 2J. Function set_cur_pos() sets the cursor to row r and column c by outputting \x1b[, followed by the row number, a semicolon, the column number, and the command code H. The upper-left corner of the screen is row 1 and column 1, so r typically varies from 1 to 24 or 25 and c from 1 to 80.

Class figure

Class figure is the abstract base class for all figures. Functions show(), which draws a figure, and hide(), which erases a figure, are pure virtual functions that must be redefined in each derived class:

```
class figure {
protected:
    int row;
    int col;
public:
    figure( int r, int c ) { row = r; col = c; }
    virtual ~figure() {};
    virtual void show() = 0;
    virtual void hide() = 0;
    void move_by( int dr, int dc )
        { hide(); row += dr; col += dc; show(); }
};
```

Class `figure` has a virtual destructor, which does nothing. Only class `label` needs a nontrivial destructor, which must delete a string when a label is destroyed. Because the base class `figure` has a virtual destructor, the destructor for class `label` overrides the do-nothing destructor for `figure` and is called whenever an object of class `label` is destroyed.

Every figure has an *anchor point* whose position determines the position of the entire figure; the positions of all other points in the figure are defined relative to that of the anchor point. Instance variables `row` and `col` give the row and column of the anchor point. The constructor `figure()` initializes `row` and `col` with a row number and a column number supplied as arguments.

The function `move_by()` moves a figure on the screen, changing the row number of the anchor point by amount `dr` and the column number by amount `dc` (`dr` and `dc` can be positive or negative). The function calls `hide()` to erase the existing figure, computes the new anchor point, and calls `show()` to display the figure in its new position.

The most interesting thing about `move_by()` is that it is *not* virtual, even though the actions that it takes depend on the class of the object to which it is applied. The reason that `move_by()` does not have to be virtual is that it calls two virtual functions, `show()` and `hide()`, to carry out all class-dependent actions. A member function called from another member function by its unqualified name is called via the predefined pointer `this`, which points to the object to which the calling function was applied. Thus the calls to `show()` and `hide()` in `move_by` are treated as if they were written

```
this->show();
this->hide();
```

where `this` points to the object to which `move_by()` was applied. Because `show()` and `hide()` are accessed via a pointer, the virtual function mechanism is used to select the appropriate definitions for the object to which `move_by()` was applied.

Class `block`

Class `block` defines a solid block of asterisks, such as

```
****
****
****
```

The anchor point for a block is its upper left corner. A block is specified by giving the row and column of the anchor point and the height (in rows) and width (in columns) of the block. Thus a `block` object has four instance variables: `row` and `column`, inherited from `figure`, and `height` and `width`, declared in `block`. The constructor for `block` accepts a row, column, height, and width as arguments; the row and column are passed to the constructor for `figure`; the height and width are assigned to `height` and `width`:

```
class block : public figure {
    int height;
    int width;
public:
    block( int r, int c, int h, int w )
        : figure( r, c )
      { height = h; width = w; }
    void show();
    void hide();
};
```

Class `block` must provide the virtual functions `show()` and `hide()` with definitions that draw and erase a solid block. The required definitions are given in Listing 6-3. The following code draws a block:

```
for ( int i = 0; i < height; i++ ) {
    set_cur_pos( row + i, col );
    for ( int j = 0; j < width; j++ )
        cout << "*";
}
```

The outer `for` statement steps i from 0 through `height − 1`, each value of i corresponding to one of the rows of the block. The call to `set_cur_pos()` positions the cursor at the beginning of a row, and the inner `for` statement prints the asterisks for that row. In the absence of instructions to the contrary, asterisks are printed one after another on the same row as usual; therefore, `set_cur_pos()` needs to be called only at the beginning of each row—not for every asterisk. The versions of `show()` and `hide()` given here assume that the entire figure fits on the screen. They do not handle *clipping,* which omits any parts of a figure that extend beyond the boundaries of the screen.

Function hide() is exactly the same as show() except that it prints spaces instead of asterisks, thus erasing a previously printed block.

Listing 6-3

```cpp
// File figures.cpp
// Source file for figures classes

#include <iostream.h>
#include <iomanip.h>
#include "figures.h"

// Draw a block

void block::show()
{
    for ( int i = 0; i < height; i++ ) {
        set_cur_pos( row + i, col );
        for ( int j = 0; j < width; j++ )
            cout << "*";
    }
}

// Erase a block

void block::hide()
{
    for ( int i = 0; i < height; i++ ) {
        set_cur_pos( row + i, col );
        for ( int j = 0; j < width; j++ )
            cout << " ";
    }
}

// Draw a box
```

```cpp
void box::show()
{
    int imax = height - 1;
    int jmax = width - 1;
    for ( int i = 0; i < height; i++ ) {
        set_cur_pos( row + i, col );
        for ( int j = 0; j < width; j++ )
            if ( i == 0 || i == imax || j == 0 || j == jmax )
                cout << "*";
            else
                cout << " ";
    }
}

// Erase a box

void box::hide()
{
    int imax = height - 1;
    int jmax = width - 1;
    for ( int i = 0; i < height; i++ )
        for ( int j = 0; j < width; j++ )
            if ( i == 0 || i == imax || j == 0 || j == jmax ) {
                set_cur_pos( row + i, col + j );
                cout << " ";
            }
}

// Draw a triangle

void triangle::show()
{
    for ( int i = 0; i < height; i++ ) {
        set_cur_pos( row + i, col - i );
        for ( int j = -i; j <= i; j++ )
            cout << "*";
    }
}

// Erase a triangle
```

(continued)

```
void triangle::hide()
{
    for ( int i = 0; i < height; i++ ) {
        set_cur_pos( row + i, col - i );
        for ( int j = -i; j <= i; j++ )
            cout << " ";
    }
}

// Print a label

void label::show()
{
    set_cur_pos( row, col );
    cout << text;
}

// Erase a label

void label::hide()
{
    set_cur_pos( row, col );
    cout << setw( strlen(text) ) << " ";
}
```

Class box

Class box defines an open block such as

```
****
*  *
*  *
****
```

Except for the names of the class and the constructor, the declaration for box is identical to that of block. The definitions of the virtual functions show() and hide() are different, however, because the functions for box must print an open box rather than a solid block.

Function show() for box is similar to the corresponding function for block, except that asterisks are to be printed only on the boundary of the box—that is, when i or j has its minimum or maximum value. The minimum values of i and j are 0; their maximum values are assigned to `imax` and `jmax`:

```
int imax = height - 1;
int jmax = width - 1;
```

In the nested `for` statements that print the box, an `if` statement assures that asterisks are printed on the boundary and spaces are printed in the interior:

```
for ( int i < 0; i < height; i++ ) {
    set_cur_pos( row + i, col );
    for ( int j = 0; j < width; j++ )
        if ( i == 0 || i == imax || j == 0 || j == jmax )
            cout << "*";
        else
            cout << " ";
}
```

The code for `hide()` is similar, except that only the asterisk boundary is erased—not the blank interior. Therefore, a space is printed for each boundary point:

```
int imax = height - 1;
int jmax = width - 1;
for ( int i = 0; i < height; i++ )
    for ( int j = 0; j < width; j++ )
        if ( i == 0 || i == imax || j == 0 || j == jmax ) {
            set_cur_pos( row + i, col + j );
            cout << " ";
}
```

If we had chosen to erase the interior points as well (thus erasing anything that might have been placed inside the box), then `box::hide()` would be the same as `block::hide()`.

Class `triangle`

Class `triangle` defines a solid triangle such as

```
   *
  ***
 *****
******
```

The anchor point for a triangle is the top vertex. To assure that the slanting sides will be smooth, the user is allowed to choose only the height of the triangle; the slope of the sides — and hence the width of the base — is chosen to produce a pleasing appearance. With better graphics, of course, we could allow the user to choose the width of the base as well as the height. Class `triangle` thus differs from `block` and `box` in that it declares only one instance variable, `height`. Accordingly, the constructor takes only three arguments: the row and column of the anchor point and the height of the triangle:

```
class triangle : public figure {
    int height;
public:
    triangle( int r, int c, int h )
              : figure( r, c )
        { height = h; }
    void show();
    void hide();
};
```

As usual, `triangle` has to provide its own definitions for `show()` and `hide()`. The code for `triangle::show()` is similar to that for `block::show()`, except in two respects. First, the anchor point is on the centerline of the triangle, and successive rows after the first begin increasingly farther to the left of the anchor point; the asterisks in row `row + i` begin in column `col - i`. Second, the number of asterisks vary from row to row; row `row + i` contains `2*i - 1` asterisks. We count the asterisks in row `row + i` by letting j vary from −i to i:

```
for ( int i = 0; i < height; i++ ) {
    set_cur_pos( row + i, col - i );
    for ( int j = -i; j <= i; j++ )
        cout << "*";
}
```

The code for `hide()` is the same as for `show()`, except that spaces are printed instead of asterisks.

Class label

Class `label` defines not a geometrical figure but a character string, which can label a figure or convey a message to the user. The anchor point for a label is its left-most character. Class `label` declares one instance variable, `text`, which is a pointer to the string:*

* For Release 2.1, delete text should be delete [ ] text.

```
class label : public figure {
   char* text;
public:
   label( int r, int c, char* t ) : figure( r, c )
      { text = new char[ strlen( t ) + 1 ];
         strcpy( text, t ); }
   ~label() { delete text; }
   void show();
   void hide();
};
```

The constructor label() takes as arguments the row and column of the anchor point and the text string to be printed. The constructor makes a private copy of the text string for the class object and sets the instance variable text to point to it. Because it "owns" a string, a label object needs a destructor to delete the string when the object is destroyed. The destructor ~label() redefines the virtual destructor in figure and so is invoked whenever a label object is destroyed (even if the object is accessed via a pointer of type figure*).

As usual, class-specific definitions must be provided for the virtual functions show() and hide(); show() just positions the cursor at the anchor point and prints the text string:

```
set_cur_pos( row, col );
cout << text;
```

Function hide() must print the same number of spaces as there are characters in the label string. A simple way to do this uses the parameterized manipulator setw(), which we have already used with the insertion operator >>. When used with the extraction operator <<, setw() causes the next output value to be printed in a field of a given width. For example,

```
cout << setw( 10 ) << 100;
```

prints seven spaces followed by 100, so that the spaces and the digits together occupy a 10-character field. We can print a given number of spaces by using setw() to print the null string; because the null string does not contain any characters, the entire field will be filled with spaces. Thus the statement

```
cout << setw( strlen(text) ) << " ";
```

prints one space for each character in the string text. As mentioned before, we must include the header file iomanip.h in order to use setw().

Example Program Heterogeneous Linear List

Listing 6-4 is a demonstration program for the class hierarchy based on `figure`. The program begins by displaying an arrangement of figures near the upper left corner of the screen. In response to the user pressing the return key, the arrangement is moved successively to the lower left, lower right, and upper right. The figures making up the arrangement are kept on heterogeneous list, and calls to virtual functions show and hide the figures in each position. The program in Listing 6-4 uses a heterogeneous *linear* list—that is, one implemented with an array. (The program in Listing 6-6—page 297—is identical except that it uses a heterogeneous *linked* list.)

We will use the following arrangement of figures for our experiments:

```
* * * * * * *          *        * * * * * *
*         *         * * *        * * * * * *
*         *        * * * * *      * * * * * *
* * * * * *      * * * * * * *    * * * * * *
* * * * * * * * * * * * * * * * * * * * * * * * *
* * * * * * * * * * * * * * * * * * * * * * * * *
             Press Return
```

The label `Press Return` invites the reader to press the Return key to see the arrangement moved to another position. The following declarations create the arrangement:

```
box       bx( 3, 5, 4, 7 );
triangle tr( 3, 17, 4 );
block     b1( 3, 23, 4, 7 );
block     b2( 7, 3, 2, 29 );
label     lb( 9, 11, "Press Return" );
```

The anchor points are chosen so that the arrangement is positioned near the upper left corner of the screen. Of the two blocks, `b1` is the square block at the right and `b2` consists of the two horizontal lines at the bottom.

We create a heterogeneous list by declaring the array `list` with elements of type `figure*`, and initialize it with pointers to the figures in the arrangement:

```
const int SIZE = 5;
figure* list[ SIZE ] = { &bx, &tr, &b1, &b2, &lb };
```

Listing 6-4

```
// File testf.cpp
// Demonstration program using heterogeneous linear list

#include "figures.h"

// Create arrangement of figures and label

//      *******        *        *******
//      *     *    *        ***        *******
//      *     *    *      *****        *******
//      *******  *******  *******
//      *****************************
//      *****************************
//               Press Return

box        bx( 3, 5, 4, 7 );
triangle tr( 3, 17, 4 );
block      bl( 3, 23, 4, 7 );
block      b2( 7, 3, 2, 29 );
label      lb( 9, 11, "Press Return");

// Create heterogeneous linear list of figures

const int SIZE = 5;
figure* list[ SIZE ] = { &bx, &tr, &bl, &b2, &lb };

// Program to display arrangement of figures

main()
{
    char ch;
    clear_screen();

    // Draw figures in upper left corner of screen

    for ( int i = 0; i < SIZE; i++ )
        list[ i ]->show();
    cin.get( ch );
```

(continued)

```
// Move figures to lower left corner

for ( i = 0; i < SIZE; i++ )
    list[ i ]->move_by( 14, 0 );
cin.get( ch );

// Move figures to lower right corner

for ( i = 0; i < SIZE; i++ )
    list[ i ]->move_by( 0, 47 );
cin.get( ch );

// Move figures to upper right corner

for ( i = 0; i < SIZE; i++ )
    list[ i ]->move_by( -14, 0 );
cin.get( ch );

clear_screen();
}
```

The figures are not displayed when the corresponding objects are declared; instead, each object must be sent a `show` message to display the corresponding figure. Therefore, after clearing the screen, function `main()` calls the virtual function `show()` for each object on the heterogeneous list:

```
for ( int i = 0; i < SIZE; i++ )
    list[ i ]->show();
cin.get( ch );
```

The member function `get()` reads one character, waiting for it to be typed if, necessary. Thus the statement

```
cin.get( ch );
```

causes the program to pause until the user presses the Return key, thereby giving the user time to view the figures that have just been displayed.

After the user presses the Return key, the program sends each object the message `move_by( 14, 0 )`, thereby moving the entire arrangement down by 14 rows, to near the lower left corner of the screen:

```
for ( i = 0; i < SIZE; i++ )
    list[ i ]->move_by( 14, 0 );
cin.get( ch );
```

Although `move_by()` is not a virtual function, it calls virtual functions `show()` and `hide()`. Thus as each figure is moved, the appropriate definition of `hide()` is used to erase the figure, and the appropriate definition of `show()` is used to redraw the figure in its new position.

The remaining two `for` statements in the program use calls to `move_by()` to move the arrangement first to the lower right and then to the upper right part of the screen.

Example Program: *Heterogeneous* **Linked** *List*

We need to modify class `figure` slightly so that figure objects can be placed on linked lists; Listing 6-5 shows the modified declaration of `figure`. We equip `figure` with a member variable `next`, which points to the next element on a linked list:

```
figure* next;
```

The variable `next` is inherited by all classes in the hierarchy; therefore, every object of a class in the hierarchy has an instance variable for pointing to the next element on a linked list. What's more, because `next` is of type `figure*`, it can point to objects of any class in the hierarchy. Therefore, we can build a heterogeneous linked list whose objects can belong to any class in the figures hierarchy.

In addition to declaring `next`, we modify the constructor of `figure` to initialize `next` to the null pointer. We also define functions `set_next()` and `get_next()` for setting and returning the value of `next`:

```
figure( int r, int c )
    { row = r; col = c; next = 0; }
void set_next( figure* nxt )
    { next = nxt; }
figure* get_next()
    { return next; }
```

Function `set_next()` sets `next` to the value of argument `nxt`; `get_next()` returns the value of `next`.

Listing 6-5

```
// File figuresl.h (excerpt)
// Declaration of class figure modified to include
// next-object pointer for building linked lists

class figure {
protected:
    int row;
    int col;
    figure* next;   // Pointer to next object on list
public:
    figure( int r, int c ) { row = r; col = c; next = 0; }
    void set_next( figure* nxt )         // set value of next
        { next = nxt; }
    figure* get_next() { return next; } // get value of next
    virtual ~figure() {};
    virtual void show() = 0;
    virtual void hide() = 0;
    void move_by( int dr, int dc )
        { hide(); row += dr; col += dc; show(); }
};
```

Listing 6-6 is the linked-list version of the demonstration program. The figure objects are declared exactly as in the linear-list version. The following statements join the objects into a linked list with list pointing to the first object:

```
figure* list = &bx;
bx.set_next( &tr );
tr.set_next( &bl );
bl.set_next( &b2 );
b2.set_next( &lb );
```

We recall that the constructor for a figure object initializes next to the null pointer. Therefore, we do not have to set the value of next for lb, the last object on the list; for lb, next retains the null value it was assigned when the object was created.

Listing 6-6

```
// File testfl.cpp
// Demonstration program using heterogeneous linked list

#include "figuresl.h"

// Create arrangement of figures and label

//      ******      *        ******
//      *    *     ***       ******
//      *    *    *****       ******
//      ******   *******      ******
//    ****************************
//    ****************************
//             Press Return

box       bx( 3, 5, 4, 7 );
triangle tr( 3, 17, 4 );
block    bl( 3, 23, 4, 7 );
block    b2( 7, 3, 2, 29 );
label    lb( 9, 11, "Press Return");

// Program to create list and display figures

main()
{
   char ch;
   clear_screen();

   // Create heterogeneous linked list of figures

   figure* list = &bx;
   bx.set_next( &tr );
   tr.set_next( &bl );
   bl.set_next( &b2 );
   b2.set_next( &lb );

   figure* p;  // pointer to figure on list

   // Draw figures in upper left corner of screen
```

(continued)

```
for ( p = list; p != 0; p = p->get_next() )
    p->show();
cin.get( ch );

// Move figures to lower left corner

for ( p = list; p != 0; p = p->get_next() )
    p->move_by( 14, 0 );
cin.get( ch );

// Move figures to lower right corner

for ( p = list; p != 0; p = p->get_next() )
    p->move_by( 0, 47 );
cin.get( ch );

// Move figures to upper right corner

for ( p = list; p != 0; p = p->get_next() )
    p->move_by( -14, 0 );
cin.get( ch );

clear_screen();
}
```

We use the `figure*` pointer p as a control variable for stepping through the list. The following code displays the arrangement by executing `show()` for each object and then waiting for the user to hit the Return key:

```
for ( p = list; p != 0; p = p->get_next() )
    p->show();
cin.get( ch );
```

Likewise, the following code moves the arrangement by sending the same `move_by` message to each object:

```
for ( p = list; p != 0; p = p->get_next() )
    p->move_by( 14, 0 );
cin.get( ch );
```

As in the linear-list version, each of the remaining `for` statements moves the arrangement to another screen position.

EXAMPLE: EXPRESSION TREES

Figure 6-3 shows how expressions such as 10 + 20 and 10 * 20 + 30 * 40 can be represented as *expression trees*. A *tree* is a branching structure made up of *nodes* (represented by circles) and *branches* (represented by lines). Computer-science trees are drawn upside down compared to living trees: the topmost node is the *root* of the tree and the bottommost nodes are its *leaves*. Some terminology comes from family trees: the nodes below a given node and joined to it by branches are its *children*; the given node is their *parent*. The root of a tree has no parent; the leaves have no children. A node's children, children's children, and so on, are its *descendants*. Any part of a tree that itself forms a tree is called a *subtree*. Any node together with all its descendants constitutes a subtree.

The simplest expression is a constant such as 10; we can represent it by the tree in Figure 6-3a, which consists of a single node that is both a root and a leaf. The next most complex expression is an operator applied to two constants, as in 10 + 20. We can represent this expression by the tree in Figure 6-3b; the operator node has two children, one for each operand.

The operands of an operator can be computed by arbitrarily complicated subexpressions. In 10 * 20 + 30 * 40, for example, the operands for + are the values of the subexpressions 10 * 20 and 30 * 40; in the corresponding tree, Figure 6-3c, the operands for + are represented by the subtrees for 10 * 20 and 30 * 40. This principle can be applied to even more complicated expressions. For example, Figure 6-3d shows the tree for 10 * 20 + 30 * (40 + 50), where the second operand of the right-most * is also represented by a subtree.

We have two aims in this section. First, we wish to see how to represent an expression tree with a linked structure in which the nodes are represented by objects and the branches by pointers. Second, we wish to see how to evaluate expressions using message passing: a message sent to the root object will trigger additional message passing among the node objects of the tree; when this message passing is completed, the root will be able to reply to the original message with the value of the expression. This object-oriented approach to trees representing language constructions has important applications to language processors such as compilers and interpreters.

If we look up the formal definition of an expression in a programming language, we will find that it can have a number of

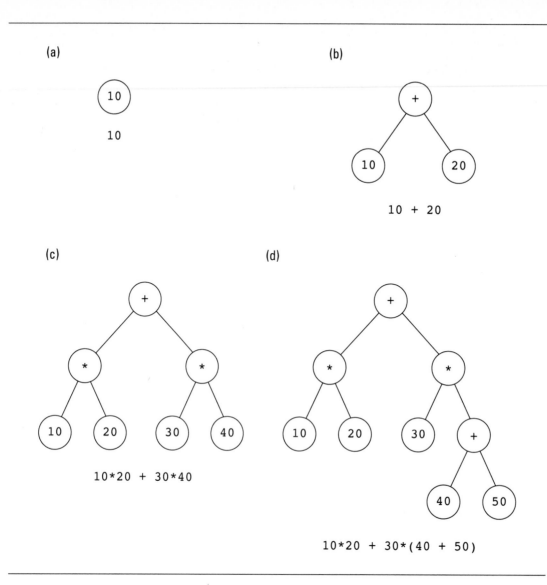

10

10

(b)

+

10   20

10 + 20

(c)

+

*   *

10   20   30   40

10*20 + 30*40

(d)

+

*   *

10   20   30   +

40   50

10*20 + 30*(40 + 50)

Figure 6-3
Some examples of expression trees

alternative structures. For example, the definition might say that an expression is a constant *or* a sum *or* a difference *or* a product *or* a quotient, and so on. Objects are natural for representing anything that can have several alternative forms: we define a base class for the generic entity and a derived class for each particular form. For expressions, we use the abstract base class **expr** for a generic expression and derived classes **constant, sum,** difference, product, and quotient for particular kinds of expressions.

Listing 6-7 shows the declarations of these classes as well as a simple program illustrating the construction and evaluation of several expression trees. We will look at these classes from two points of view: first, how is the structure of the expression tree represented, and second, how is the value of an expression computed.

Listing 6-7

```
// File expr.cpp
// Classes and demonstration program for
// evaluating expressions

#include <iostream.h>

// Abstract base class for all expressions

class expr {
public:
   virtual double value() = 0;
};

// Classes for particular kinds of expressions

class constant : public expr {
   double v;  // value of constant
public:
   constant( double vv ) { v = vv; }
   double value() { return v; }
};

class sum : public expr {
   expr* left;   // pointer to expression for left operand
   expr* right;  // pointer to expression for right operand
public:
   sum( expr* l, expr* r ) { left = l; right = r; }
   double value() { return left->value() + right->value(); }
};
```

(continued)

```cpp
class difference : public expr {
   expr* left;    // pointer to expression for left operand
   expr* right;   // pointer to expression for right operand
public:
   difference( expr* l, expr* r ) { left = l; right = r; }
   double value() { return left->value() - right->value(); }
};

class product : public expr {
   expr* left;    // pointer to expression for left operand
   expr* right;   // pointer to expression for right operand
public:
   product( expr* l, expr* r ) { left = l; right = r; }
   double value() { return left->value() * right->value(); }
};

class quotient : public expr {
   expr* left;    // pointer to expression for left operand
   expr* right;   // pointer to expression for right operand
public:
   quotient( expr* l, expr* r ) { left = l; right = r; }
   double value() { return left->value() / right->value(); }
};

// Demonstration of expression evaluation
#include <iostream.h>

main()
{

   // Create expression trees

   constant a( 10 );        // 10
   constant b( 20 );        // 20
   constant c( 30 );        // 30
   constant d( 40 );        // 40

   product e( &a, &b );     // 10*20
   product f( &c, &d );     // 30*40

   sum g( &e, &f );         // 10*20 + 30*40
   difference h( &e, &f );  // 10*20 - 30*40
   quotient k( &e, &f );    // (10*20) / (30*40)
```

```
// Evaluate each expression by sending value message
// to root of expression tree

cout << "10*20 + 30*40 = " << g.value() << "\n";
cout << "10*20 - 30*40 = " << h.value() << "\n";
cout << "(10*20) / (30*40) = " << k.value() << "\n";
}
```

Class Declarations: Structure of Expression Trees

As to the structure of the expression tree, an object of class constant has no children but must store the value of the constant. Class constant thus declares a single instance variable

```
double v;
```

for holding the value of the constant. An object of class sum, difference, product, or quotient has two children representing its operands; therefore, each of these classes defines two instance variables

```
expr* left;
expr* right;
```

that serve as pointers to the object's children. As in our previous examples, a pointer of type expr* can point to objects of any of the classes derived from expr. Each class is equipped with a constructor whose arguments are used to assign initial values to the instance variables.

Function main() at the end of Listing 6-7 shows how to construct several expression trees. The declarations

```
constant a( 10 );
constant b( 20 );
constant c( 30 );
constant d( 40 );
```

define a, b, c, and d as objects of class constant with the respective values 10, 20, 30, and 40. Likewise, the declarations

```
product e( &a, &b );
product f( &c, &d );
```

define e and f as objects of type product. Object e has a and b as children and so represents the expression 10*20; f has c and d as children and so represents the expression 30*40.

Finally, we define objects of classes sum, difference, and quotient:

```
sum g( &e, &f );
difference h( &e, &f );
quotient k( &e, &f );
```

Object g is of class sum and has children e and f; it therefore represents the expression 10*20 + 30*40. Likewise, object h represents 10*20 − 30*40 and object k represents (10*20) / (30*40).

Class Declarations: Expression Evaluation

We have seen how to represent the structure of an expression tree; now let's see how to evaluate an expression so represented. Class expr declares a pure virtual function value() that is redefined in each of the derived classes. For any object of a derived class, value() returns the value of the expression represented by the object and its descendants. That is, when value() is applied to the root of a tree or subtree, it returns the value of the expression represented by that tree or subtree.

For an object of class constant, value() simply returns the value stored in the object:

```
double value() { return v; }
```

When value() is applied to an object of class sum, difference, product, or quotient, the object sends value messages to its children. The values received from the object's children are combined with the corresponding C++ operator, +, −, *, or /; the result produced by the C++ operator is returned as the object's reply to the value message that it received. All this is easier to represent in C++ than it is to describe, as we see from the definitions of value() for class sum

```
double value()
    { return left->value() + right->value(); }
```

for class difference

```
double value()
    { return left->value() - right->value(); }
```

for class `product`

```
double value()
    { return left->value() * right->value(); }
```

and for class `quotient`

```
double value()
    { return left->value() / right->value(); }
```

When we send a `value` message to the root of an expression tree, it sends `value` messages to its children, which in turn send `value` messages to their children, and so on. Thus `value` messages spread outward from the root and flow downward throughout the tree. When a `value` message reaches a leaf node, the value of the node is returned in reply. Thus replies start at the leaf nodes and move upward toward the root. When an operator node receives the replies to its value messages, it applies the corresponding operator and returns the result to its parent. Ultimately, the root (if it is an operator node) will receive replies to its `value()` messages, will apply its operator to them, and will return the result (which is the value of the entire expression) as the reply to the original value message that triggered the evaluation.

The function `main()` computes the values of three expressions by sending `value` messages to objects g, h, and k:

```
cout << "10*20 + 30*40 = " << g.value() << "\n";
cout << "10*20 - 30*40 = " << h.value() << "\n";
cout << "(10*20) / (30*40) = " << k.value() << "\n";
```

These statements produce the following output:

```
10*20 + 30*40 = 1400
10*20 - 30*40 = -1000
(10*20) / (30*40) = 0.166667
```

EXAMPLE: STATE MACHINES

Some hardware and software components are best modeled as *state machines*, also called *finite state machines* or *finite automata*. As its name implies, a state machine can be in any of several internal states. The machine is driven by input symbols (such as characters or bits), each of which changes the machine's internal state and possibly causes it to produce output. In state-machine theory, the output consists of symbols similar those used for input.

Figure 6-4

State diagram for a state machine that counts words and sequences of punctuation marks. S, W, and P are the states in which, respectively, spaces, a word, and a punctuation-mark sequence are being scanned. The small letters represent possible inputs: s represents a space, w a letter or digit, and p a punctuation mark.

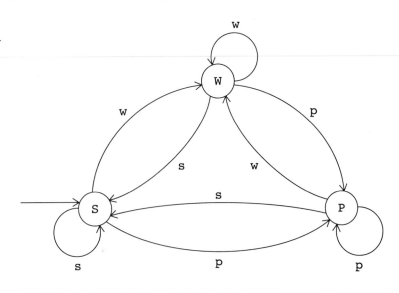

In practical applications, however, the output of a state machine often consists of actions, such as computing new values for designated variables.

For example, suppose we wish to count the number of words in a piece of text as well as the number of times the text is interrupted by sequences of one or more punctuation marks. We need to analyze the text into sequences of spaces, words (sequences of letters and digits), and sequences of punctuation marks, counting the number of words and punctuation-mark sequences. We can do this with a state machine having three states: S if the machine is scanning a sequence of spaces, W if it is scanning a word, and P if it is scanning a sequence of punctuation marks.

We will use lowercase letters to designate various kinds of input characters: s designates a nonprinting character such as the space character or a control character, w designates a letter or digit (which can occur in a word), and p designates a punctuation mark. Each input character causes the machine to go to a new state, which can be the same as or different from its previous state. The transitions between states can be represented by a *state graph* such as that shown in Figure 6-4. In the state graph, the circles represent states and the lines connecting the states represent transitions. Each transition is labeled with the kind of input character that will cause that transition to take place. A short arrow points to the *initial state*, the state of the machine when it is first put into operation. We start our machine in state S, which is equivalent to assuming that the first character of text is preceded by a blank space.

Thus if the machine diagrammed in Figure 6-4 is in state S, then a space (s) will cause it to remain in state S, a letter or digit (w) will cause it to go to state W, and a punctuation mark (p) will cause it to go to state P. In fact, all the transitions depicted in Figure 6-4 can be summarized very simply: regardless of the current state of the machine, input of a space will cause it to go to state S; input of a letter or digit will cause it to go to state W; and input of a punctuation mark will cause the machine to go to state P.

The state graph in Figure 6-4 is incomplete in that it does not indicate the output produced by the machine. The output consists of three possible actions:

- Do nothing

- Count a word

- Count a punctuation-mark sequence

The machine will count a word on input of the first character of the word, and count a punctuation-mark sequence on input of the first character of the sequence. For all other input characters—those that are not the first character of a word or punctuation-mark sequence—the machine will take no action.

Let the integer variables wc and pc be, respectively, the word counter and the punctuation counter. Then the actions of counting a word and counting a punctuation-mark sequence can be represented by the C++ expressions wc++ and pc++. We associate outputs with transitions, so that each action will be taken when a corresponding transition occurs. Thus each transition must be labeled both with the kind of input character that will cause the transition and the action (if any) to be taken for that transition. The input and the action are normally separated by a slash; For example, the label

```
w/wc++
```

indicates that the corresponding transition takes place on input of a letter or digit, and that it causes the word counter to be incremented. Likewise, the transition labeled

```
p/pc++
```

Figure 6-5

This is the same state diagram as in Figure 6-4, but we have added the action, if any, that the machine takes on each transition. If a transition takes an action, the input character is followed by a / and the C++ notation for the action. Thus the notation w/wc++ indicates that a transition takes place on input of a letter or digit (w) and that the transition causes the counter wc to be incremented (wc++).

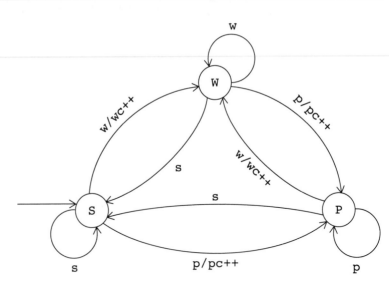

takes place on input of a punctuation mark and causes the punctuation counter to be incremented. When no action is to be taken, the slash is also omitted; the transition labeled

s

takes place on input of a space and causes no action to be taken.

Figure 6-5 results from including the actions in the state graph of Figure 6-4. Each transition from another state into state W or state P increments the corresponding counter; thus a word or punctuation-mark sequence is counted on input of its first character. On the other hand, transitions from state W to itself or from state P to itself do not increment a counter, because a character that causes one of these transitions is not the first character of a word or punctuation-mark sequence (why?).

There are a number of methods of representing state machines in computer programs. We will look here at an unusual method described by Wiener:* each state is represented by an object, and objects representing different states belong to different derived classes of a common base class `state`. A virtual function `next()` returns the next state following a transition and also takes any action associated with the transition.

---

* Richard S. Wiener, "Object-Oriented Programming in C++ —A Case Study," *SIGPLAN Notices*, June 1987, pp. 59–68.

Static Class Members: Class Variables and Functions

The member variables declared in a class declaration are normally *instance variables*—a separate copy of them is created for each class object. Sometimes, however, it is convenient to have *class variables* that are associated with the class itself rather than with any class object. Every instance of a class accesses the same class variables, although each has its own private copy of any instance variables.

In C++, class variables are declared as `static`. Thus in

```
class c {
    int i;
    int j;
    static int m;
    static int n;
public:
    void zap()
        { i = 0; j = 0; m = 0; n = 0; }
    static void clear() { m = 0; n = 0; }

    //...

};
```

`i` and `j` are instance variables and `m` and `n` are class variables. Every object of class `c` will have its own private `i` and `j`, which can have different values for different objects; however, all objects will access the same `m` and `n`, which will, of course, have the same values for all objects.

Static variables are like non-inline member functions in that they are declared in a class declaration and defined in the corresponding source file. To define the static variables `m` and `n`, the source file for class `c` must contain the following declarations (which are also definitions):

```
int c::m;
int c::n;
```

These definitions can also be used to assign initial values to the static member variables. For example, the following definitions give `m` the initial value 5 and `n` the initial value 6:

```
int c::m = 5;
int c::n = 6;
```

The accessibility rules for class variables are the same as for instance variables. Thus private and protected class variables can be accessed by member and friend functions, but not by functions that are not associated with the class. Likewise, a derived class with a public base class inherits access to the protected and public class variables of the base class.

In addition, we can define *static member functions* that can manipulate only static member variables — they cannot access the instance variables of class objects. Like static member variables, static member functions are associated with a class rather than with any class object. A static member function is invoked via the name of the class rather than via the name of a class object.

The preceding example defines an ordinary member function `zap()` and a static member function `clear()`. To invoke the ordinary member function `zap()`, we must declare a class object `cc` and apply `zap()` to it with the dot operator:

```
c cc;       // declare cc as c object
cc.zap();   // apply zap() to class object cc
```

From the definition of `zap()`, we note that it can manipulate the instance variables i and j of cc as well as the class variables m and n.

In contrast, the static member function `clear()` is invoked using the name of the class and the `::` operator:

```
c::clear();
```

We can call `clear()` even if no class objects have been created. From the definition of `clear()`, we note that it manipulates only the class variables m and n; `clear()` does not have access to the instance variables i and j of any class object.

Class state

The header file in Listing 6-8 and the source file in Listing 6-9 show how our state machine can be represented in C++. As mentioned before, each state of the machine is represented by a class object. Figure 6-6 shows the hierarchy of state classes, with base class `state` and derived classes `state_S`, `state_W`, and `state_P`; `state_S` is the class of S states, `state_W` is the class of W states, and so on.

Because the counters that the machine manipulates must be accessible in all states, they are declared as class variables of class

Figure 6-6

Each state of a state machine belongs to a different class, all of which are derived from the common base class state.

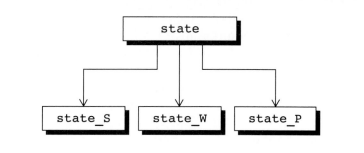

state; wc holds the current word count and pc holds the current count of punctuation-mark sequences:

```
static int wc;
static int pc;
```

To compute the state that results from a transition, we need pointers to all the objects that are used to represent states. These pointers must be accessible in all states and so are also represented by class variables; sp points to the object representing state S, wp points to the object representing state W, and so on:

```
static state* sp;
static state* wp;
static state* pp;
```

All the class variables of state are given protected status so that they can be accessed by member functions of the three derived classes.

The static member variables of class state, which are declared in the header file, must be defined in the source file:

```
int state::wc;
int state::pc;
state* state::sp;
state* state::wp;
state* state::pp;
```

Class state defines four public functions, three of which are static and one of which is pure virtual. The static function init() clears the two counters and initializes the pointers to the state objects:

```
static void init( state* spp, state* wpp, state* ppp )
    { wc = pc = 0; sp = spp; wp = wpp; pp = ppp; }
```

Listing 6-8

```
// File counts.h
// Header file for state-machine classes

// Base class for all state classes

class state {
protected:
   static int wc;       // word counter
   static int pc;       // punctuation-sequence counter

   static state* sp;   // pointer to state S
   static state* wp;   // pointer to state W
   static state* pp;   // pointer to state P
public:
   static void init( state* spp, state* wpp, state* ppp )
      { wc = pc = 0; sp = spp; wp = wpp; pp = ppp; }
   static int get_wc() { return wc; }
   static int get_pc() { return pc; }
   virtual state* next( char ch ) = 0;  // next state
};

// There is one derived class for each state; derived
// classes differ only in definition of next-state function

class state_S : public state {   // class for state S
public:
   state* next( char ch );
};

class state_W : public state {   // class for state W
public:
   state* next( char ch );
};

class state_P : public state {   // class for state P
public:
   state* next( char ch );
};
```

Thus, `init()` can be called only after all the objects representing states have been declared. The static functions `get_wc()` and `get_pc()` return the current values of the corresponding counters:

```
static int get_wc() { return wc; }
static int get_pc() { return pc; }
```

The heart of the state-machine representation is the transition function `next()`, which takes the current input character as its argument and returns a pointer to the next state; as a side effect, `next()` increments any counter that is affected by the transition. In general, the effect of a transition depends on the state from which the transition takes place; therefore, the transition function `next()` is a pure virtual function that has a different definition for each of the three state classes, `state_S`, `state_W`, and `state_P`.

Listing 6-9

```
// File counts.cpp
// Definitions of data and function members
// for state-machine classes

#include <ctype.h>
#include "counts.h"

// Definitions of static data members

int state::wc;
int state::pc;
state* state::sp;
state* state::wp;
state* state::pp;

// Compute next state when current state is S
```
(continued)

```
state* state_S::next( char ch )
{
    if ( isalnum( ch ) ) {
        wc++;
        return wp;
    }
    else if ( ispunct( ch ) ) {
        pc++;
        return pp;
    }
    else
        return sp;
}

// Compute next state when current state is W

state* state_W::next( char ch )
{
    if ( isalnum( ch ) )
        return wp;
    else if ( ispunct( ch ) ) {
        pc++;
        return pp;
    }
    else
        return sp;
}

// Compute next state when current state is P

state* state_P::next( char ch )
{
    if ( isalnum( ch ) ) {
        wc++;
        return wp;
    }
    else if ( ispunct( ch ) )
        return pp;
    else
        return sp;
}
```

Classes state_S, state_W, *and* state_P

The purpose of the three derived classes is to provide three definitions of the transition function `next()`. The definition in class `state_S` will be used when the machine is in state S, the definition in class `state_W` will be used when the machine is in state W, and so on.

To write definitions for `next()` we need to classify input characters as alphanumeric characters (letters or digits), punctuation marks, or spaces. The *ctype* library (header file `ctype.h`) provides functions* for this purpose: `isalnum()` returns 1 (*true*) if its argument is an alphanumeric character and 0 (*false*) otherwise; `ispunct()` returns 1 when its argument is a punctuation mark—any printing character that is not alphanumeric—and 0 otherwise. We will consider a space to be any nonprinting character, that is, any character that is neither alphanumeric nor a punctuation mark.

Because of the symmetrical structure of the state graph, the three definitions of `next()` differ only in the way the counters are updated. If we omitted the statements that update the counters, then all three versions of `next()` would have the same definition:

```
state* next( char ch )
{
    if ( isalnum( ch ) )
        return wp;
    else if ( ispunct( ch ) )
        return pp;
    else
        return sp;
}
```

This function implements the state-transition rule discussed earlier. If the input character is alphanumeric, the next state will be W and so the value of `wp`—the pointer to the object representing state W—is returned. Likewise, if the input character is a punctuation mark, the value of `pp` is returned. If the input character is a space—that is, neither alphanumeric nor a punctuation mark—then the value of `sp` is returned.

---

* If the *ctype* library were written in C++, inline functions would be used for character classification. For historical reasons, however, this library is usually written in C and so must use preprocessor macros, a more primitive method of producing inline code. We can use these macros as if they were functions.

After we insert the statements for manipulating the counters, the three versions of `next()` will differ. The basis for the difference is this: we increment the corresponding counter when entering either W or P *from another state*. We do not, however, increment a counter for transitions that do not change the state. Thus `state_S::next()` increments wc before returning wp and increments pc before returning pp. On the other hand, `state_W::next()` only increments pc before returning pp; it does not increment wc before returning wp because that transition does not change the state — the machine is already in the state pointed to by wp. Likewise, `state_P::next()` only increments wc before returning wp; it does not increment pc before returning pp because, again, that transition does not change the state.

Demonstration Program

Listing 6-10 gives a short program for demonstrating the state-machine implementation. The program declares a text buffer large enough to hold a little more than one typewritten page:

```
const SIZE = 4096;
char buffer[ SIZE ];
```

Function `main()` begins by declaring objects to represent the three machine states:

```
state_S S;
state_W W;
state_P P;
```

We call `init()` to initialize the class variables; the arguments for `init()` are the addresses of the three state objects that were just declared. Because `init()` is a static member function, we call it via the class name and the `::` operator:

```
state::init( &S, &W, &P );
```

The program asks the user to enter the text to be analyzed and reads the text into `buffer`. The user must terminate the text with a dollar sign.

```
cout << "Enter text:\n";
cin.getline( buffer, SIZE, '$' );
```

Listing 6-10

```
// File testc.cpp
// Count words and punctuation sequences
// using a state machine

#include <iostream.h>
#include "counts.h"

const SIZE = 4096;
char buffer[ SIZE ];   // array to hold input text

main()
{
   // Create state objects

   state_S S;
   state_W W;
   state_P P;

   // Initialize class variables

   state::init( &S, &W, &P );

   // Input text

   cout << "Enter text:\n";
   cin.getline( buffer, SIZE, '$' );

   // Process text with state machine
   // Machine starts off in state S

   char ch;
   state* cur_state = &S;
   for ( char* p = buffer; (ch = *p) != 0; p++ )
      cur_state = cur_state->next( ch );

   // Print statistics collected by state machine

   cout << "\nWords: " << state::get_wc() << "\n";
   cout << "Punct Seqs: " << state::get_pc() << "\n";
}
```

We use the variable `cur_state` to point to the object representing the current state of the machine; `cur_state` is set initially to point to S, which is designated as the initial state on the state graph. A `for` statement calls `next()` for every character in the text buffer. Each call to `next()` updates the counters as needed and returns a pointer to the next state:

```
char ch;
state* cur_state = &S;
for ( char* p = buffer; (ch = *p) != 0; p++ )
    cur_state = cur_state->next( ch );
```

Finally, we use the static member functions `get_wc()` and `get_pc()` to print the results of the counting:

```
cout << "\nWords: " << state::get_wc() << "\n";
cout << "Punct Seqs: " << state::get_pc() << "\n";
```

Running the program with the input text

```
"Halt!" shouted the guard.$
```

yields the output

```
Words: 4
Punct Seqs: 3
```

EXERCISES

1. To aid in positioning figures relative to one another, it is useful to have functions that will return the row and column numbers of certain distinctive points on a figure, such as the four corners of a box or the three vertices of a triangle. Equip the figures classes with the following four virtual functions:

```
void upper_left( int& r, int& c );
void upper_right( int& r, int& c );
void lower_left( int& r, int& c );
void lower_right( int& r, int& c );
```

Each function returns the row and column numbers of the designated point via the reference parameters r and c; for some figures, the points returned by the four functions will not all be distinct. For a block or a box, the designated points are the four corners of the corresponding rectangle. For a triangle, both `upper_left()` and `upper_right()` return the coordinates of the top vertex; `lower_left()` and `lower_right()` return the coordinates of the lower left and lower right vertices. For a label, both `upper_left()` and `lower_left()` return the coordinates of the left-most character of the label field; `upper_right()` and `lower_right()` return the coordinates of the right-most character.

2. Some implementations of C++ provide a graphics library that offers functions for drawing common figures such as points, lines, arcs, circles, and ellipses. Write your own version of the figures hierarchy, providing classes for those figures that can be readily drawn by calls to library functions. Try to take full advantage of the options offered by your graphics library. For example, some libraries allow figures to be drawn in different colors and with different line styles (solid, broken, dotted, etc.), and some allow solid areas to be filled in with different patterns. Write a program to demonstrate some of the capabilities of your figures classes.

3. Extend the expression class-hierarchy to include classes for variables and assignment operators. Like a constant object, a variable object will contain an instance variable for storing a value, and class `variable` will implement the virtual function `value()` so that it returns the stored value. However, class `variable` will also provide a member function

```
void store( double v );
```

that stores a given value in a variable object. Class `assign_op` declares pointers to the left and right operands of an assignment operator:

```
variable* left;
expr* right;
```

Thus, the right operand of an assignment operator can be any expression, but the left operand *must* be a variable. In response to a `value` message, an assignment operator obtains the value of its right operand, stores that value in its left operand, and returns that value as its own value. Write a program that carries out a computation by evaluating several expression trees representing assignment statements.

4. Write C++ classes for a *serial adder*—a state machine that carries out a binary addition such as

```
  1001
+ 0011
  ‾‾‾‾
  1100
```

using the binary addition table

```
0 + 0 = 0
0 + 1 = 1
1 + 0 = 1
1 + 1 = 0 and 1 to carry
```

A serial adder is a state machine with two inputs and one output. The bit strings representing the two operands are fed bit by bit, in right-to-left order, into the machine's two inputs; the string representing the sum is generated bit by bit, in right-to-left order, at the machine's output. (This bit-by-bit operation is the reason the machine is classified as a *serial* adder.)

The machine has two states, C (carry) and NC (no carry), corresponding to whether or not the addition in the column to the right produced a carry; the reason the bit strings must be processed in right-to-left order is so that carries will propagate in the correct direction. Figure 6-7 shows the state graph for the machine. A label such as

```
11/0
```

designates a transition that can take place only if both of the machine's inputs are 1 and indicates that the transition produces an output of 0. The loops at left and right in the state graph each have three labels and so each represents three different transitions.

Because the adder has two inputs, `next()` must have two arguments

```
state* next( int input1, int input2 );
```

Figure 6-7

State diagram of a serial adder. The two digits before each slash represent the machine's two inputs; the digit following the slash represents the output produced by the transition. Thus the transition labeled 11/0 takes place when both inputs are 1 and produces an output of 0. Note that each of the loops at bottom has three labels and so represents three distinct transitions.

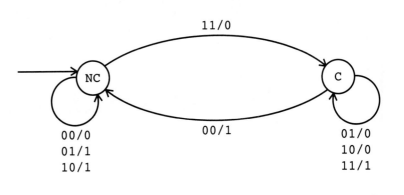

One way to handle output is for `next()` to store the output value in a class variable `out`; a static member function `output()` can return the output produced by the most recent transition.

7
Case Study:
Event-Driven Simulation

S IMULATION IS a rich source of applications for object-oriented programming. A simulation program mimics the behavior of a system of real-world objects; we find it natural to model the real-world objects by program objects and to model the interactions of the real-world objects by exchanges of messages. The ties between simulation and object-oriented programming are long standing. The first object-oriented language, Simula, was designed to aid simulation programming. The object-oriented features of Simula inspired Smalltalk, which has been the inspiration for all other object-oriented languages.

In this chapter we use a simulation program as a case study to further illustrate such important concepts as data abstraction, message passing, inheritance, and polymorphism. A notable feature of the program is that the simulation is carried out entirely by interacting objects. In most of our previous examples, a conventional main program sent messages to objects and received their replies; only in the expression-tree example was there substantial interaction among objects. In the simulation program, on the other hand, the conventional main program serves only to create and initialize objects and to collect statistics; the simulation itself is triggered by a single message from the main program and is thereafter carried out entirely by objects interacting via message passing.

THE MACHINE-ADJUSTMENT PROBLEM

Figure 7-1 illustrates the system that our program will simulate. A factory has a certain number of *machines* that require relatively frequent adjustment and repair; a certain number of *adjusters* are employed to keep the machines running. A *service manager* coordinates the activities of the adjusters. If there are machines waiting to be repaired, the service manager maintains a queue of inoperative machines and assigns the machine at the front of the queue to the next adjuster to become available. Likewise, when some adjusters are not busy, the service manager maintains a queue of idle adjusters and assigns the adjuster at the front of the queue to the next machine that breaks down.

At any given time, one of the two queues will be empty: if machines are waiting to be repaired, there is no reason for an adjuster to wait for an assignment, and if adjusters are waiting for work, there is no reason for a machine to wait for a repair. Thus the service manager needs to maintain only a single queue, which when it is not empty contains only machines or only adjusters.

The factory management wishes to get as much use as possible out of its machines and its adjusters. It is therefore interested in the *machine utilization*—the percentage of time a machine is up and running—and in the *adjuster utilization*—the percentage of time an adjuster is busy. The goal of our simulation, then, is to see how the average machine and adjuster utilizations depend on such factors as the number of machines, the number of adjusters, the reliability of the machines (the mean time between failures), and the productivity of the adjusters (measured by the mean time required for a repair).

Discrete, Event-Driven Simulations

Our simulation will be *discrete* rather than *continuous*. This means that it will be concerned with isolated events, such as the failure of a machine or the completion of a repair, rather than with continuously varying quantities such as currents, pressures, and flow rates.

In a discrete simulation, time itself is discrete: all events take place at regularly spaced instants that we will refer to as *clock ticks*. The time interval between successive clock ticks must be small enough so that no appreciable error occurs from assuming that events occur only on clock ticks (and not between them).

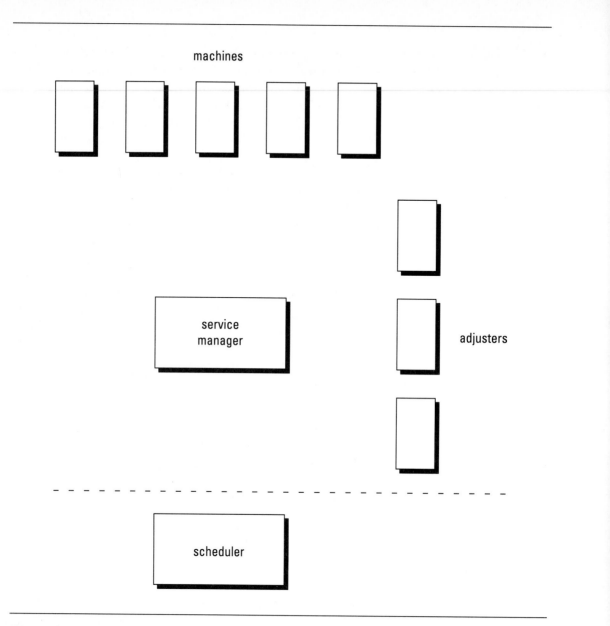

Figure 7-1

Components of the machine-adjustment simulation. The machines break down at random intervals; the adjusters are responsible for adjusting or repairing nonfunctioning machines. The service manager is responsible for assigning machines to adjusters; machines waiting for repair are handled on a first-come-first-served basis, as are adjusters waiting for work assignments. The scheduler drives the simulation by sending event messages to machines and adjusters. All the objects above the dotted line represent real-world entities that would be found in a real factory; below the dotted line is the scheduler, an artifact of the simulation that does not correspond to any real-world entity.

Depending on the time scale of the simulation, the time between clock ticks can range from a fraction of a second to days, weeks, or years. For the example in this chapter, 15 minutes between clock ticks is a reasonable choice.

Some simulation objects are *passive*, in that they originate no actions of their own but merely respond to messages from other simulation objects. Other simulation objects are *active*, in that they take actions on their own initiative without prompting from any other simulation object. In our example, the machines and adjusters are active objects: a machine will break down after it has been in service for a certain period, and an adjuster will complete a repair after a certain period of time. Neither breakdowns nor repair completions are triggered by messages from any other simulation object.

Although breakdowns and repair completions are not triggered by messages from other simulation objects, they must be triggered somehow. This can be done by messages from a simulation control object that is not itself part of the simulation — that is, it doesn't correspond to any real-world object that is being simulated. Depending on the kind of messages received from the control object, a simulation may be classified as *clock driven* or *event driven*.

In a clock-driven simulation, each active object is sent the current time on each clock tick. The active object compares the current time with the time at which it is supposed to take some action, such as breaking down or completing a repair. If the time for an action has arrived, the active object takes that action; otherwise, it just ignores the clock-tick message. The problem with clock-driven simulation is that most of the clock-tick messages trigger no action, so active objects waste a lot of real computer time determining whether the simulation time for the next action has arrived.

An event-driven simulation uses a simulation-control object called a *scheduler*. Before completing its current event and "going to sleep," an active object determines the time of its next event and sends a message with this information to the scheduler. The latter schedules the event and at the requested time sends a "wake-up call" to the active object. Thus an active object receives a message from the simulation-control object not on each clock tick but only when an event is scheduled to occur.

For example, when a machine is placed in service, it determines when it will fail and requests a wake-up call at that time; the scheduler then sends the machine an **event** message when it is time for the machine to fail. Likewise, when an adjuster begins a repair, it schedules the time at which the repair will be completed, and receives an **event** message from the scheduler at that time.

THE WORKINGS OF CHANCE

Of course, we have no way of knowing exactly when a machine will break down or an adjuster will complete a repair. When such events must be simulated, we use *pseudorandom numbers* to simulate the workings of chance. Pseudorandom numbers (often just called *random numbers*) appear to have been drawn at random but are in fact generated by a computer algorithm — that is, by a C or C++ function. Pseudorandom numbers are preferred over true random numbers (generated by a hardware device) because it would be difficult to debug a program whose operation could not be reproduced from one run to the next.

C and C++ provide a (pseudo-) random number generator in the *stdlib* library, which is accessed via the header file `stdlib.h`. Each call to the function

```
int rand();
```

returns a random integer in the range 0 through RAND_MAX, where RAND_MAX (defined in `stdlib.h`)* is most commonly 32767. The integers returned by `rand()` are said to be *uniformly distributed* in that any integer in the range 0 through RAND_MAX is equally likely to be chosen. The effect is as if we drew a numbered ball at random from a huge urn containing RAND_MAX + 1 balls, each bearing a distinct integer in the range 0 through RAND_MAX.

We can provide a random number generator with a *seed* that serves as a starting point for its computations and thus determines the sequence of random numbers that will be generated. The function

```
void srand( unsigned s );
```

* Some C++ implementations do not define RAND_MAX in `stdlib.h` (or in any other header file); therefore a definition for RAND_MAX has been placed near the beginning of Listing 7-2 (page 333), the source file for class `geometric`. The directives `#ifndef RAND_MAX` and `#endif` cause this definition to be ignored if RAND_MAX was indeed defined in `stdlib.h` (which was included earlier in the source file).

allows the user to provide any value of type `unsigned` as a seed for the random number generator `rand()`.

The Geometric Distribution

The probability distribution of the random numbers—the probability that each particular number will occur—must be chosen for the problem at hand. If the uniform distribution provided by `rand()` is not appropriate, then the output of `rand()` must be modified to provide the required distribution.

Consider the probability that a machine will break down `t` clock ticks after it has been placed in service. Frequently, the only information about reliability that we have is the *mean time between failures*, the average number of clock ticks required for the machine to fail. Let `mean` be the mean time between failures. In the absence of more detailed information, the most general assumption we can make is that the probability of the machine failing on any particular clock tick is `1/mean`. For example, if the mean time between failures is 10 clock ticks, then there is 1 chance in 10 (probability 1/10) that the machine will fail on the first clock tick, 1 chance in 10 it will fail on the second clock tick, and so on. The probabilities on different clock ticks are independent of one another, so the chance of failing on the next clock tick will remain 1 in 10 regardless of how many ticks have transpired without a failure.

We might expect that this uniform probability of failure will lead to a uniform probability distribution, but the following shows that it does not. Let `p = 1/mean` be the probability that the machine fails on the current tick; then the probability that the machine *does not* fail on the current tick is `1 - p`. The probability that the machine fails on the first tick after it is put into service is just

```
p
```

The probability that the machine fails on the second tick after it is put into service is more complicated: it is the probability that the machine failed on tick 2 *and* did not fail on tick 1. The probability of failing on tick 2 is `p` and the probability of not failing on tick 1 is `1 - p`; thus the probability that the machine runs until tick 2 and then fails is

```
p * (1 - p)
```

(Because events on tick 1 and tick 2 are independent, their probabilities are multiplied.) Likewise, the probability that the machine runs to tick 3 and then fails is

```
p * (1 - p) * (1 - p)
```

The probability that the machine runs to tick 4 and then fails is

```
p * (1 - p) * (1 - p) * (1 - p)
```

And so on.

In general, then, the probability that the machine runs until tick t and then fails is

$$p * (1 - p)^{t-1}$$

This probability formula is known as the *geometric distribution*. The preceding discussion also applies to many other time intervals occurring in simulations, such as the time required for a repair or the time between customers arriving at a store. In each case, we are given the mean time interval between events, and we choose the actual times at random using the geometric distribution.

Class geometric

There is a simple, easy-to-understand mechanism for generating geometrically distributed random numbers. Suppose we have an urn containing n balls, of which n/mean are white and the rest are black. The probability of drawing a white ball from this urn is p = 1/mean and the probability of drawing a black ball is 1 - p. Thus we can use draws from this urn to determine when a machine fails: if we draw a white ball, the machine fails on the current clock tick; if we draw a black ball, the machine will run until at least until the next clock tick.

We can use the urn to generate geometrically distributed random numbers as follows. Thinking in terms of machine failures, the random number will be the clock tick on which the machine fails. Our first draw determines if the machine fails on the first clock tick after it is placed in service: if the ball is white, the machine fails and the random number is 1. If the ball is black, we replace it in the urn and draw again to determine if the machine fails on the second clock tick. If the second draw yields a white ball, the random number is 2; otherwise, we replace the black ball and draw again to see if the machine fails on the third clock tick, and so on.

In general, the geometrically distributed random number will be the number of times we must draw in order to draw a white ball. If the random number is `t`, then we drew `t - 1` black balls (each with probability `1 - p`) and one white ball (with probability `p`). Thus the probability of the random number having the value `t` is

$$p * (1 - p)^{t-1}$$

which is the desired geometric distribution.

For our urn, we will use the library-supplied random number generator `rand()`, which we can think of as drawing from an urn containing `RAND_MAX + 1` balls numbered from 0 through `RAND_MAX`. For a given value of `mean`, the number of white balls is `(RAND_MAX + 1)/mean`; this computation should be carried out using floating-point arithmetic and then rounded to the nearest integer. The number of white balls is, more generally, the number of different possible outcomes of a draw that correspond to the occurrence of the event in question; we will thus designate this number as `ways_to_occur`. We assume that we start out with ball 0 and color balls white until `ways_to_occur` balls have been colored, after which we color the remaining balls black. Thus, if the value returned by `rand()` is in the range 0 through `ways_to_occur - 1`, the event in question occurs. If the value returned by `rand()` is in the range `ways_to_occur` through `RAND_MAX`, the event in question does not occur.

Objects serve well as random number generators; we can think of such objects as modeling the devices, such as dice and roulette wheels, that we use in everyday life to generate random numbers. From a computational point of view, a random number generator generally has parameters, such as `ways_to_occur`, that determine the properties of the generated numbers. Such parameters can be stored conveniently in the instance variables of a random-number-generator object.

Objects of class `geometric` generate geometrically distributed random numbers. All the class definitions for our simulation are in the header file `repair.h`, which is shown in Listing 7-1. The function definitions, however, are collected in several different source files. Thus, the definition of class `geometric` is in `repair.h` (Listing 7-1), but the corresponding function definitions are in file `geometrc.cpp` (Listing 7-2).

Class `geometric` defines two instance variables:

```
int geo_max;
int ways_to_occur;
```

We have already discussed `ways_to_occur`; `geo_max` is the largest possible value for a geometrically distributed random number. The geometric distribution allows arbitrarily large random numbers, although values larger than `10 * mean` are extremely rare. Because we are using random numbers to represent time intervals, it will simplify the design of the scheduler if we place an arbitrary limit, `geo_max`, on geometrically distributed random numbers. If this limit is `10 * mean` or larger, it will have negligible effect on the probability distribution.

Class `geometric` defines two public functions:

```
geometric( double mean, int max );
int draw();
```

The constructor `geometric()` creates an object that generates random numbers with a given mean and maximum value. Note that the mean is not restricted to being an integer. The function `draw()` returns the next random number.

Listing 7-1

```
// File repair.h
// Header file for machine-adjustment simulation

enum Boolean { FALSE, TRUE };

class scheduler;
class manager;

// Class of geometric-distribution random number generators

class geometric {
    int geo_max;          // maximum value of random number
    int ways_to_occur;    // no. ways desired event can occur
public:
    geometric( double mean, int max );
    int draw();           // return next random number
};

// Abstract base class of active objects
```

```
class active {
   active* next;   // next-object pointer for linked lists
public:
   void set_next( active* p ) { next = p; }
   active* get_next() { return next; }
   virtual void event() = 0;   // trigger scheduled event
};

// Class for machine objects

class machine : public active {
   scheduler* sp;      // pointer to scheduler
   manager* mp;        // pointer to service manager
   geometric g;        // random number generator
   Boolean is_up;      // state variable
   int up_time_start;  // start of most recent up-period
   int tot_up_time;    // total up-time
public:
   machine( double mean, int max,
            scheduler* s, manager* m );
   void event();       // time to break down
   void adjusted();    // repairs complete
   int up_time();      // return total up-time
};

// Class for adjuster objects

class adjuster : public active {
   scheduler* sp;       // pointer to scheduler
   manager* mp;         // pointer to service manager
   geometric g;         // random number generator
   machine* workp;      // pointer to machine under repair
   Boolean is_busy;     // state variable
   int busy_time_start; // start of most recent busy period
   int tot_busy_time;   // total busy time
public:
   adjuster( double mean, int max,
            scheduler* s, manager* m );
   void event();           // time to complete repair
   void adjust( machine* p );  // accept work assignment
   int busy_time();        // return total busy time
};
```

(continued)

```
// Class for service manager

class manager {
    enum who { MACHINES, ADJUSTERS, NONE };

    who waiting;      // kind of objects in queue
    active* first;    // points to first object in queue
    active* last;     // points to last object in queue

    // Private functions for manipulating queue

    void insert_first( active* p )
        { first = last = p; p->set_next( 0 ); }
    void insert( active* p )
        { last->set_next( p ); p->set_next( 0 ); last = p; }
    void remove()
        { first = first->get_next(); }
public:
    manager() { first = last = 0; waiting = NONE; }
    void request_service( machine* p );       // service request
    machine* request_work( adjuster* p );  // work request
};

// Class for scheduler

class scheduler {
    int clock;            // simulation clock
    int calendar_size;    // size of calendar-queue array
    active** calendar;    // pointer to calendar-queue array
    int index;            // calendar-queue array subscript
                          //     for current time
public:
    scheduler( int sz );
    int time() { return clock; }              // return time
    void schedule( active* p, int delay );  // schedule event
    void run( int ticks );                    // run simulation
};
```

Listing 7-2

```
// File geometrc.cpp
// Source file for class geometric

#include <stdlib.h>
#include "repair.h"

#ifndef RAND_MAX
#define RAND_MAX  32767
#endif

// RAND_COUNT is number of different values that
// rand() can return

const double RAND_COUNT = double( RAND_MAX ) + 1.0;

// Initialize geometric-distribution object

geometric::geometric( double mean, int max )
{
   ways_to_occur = int( RAND_COUNT / mean + 0.5 );
   geo_max = max;
}

// Return next geometrically distributed random number

int geometric::draw()
{
   for ( int i = 1; i < geo_max; i++ )
      if ( rand() < ways_to_occur ) return i;
   return geo_max;
}
```

Turning to Listing 7-2, the source file for class `geometric` includes the header file `stdlib.h`, which contains the declarations for `rand()` and RAND_MAX. All of our geometric-distribution objects will use `rand()` as an underlying source of random numbers. As previously mentioned, a definition of RAND_MAX is provided in this file because some C++ implementations do not define RAND_MAX in `stdlib.h`. This definition will have to be modified for implementations in which the maximum random number is other than 32767.

The constant RAND_COUNT is the number of different values that rand() can return; in terms of the urn analogy, RAND_COUNT is the number of balls in the urn. RAND_COUNT is equal to RAND_MAX + 1; however, it is defined as a floating-point constant because it will be used in a floating-point calculation:

```
const double RAND_COUNT = double( RAND_MAX ) + 1.0;
```

The constructor geometric() computes ways_to_occur from the argument mean and initializes geo_max from the argument max. As previously discussed, ways_to_occur is computed by dividing mean into "the number of balls in the urn," which here is RAND_COUNT. The computation is done with floating-point arithmetic and then rounded to the nearest integer:

```
ways_to_occur = int( RAND_COUNT / mean + 0.5 );
geo_max = max;
```

The function draw() uses the method of repeated drawings to generate geometrically distributed random numbers:

```
for ( int i = 1; i < geo_max; i++ )
   if ( rand() < ways_to_occur ) return i;
return geo_max;
```

The for statement makes repeated calls to rand() to simulate repeated drawings of balls from an urn; the value of i gives the number of the drawing (first, second, third, etc.). If the value returned by rand() is less than ways_to_occur, then a white ball was drawn, and the drawing number i is returned as the random number. Otherwise, another drawing is carried out. If, however, no white ball is drawn in the first geo_max - 1 attempts, the drawing process is abandoned, and geo_max is returned as the random number.

ACTIVE OBJECTS

We recall that active objects are those that can originate spontaneous actions such as the breakdown of a machine or the completion of a repair. In the simulation, such "spontaneous" actions are scheduled in advance and then triggered by an **event** mes-

Figure 7-2

Class hierarchy for active objects.

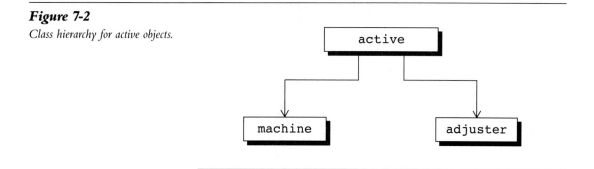

sage from the scheduler. Thus active objects are those that can receive `event` messages; their classes are all derived from the abstract base class `active`, which declares the pure virtual function `event()` for sending event messages to active objects. Figure 7-2 shows the class hierarchy for active objects: `machine` is the class of objects representing machines and `adjuster` is the class of objects representing adjusters.

Before discussing `active`, `machine`, and `adjuster`, we need to mention the remaining two classes of the simulation: `manager` (the class of the service manager) and `scheduler` (the class of the scheduler). Classes `machine` and `adjuster` refer to `manager` and `scheduler`, `scheduler` refers to `active`, and `manager` refers to `active`, `machine`, and `adjuster`. Therefore, there is no way in which we can order the class definitions so that each class is defined before it is referred to. We get around this problem by supplying incomplete definitions for `manager` and `scheduler` near the beginning of `repair.h`:

```
class scheduler;
class manager;
```

These incomplete definitions will allow us to refer to `scheduler` and `manager`, and to their member functions, while defining `machine` and `adjuster`. The complete definitions of the classes must be and are supplied later in `repair.h`.

We will face a similar problem in our discussion in that we will have to refer to member functions of `scheduler` and `manager` before those classes have been discussed. We will describe the use of such a function when we first encounter it and then discuss how it works when we come to the class in which it is defined.

Class active

The defining property of active objects is that they can receive event messages via the function event(). Therefore, class active defines event() as a pure virtual function that will be redefined in each derived class. Another common property of active objects is that they will be placed on linked lists by both the scheduler and the service manager. Therefore, class active declares a next pointer next and provides functions set_next() and get_next() for manipulating it:

```
class active {
    active* next;
public:
    void set_next( active* p ) { next = p; }
    active* get_next() { return next; }
    virtual void event() = 0;
};
```

Function set_next() assigns its argument value to next; get_next() returns the value of next.

Class machine

Class machine defines six instance variables:

```
scheduler* sp;
manager* mp;
geometric g;
Boolean is_up;
int up_time_start;
int tot_up_time;
```

An object often needs pointers to objects to which it will send messages; such pointers serve as "mailing addresses" for the objects to which they point. Instance variables sp and mp point respectively to the scheduler and manager objects, enabling a machine to send messages to the manager and the scheduler.

Instance variable g is a geometric-distribution random number generator, which will be used for generating the times between failures. As mentioned in Chapter 5, a constructor's initialization list is used not only to call constructors for base classes but to call constructors for any instance variables that require such initialization. Thus the constructor for g is called from the initialization list of the constructor for machine.

Type `Boolean` is defined as an enumerated type at the beginning of `repair.h`. The Boolean variable `is_up` is a *state variable*: its value distinguishes the two possible states of a machine object. When the value of `is_up` is TRUE, the machine is up, that is, running; when the value of `is_up` is FALSE, the machine is down, that is, awaiting repair. A state variable often plays the crucial role of determining what action will be taken when an `event` message is received. In our example, however, `is_up` is used only in collecting statistics: the total up-time for a machine must be adjusted if the machine is in the up state when that statistic is collected.

It is the responsibility of every simulation object to collect any needed statistics about its operation. For machines, the statistic we are interested in is the total up-time, which will be used to compute the machine utilization. Instance variables `up_time_start` and `tot_up_time` are used for collecting up-time statistics: `up_time_start` is the most recent time at which the machine went into the up state — that is, the most recent time at which it was created or repaired; `tot_up_time` is the total up-time for all previous periods during which the machine was up (it does not include the current period if the machine is currently up).

Class `machine` has four member functions:

```
machine( double mean, int max,
         scheduler* s, manager* m );
void event();
void adjusted();
int up_time();
```

The arguments for the constructor `machine()` specify mean and maximum times between failures and provide pointers to the scheduler and the manager; the values of `mean` and `max` must be passed on to the random number generator `g`. The constructor places the newly created machine into normal operation, which it does by scheduling the machine's first breakdown. Function `event()` informs a machine that a previously scheduled event (a breakdown) has occurred; `adjusted()` informs a machine that work on it has been completed and it can return to normal operation, which it does by scheduling its next breakdown. The statistical function `up_time()` returns the current total up-time for the machine.

Listing 7-3 shows the file `active.cpp`, which contains the function definitions for classes `active`, `machine`, and `adjuster`.

Listing 7-3

```cpp
// File active.cpp
// Source file for classes machine and adjuster

#include "repair.h"

// Initialize machine object and schedule first breakdown

machine::machine( double mean, int max, scheduler* s,
                  manager* m ) : g( mean, max )
{
    sp = s;
    mp = m;
    tot_up_time = 0;
    is_up = TRUE;
    up_time_start = sp->time();
    sp->schedule( this, g.draw() );
}

// Request service for disabled machine

void machine::event()
{
    is_up = FALSE;
    tot_up_time += sp->time() - up_time_start;
    mp->request_service( this );
}

// Return repaired machine to service

void machine::adjusted()
{
    is_up = TRUE;
    up_time_start = sp->time();
    sp->schedule( this, g.draw() );
}

// Return total up-time
```

```
int machine::up_time()
{
    int t = tot_up_time;
    if ( is_up ) t += sp->time() - up_time_start;
    return t;
}

// Initialize adjuster object and, if possible, get object's
// first work assignment

adjuster::adjuster( double mean, int max, scheduler* s,
                    manager* m ) : g( mean, max )
{
    sp = s;
    mp = m;
    tot_busy_time = 0;
    workp = mp->request_work( this );
    if ( workp == 0 )
        is_busy = FALSE;
    else {
        is_busy = TRUE;
        busy_time_start = sp->time();
        sp->schedule( this, g.draw() );
    }
}

// Complete repair on current machine; if possible get
// new work assignment

void adjuster::event()
{
    tot_busy_time += sp->time() - busy_time_start;
    workp->adjusted();
    workp = mp->request_work( this );
    if ( workp == 0 )
        is_busy = FALSE;
    else {
        is_busy = TRUE;
        busy_time_start = sp->time();
        sp->schedule( this, g.draw() );
    }
}
```

(continued)

```
// Accept work assignment

void adjuster::adjust( machine* p )
{
    workp = p;
    is_busy = TRUE;
    busy_time_start = sp->time();
    sp->schedule( this, g.draw() );
}

// Return total busy time

int adjuster::busy_time()
{
    int t = tot_busy_time;
    if ( is_busy ) t += sp->time() - busy_time_start;
    return t;
}
```

The constructor machine() uses its initialization list to pass arguments mean and max to the constructor for the class object g; because class active does not define a constructor, no arguments have to be passed to the constructor of a base class. In

```
machine::machine( double mean, int max, scheduler* s,
                  manager* m ) : g( mean, max )
```

g(mean, max) calls the constructor for g with arguments mean and max. The call to the constructor takes place before the statements of machine() are executed, thus allowing the code for machine() to use the initialized object g.

The constructor assigns values to pointers sp and mp, and it initializes tot_up_time to 0. Because a newly created machine is started off in the up state, is_up is initialized to TRUE:

```
sp = s;
mp = m;
tot_up_time = 0;
is_up = TRUE;
```

To initialize up_time_start, the constructor needs to know the current simulation time; the scheduler, which is responsible for all timekeeping, has a member function time()

that returns the reading of the simulation clock. Because `sp` points to the scheduler object, the expression `sp->time()` returns the current simulation time. Thus, `machine()` uses the following statement to initialize `up_time_start`:

```
up_time_start = sp->time();
```

Finally, the constructor needs to place the machine in normal operation, which—somewhat paradoxically—is done by scheduling its first breakdown. Scheduling is done with the function

```
void schedule( active* p, int delay );
```

which is a member function of class `schedule`. Argument `p` is a pointer to the object that is doing the scheduling—the one that will eventually receive an `event` message—and argument `delay` is the time that should elapse before the event takes place. When an object is scheduling itself, then `this`—the predefined pointer to the current object—can be used for the first argument to `schedule`. For the second argument, we use the random number generator `g` to provide a randomly chosen time interval, which will be the up-time for the machine. Thus the call

```
sp->schedule( this, g.draw() );
```

schedules the newly created machine to break down after the randomly chosen time `g.draw()` has elapsed.

The function `event()` is called when it is time for a machine to break down. Breakdowns are scheduled—and hence `event()` is called—only when a machine is in the up state. Therefore, the code for `event()` does not have to check the state variable to determine the current state, as it would have to do if `event` messages could be received in both the up and down states.

The code for `event()` sets `is_up` to `FALSE` and updates `tot_up_time` with the time for the up period just completed. The latter time is computed by subtracting `up_time_start` from `sp->time()`, the current time obtained from the scheduler:

```
is_up = FALSE;
tot_up_time += sp->time() - up_time_start;
```

Finally, `event()` must request service for the disabled machine. Service is requested from the service manager by calling the member function

```
void request_service( machine* p );
```

where p is a pointer to the machine requesting service. Recalling that mp points to the service manager and this points to the machine object in question, we see that

```
mp->request_service( this );
```

requests service for the newly disabled machine.

When an adjuster completes work on a machine, it calls the member function adjusted() to put the machine back into normal operation. This is done by executing the same three statements that occur at the end of the constructor:

```
is_up = TRUE;
up_time_start = sp->time();
sp->schedule( this, g.draw() );
```

The state variable is_up is set to TRUE, up_time_start is set to the current time, and the machine is scheduled to break down again after a randomly chosen time has elapsed.

The function up_time() returns the current up-time. The temporary variable t is set to the value of tot_up_time:

```
int t = tot_up_time;
```

If the machine is currently up, the time into the current up period is not included in tot_up_time, which is updated only when a machine breaks down. In this case, the value of t must be adjusted to reflect the time into the current up period:

```
if ( is_up ) t += sp->time() - up_time_start;
```

The adjusted value of t is returned as the value of the function:

```
return t;
```

Class adjuster

Adjusters are similar to machines in several respects. Just as a machine has up and down periods, an adjuster has busy periods (when it is repairing a machine) and idle periods (when it is waiting for an assignment). At the beginning of a busy period the adjuster schedules the repair to be completed after a randomly chosen time has elapsed. An event message from the scheduler signals when the repair is complete. Just as we keep track of the total up-time for a machine, we will keep track of the total busy-time for an adjuster.

The first three instance variables are the same for machines and adjusters:

```
scheduler* sp;
manager* mp;
geometric g;
```

Note, however, that g will be initialized differently for machines and adjusters, so that up-times and busy times will have different means. Indeed, we could initialize g differently for each class object if we had machines with different reliabilities and adjusters with different productivities. For adjusters, the constructor for g is called from the initialization list of the constructor for adjuster.

The instance variable declared by

```
machine* workp;
```

points to the machine that the adjuster is currently repairing. When the repair is complete, the adjuster must send this machine an adjusted message to return it to normal operation.

The remaining three instance variables

```
Boolean is_busy;
int busy_time_start;
int tot_busy_time;
```

are the same as for class machine except that the word *busy* has been substituted for *up*. Thus the value of is_busy is TRUE if the adjuster is busy and FALSE if it is idle, busy_time_start is the starting time for the most recent busy period, and tot_busy_time is the total busy time for all previous busy periods.

Like machine, class adjuster defines four member functions:

```
adjuster( double mean, int max,
          scheduler* s, manager* m );
void event();
void adjust( machine* p );
int busy_time();
```

The constructor adjuster() creates an adjuster with a given mean and maximum time for completing a repair and with pointers to the scheduler and manager objects. Function event() signals that a repair is complete, adjust() provides the adjuster with a machine to work on, and busy_time() returns the current total busy time.

As for machines, the constructor adjuster() uses its initialization list to pass the values of mean and max to the constructor for the random number generator g. The function `adjust()` then sets pointers `sp` and `mp` to their proper values and clears `tot_busy_time`:

```
sp = s;
mp = m;
tot_busy_time = 0;
```

The newly created adjuster reports for duty by sending a `request_work` message to the service manager:

```
workp = mp->request_work( this );
```

If work is currently available, `request_work()` returns a pointer to a machine to be repaired. If no machines are currently waiting to be repaired, `request_work()` returns the null pointer; in that case, the service manager will "call back later" via `adjust()` when work for this adjuster is available. The remaining actions of the constructor depend on whether `request_work()` returned the null pointer:

```
if ( workp == 0 )
    is_busy = FALSE;
else {
    is_busy = TRUE;
    busy_time_start = sp->time();
    sp->schedule( this, g.draw() );
}
```

If `request_work()` returned the null pointer, `is_busy` is set to `FALSE` to indicate that the adjuster starts off in the idle state. Nothing more need be done for now: the service manager knows that this adjuster is idle (a pointer to the adjuster was included in the `request_work` message) and will send it an `adjust` message when work is available.

On the other hand, if `request_work()` returned a pointer to a machine, the adjuster begins work immediately on that machine: `is_busy` is set to `TRUE`, `busy_time_start` is set to the current simulation time, and `schedule()` is called to schedule the repair to be completed after the elapse of a random time interval provided by `g`.

A repair is completed when the scheduler calls `event()`, which updates `tot_busy_time` and sends an `adjusted` message to the newly repaired machine:

```
tot_busy_time += sp->time() - busy_time_start;
workp->adjusted();
```

The adjuster then requests more work from the service manager, using the same code as in the constructor. As already discussed, if `request_work()` returns the null pointer, the adjuster becomes idle. Otherwise, it remains busy and schedules a new completion time.

The function `adjust()` provides a means for the service manager to call back with an assignment if no work was available the last time the adjuster reported in. The function sets `workp` to point to the machine to be repaired, sets `is_busy` to TRUE, sets `busy_time_start` to the current time, and schedules the completion of the repair:

```
workp = p;
is_busy = TRUE;
busy_time_start = sp->time();
sp->schedule( this, g.draw() );
```

The statistics function `busy_time()` works just like the function `up_time()` for machines. If the adjuster is busy when the function is called, the time for the current busy period must be added to the value of `tot_busy_time`:

```
int t = tot_busy_time;
if ( is_busy ) t += sp->time() - busy_time_start;
return t;
```

MANAGING AND COORDINATING RESOURCES

The real-world entities corresponding to active objects typically require certain *resources*. Examples of resources are seats for a theater, cars for an automobile rental agency, airplanes and fuel for an airline, tables for a restaurant, rooms for a hotel, and main memory, disk space, and input/output devices for a computer program. Resource management is a crucial feature of many real-world systems and so must be represented in any simulation of them.

Often, control of a resource is given to a *resource manager* object, which contains a counter representing the number of units of the resource that are currently available—the number of cars in a rental agency parking lot, for example. The resource manager can accept two kinds of messages: one for supplying resources to the resource manager and one for requesting resources from the resource manager. When an object requests a certain number of units of a resource, the resource manager checks its counter to see if the request can be satisfied. If it can, the object is informed that its request has been fulfilled and the count of available units is decreased appropriately. Otherwise, the request is denied, and the requesting object is placed on a waiting list—a queue—until the requested amount of resource becomes available.

If a resource is consumed by the objects that request it, then new supplies must be ordered from time to time. If it is not consumed, the objects that request it must eventually return it to the resource manager. In either case, the manager will from time to time receive supply messages indicating the availability of units of the resource. If the newly available units allow a pending request to be satisfied, the requesting object will be removed from the queue and sent a message granting its request. The counter will be adjusted to reflect the number of units available after all possible pending requests have been satisfied.

A resource manager is typically a *passive object*—it is not driven directly by `event` messages from the scheduler but indirectly by supply and request messages from active objects. Of course, those supply and request messages are triggered—directly or indirectly—by `event` messages to active objects, so ultimately `event` messages are the driving force for the entire simulation.

Resource Coordinators

The situation in our machine-repair simulation is slightly more complex. Adjusters are a nonconsumable resource for machines, in that the services of adjusters are needed to keep a machine running. However, adjusters are also active objects of the simulation. It is thus insufficient to merely keep track of the number of adjusters that are available; we must simulate the actions of each individual adjuster. What's more, if we look at the situation from another point of view, we can think of machines as a resource for adjusters, because nonfunctioning machines are needed for adjusters to perform their appointed function. Thus machines and adjusters are both represented by active objects and each regards the other as a resource.

The service manager in our simulation is a *resource coordinator* object that serves as a resource manager for both machines and adjusters. It is a passive object that is driven by repair requests from machines and work requests from adjusters. If there are more repair requests than available adjusters, the service manager maintains a queue of nonfunctioning machines and assigns them to adjusters as the latter complete their current tasks. If there are more work requests than nonfunctioning machines, the service manager maintains a queue of idle adjusters and assigns them work as machines break down.

Class manager

A manager object maintains a single queue of active objects. The queue can contain machines waiting for an adjuster or adjusters waiting for a machine, or it can be empty. If the queue is nonempty, it contains either all machines or all adjusters; we cannot have both machines and adjusters waiting at the same time. Values of the enumerated type who indicate what kind of objects, if any, are waiting:

```
enum who { MACHINES, ADJUSTERS, NONE };
```

Class manager defines three instance variables:

```
who waiting;
active* first;
active* last;
```

Type who is used to declare waiting, the value of which tells what kind of objects, if any, are waiting on the queue. The queue is implemented as a linked list using the link next that was provided for all active objects. The instance variables first and last point to, respectively, the first and last objects in the queue. When the queue is empty, the value of first is the null pointer.

The private, inline functions insert_first(), insert(), and remove() are used for manipulating the queue. These functions can be simplified somewhat because the value of waiting lets us know in advance when the queue is empty. Thus we can call insert_first() to insert the first object in an empty queue and insert() to add an object to the end of a nonempty queue. The function remove() does not have to check whether the queue is empty because—courtesy of waiting—it will never be called when the queue is empty.

Function insert_first() inserts the object *p as the first object of a previously empty queue; first and last are both set to point to *p, and the next pointer of *p is set to the null pointer:

```
        void insert_first( active* p )
          { first = last = p; p->set_next( 0 ); }
```

Function `insert()` inserts `*p` at the end of a nonempty queue. Both `last` and the next pointer of the current last object are set to point to `*p`, making `*p` the new last object; the next pointer of `*p` is set to the null pointer:

```
        void insert( active* p )
          { last->set_next( p );
            p->set_next( 0 );
            last = p; }
```

Function `remove()` removes the first element of a nonempty queue by setting `first` to `first->get_next()`—the pointer to the object following the current first object. The function does not return a pointer to the object removed; member functions refer to the first object (before it is removed) by referring to `first` directly.

Class `manager` has three public member functions:

```
manager() { first = last = 0; waiting = NONE; }
void request_service( machine* p );
machine* request_work( adjuster* p );
```

The constructor `manager()` initializes `first` and `last` to the null pointer and `waiting` to NONE. We have already seen how a machine uses `request_service()` to request the services of an adjuster and how an adjuster uses `request_work()` to request a work assignment. Listing 7-4 shows source file `manager.cpp`, which contains the code for these two functions.

Function `request_service()` requests service for machine `*p`. The function uses a `switch` statement controlled by `waiting` to handle three cases: machines are waiting, adjusters are waiting, or no objects are waiting.

Listing 7-4

```
// File manager.cpp
// Source file for class manager

#include "repair.h"

// Handle service request from disabled machine
```

```
        void manager::request_service( machine* p )
        {
            adjuster* q;

            switch ( waiting ) {
                case MACHINES:
                    insert( p );
                    return;
                case ADJUSTERS:
                    q = (adjuster*) first;
                    remove();
                    if ( first == 0 ) waiting = NONE;
                    q->adjust( p );
                    return;
                case NONE:
                    waiting = MACHINES;
                    insert_first( p );
                    return;
            }
        };

        // Handle work request from idle adjuster

        machine* manager::request_work( adjuster* p )
        {
            machine* q;

            switch ( waiting ) {
                case MACHINES:
                    q = (machine*) first;
                    remove();
                    if ( first == 0 ) waiting = NONE;
                    return q;
                case ADJUSTERS:
                    insert( p );
                    return 0;
                case NONE:
                    waiting = ADJUSTERS;
                    insert_first( p );
                    return 0;
            }
        }
```

If machines are are already waiting for service, *p is placed at the end of the queue:

```
insert( p );
return;
```

Note that because the entire function body is a switch statement, each case ends with return rather than the more usual break.

If adjusters are waiting, an adjuster is removed from the front of the queue and sent a message to adjust machine *p. If this leaves the queue empty, waiting is set to NONE:

```
q = (adjuster*) first;
remove();
if ( first == 0 ) waiting = NONE;
q->adjust( p );
return;
```

Note that a type cast is used to convert the pointer to the first object from type active* to type adjuster* (the type of q). Why must this be done? (*Hint:* In which class is adjust() defined?)

If neither adjusters nor machines are waiting, waiting is set to MACHINES and machine *p is inserted into the previously empty queue:

```
waiting = MACHINES;
insert_first( p );
return;
```

The action taken by request_work() likewise depends on the value of waiting. If machines are waiting to be repaired, a machine is removed from the front of the queue and a pointer to it is returned as the value of request_work(). If this leaves the queue empty, waiting is set to NONE:

```
q = (machine*) first;
remove();
if ( first == 0 ) waiting = NONE;
return q;
```

If adjusters are already waiting, adjuster *p is inserted at the end of the queue. The null pointer is returned, indicating that no work assignment can be made at this time:

```
insert( p );
return 0;
```

If neither adjusters nor machines are waiting, `waiting` is set to `ADJUSTERS` and adjuster `*p` is inserted into the previously empty queue. Again, the null pointer is returned, indicating that no work assignment can be made at this time:

```
waiting = ADJUSTERS;
insert_first( p );
return 0;
```

THE SCHEDULER

The scheduler does not simulate any real-world entity but instead drives the simulation via `event` messages. After the active objects have been initialized — their constructors have been called — all further simulation activities are triggered, directly or indirectly, by `event` messages.

When an event is scheduled, the scheduler must store information about the event and then send the required `event` message on the specified clock tick. A data structure for storing information about events is called the *simulation event list* or *simulation event set*. A simulation event list is an example of a *priority queue*: every item in the queue has a priority for removal; the highest priority item is removed first, then the item with next highest priority, and so on. In a simulation event list, the times at which events are scheduled to take place determine their priorities, with earlier events having higher priorities than later ones. Thus, events are removed from the simulation event list in the order in which they are scheduled to take place, regardless of the order in which the `schedule` messages were received.

A number of data structures have been proposed for representing a simulation event list. We will use a simplified version of a structure known as a *calendar queue*.★ The relevant analogy is a desk calendar with one page for each day of the year. We can schedule events (such as appointments) by writing each on the appropriate page. When we come to a page in our day-by-day progress through the calendar, we will find written on it all the events scheduled for that day.

Suppose we want to schedule events for next year but do not yet have a calendar for next year. If we erase each page when its date is past, but we do not tear it off, we can use pages preceding

★ Randy Brown, "Calendar Queues: A Fast O(1) Priority Queue Implementation for the Simulation Event Set Problem," *Communications of the ACM*, Oct. 1988, pp. 1220–1227.

the current date to record events for next year. Thus if today is September 10 and we want to schedule an event for February 21 of next year, we just thumb back to the page for February 21 and write in the event. In our day-by-day progress through the calendar, when we reach the end we just turn back to the beginning. The pages for January 1, January 2, and so on, will have been filled in with the events scheduled for those days in the new year. Following this procedure, the same desk calendar can be reused indefinitely.*

If we schedule events a year or more in advance, then a page may contain events for different years. We will have to write down the year of each event and, in our day-by-day progress through the calendar, only act on and erase events for the current year. If we only schedule events less than a year in advance, however, all events on a page will be for the current year and we will not have to write down or check the year for each event. For simplicity, we will arrange matters so that the latter situation applies to our simulation event list: we will make our "calendar" large enough so that only events for the current "date" (actually, the current clock tick) appear on each page.

Class scheduler

Class `scheduler` declares the following instance variables:

```
int clock;
int calendar_size;
active** calendar;
int index;
```

The integer variable `clock` counts the number of clock ticks since the beginning of the simulation; it retains its value between simulation runs, allowing the simulation to be stopped and restarted. The value of `clock` is not actually used in controlling the simulation; it is needed, however, for computing statistics.

Our calendar consists of an array with one element for each calendar page; each page corresponds to a clock tick. The number of pages in our calendar should be one larger than the largest time interval by which an event is scheduled ahead. This corresponds to the situation for an actual calendar in which events are

---

* For the purpose of our analogy, we are ignoring most of the structure that is specific to real calendars, such as leap years and the day of the week on which each day falls. These details, which make it impractical to use the same calendar year after year, will not affect our simulation event list.

always scheduled less than a year ahead: each page will contain events only for the current time and not those that are to be carried out on later passes through the calendar. The instance variable `calendar_size` holds the number of elements in the calendar array.

The information that must be remembered about each event is the time at which the event is to occur and which object is to receive the `event` message. Times are handled by the structure of the calendar queue, so all we have to store in the queue are the objects that are to be sent `event` messages. As in the service manager, objects are stored on linked lists using the instance variable `next` declared for all active objects. Each element of the array `calendar` is a pointer to the head of the linked list of all objects that are to receive `event` messages on the corresponding clock tick. If no objects are to receive event messages on a particular clock tick, the corresponding element of `calendar` holds the null pointer. As usual, we represent an array by a pointer to its first element; because the elements of the calendar array are pointers to active objects, they have type `active*`, and the type of `calendar` is `active**` (pointer to `active*`).

Instance variable `index` is used to step through the array `calendar`; when we step off the end of the array, `index` is reset to 0 so that we go back to the first element and start stepping through the array again (this corresponds to reusing the same calendar year after year). Both `index` and `clock` are incremented for each clock tick. However, `index` is reset to 0 whenever it equals `calendar_size`; `clock` is never reset.

Class `scheduler` defines the following member functions:

```
scheduler( int sz );
int time() { return clock; }
void schedule( active* p, int delay );
void run( int ticks );
```

The constructor `scheduler()` creates a scheduler having a calendar array of a given size. The function `time()`, which is used only in computing statistics, returns the current value of `clock`. We have already seen how `schedule()` is used to cause an object to receive an `event` message after `delay` ticks have elapsed. The function `run()` causes the simulation to run for the specified number of clock ticks; `run()` does not reset any instance variables so the simulation can be continued for additional ticks by another call to `run()`.

The code for the functions of `scheduler` (except for

time ( ) which is inline) is in file `schedule.cpp`, which is shown in Listing 7-5. The constructor `scheduler( )` executes the following code:

```
clock = 0;
calendar_size = sz;
calendar = new active* [ sz ];
for ( int i = 0; i < sz; i++ ) calendar[ i ] = 0;
index = 0;
```

The constructor initializes `clock` to 0 and sets `calendar_size` to the argument value `sz`; `calendar` is set to point to a new array with `sz` elements of type `active*`. The `for` statement initializes all elements of array `calendar` to null pointers —that is, all "calendar pages" start off empty. The subscript `index` is initialized to 0 so that the scanning of array `calendar` will begin at element 0.

Function `schedule` schedules object `*p` to receive an `event` message after `delay` clock ticks have elapsed. The value of `index` is the subscript of the current "calendar page"—the array element corresponding to the current time. The value that `index` will have after `delay` clock ticks have elapsed is given by

```
int t = index + delay;
```

However, this value of `t` may refer to an element beyond the end of the calendar array. In that case, we proceed as in the desk calendar analogy and wrap around to the beginning of the calendar array, placing the event so that it will be picked up on the next pass through the array. Accordingly, the above value of `t` is adjusted as follows:

```
if ( t >= calendar_size ) t -= calendar_size;
```

The object `*p` is now inserted in the linked list pointed to by `calendar[ t ]`. Because all the objects in this list are scheduled to receive `event` messages at the same simulated time, no guarantee is given as to the order in which those `event` messages will be sent. Thus the objects can be placed in a linked list in any order; we therefore choose the order that is simplest to implement and insert each new object at the beginning of the list; the next pointer of the new object is assigned a pointer to the current first object on the list (the current value of `calendar[ t ]`), and `calendar[ t ]` is set to point to the newly inserted object:

Listing 7-5

```cpp
// File schedule.cpp
// Source file for class scheduler

#include "repair.h"

// Create scheduler with calendar queue having sz elements

scheduler::scheduler( int sz )
{
   clock = 0;
   calendar_size = sz;
   calendar = new active* [ sz ];
   for ( int i = 0; i < sz; i++ ) calendar[ i ] = 0;
   index = 0;
}

// Schedule object *p to receive event message
// after delay ticks have elapsed

void scheduler::schedule( active* p, int delay )
{
   int t = index + delay;
   if ( t >= calendar_size ) t -= calendar_size;
   p->set_next( calendar[ t ] );
   calendar[ t ] = p;
}

// Run simulation for given number of ticks

void scheduler::run( int ticks )
{
   active* p;
   for ( int i = 0; i < ticks; i++ ) {
      while ( (p = calendar[ index ]) != 0 ) {
         calendar[ index ] = p->get_next();
         p->event();
      }
      clock++;
      if ( ++index == calendar_size ) index = 0;
   }
}
```

```
p->set_next( calendar[ t ] );
calendar[ t ] = p;
```

The function `run()` runs the simulation for the specified number of clock ticks. It accepts the current values of all instance variables — it does not initialize anything — thereby allowing it to continue a simulation that has already been run for a number of ticks by previous calls to `run()`. The body of the `for` statement is executed once for each clock tick:

```
for ( int i = 0; i < ticks; i++ ) {
    // while statement goes here
    clock++;
    if ( ++index == calendar_size ) index = 0;
}
```

On each tick, the current calendar page is `calendar[ in-dex ]`, which — if it is not the null pointer — points to the list of objects that receive `event` messages on the current tick. The `while` statement repeatedly removes objects from this list and sends each an `event` message:

```
while ( (p = calendar[ index ]) != 0 ) {
    calendar[ index ] = p->get_next();
    p->event();
}
```

After all the `event` messages for the current tick have been sent, the values of `clock` and `index` are both incremented. If this makes the value of `index` equal to `calendar_size`, however, then we are beyond the end of the array, and `index` must be reset to 0 in preparation for another pass through the array. Note that this wraparound must have exactly the same effect for `index`, which is used for removing objects from the calendar queue, and for `t` in `schedule()`, which is used for inserting objects in the queue. If these two variables wrapped around differently, objects would not be removed at their scheduled times.

One final property of class `schedule` needs attention. Because all simulation actions are ultimately triggered by `event` messages, all calls to `time()` and `schedule()` will take place during a call to `event()` — that is, after `event()` is called and before it returns. Because `event()` is called by `run()`, calls to `time()` and `schedule()` take place while the function `run()` is active — after it is called and before it returns.

This situation has the potential for causing trouble. At some times during the execution of a member function, the instance variables may represent an invalid or inconsistent state of the object; for example, the function may have updated some instance variables but not others. If another member function were called with the instance variables in an inconsistent state, it would probably take erroneous actions and return erroneous results.

Therefore, `run()` must make sure that the scheduler's instance variables are in a consistent state when `event()` is called. We can easily see that this is indeed the case: when `event()` is called, `clock` and `index` have the appropriate values for the current clock tick, and the object that is to receive the `event` message has been removed from the linked list pointed to by `calendar[ t ]`. Likewise, `time()` and `schedule()` must not interfere with the operation of `run()`; for example, it would be erroneous for either `time()` or `schedule()` to change the value of `clock` or `index`.

THE MAIN PROGRAM

Listing 7-6 shows `simulate.cpp`, the main program for our simulation example. The main program is responsible for creating the machine, adjuster, manager, and scheduler objects, for starting a simulation run, and for collecting statistics after each run. All activities during a simulation run result from the mutual interactions of the objects.

Listing 7-6

```
// File simulate.cpp
// Demonstration program for machine-adjustment simulation

#include <iostream.h>
#include <stdlib.h>
#include "repair.h"

main()
{
    // Declare variables, obtain values from user
```

(continued)

```
unsigned seed;      // seed for rand()
int num_mach;       // number of machines
int num_adj;        // number of adjusters
double m_mean;      // mean time between failures
double a_mean;      // mean adjustment time

cout << "Number of machines? ";
cin >> num_mach;
cout << "Number of adjusters? ";
cin >> num_adj;
cout << "Mean time between failures? ";
cin >> m_mean;
cout << "Mean adjustment time? ";
cin >> a_mean;
cout << "Random number seed? ";
cin >> seed;

// Seed rand(); set max_time to ten times maximum of
// m_mean and a_mean

srand( seed );
int max_time =
    10 * int( m_mean > a_mean ? m_mean : a_mean );
int i;

// Create manager and scheduler

manager mngr;
scheduler sch( max_time + 1 );

// Create machines

machine** m_list = new machine* [ num_mach ];
for ( i = 0; i < num_mach; i++ )
   m_list[ i ] =
      new machine( m_mean, max_time, &sch, &mngr );

// Create adjusters

adjuster** a_list = new adjuster* [ num_adj ];
for ( i = 0; i < num_adj; i++ )
   a_list[ i ] =
      new adjuster( a_mean, max_time, &sch, &mngr );
```

```
// Do successive runs of simulation; print cumulative
// statistics after each run

    char ch;
    do {
        // Get number of ticks for this run

        int duration;
        cout << "\nNumber of time steps? ";
        cin >> duration;

        // Run simulation

        sch.run( duration );

        // Compute and print average machine utilization

        double m_factor =
            100.0 / double( sch.time() ) / double ( num_mach );
        long tot_up_time = 0;
        for ( i = 0; i < num_mach; i++ )
            tot_up_time += m_list[ i ]->up_time();
        cout << "Average machine utilization: "
            << tot_up_time * m_factor << "%\n";

        // Compute and print average adjuster utilization

        double a_factor =
            100.0 / double( sch.time() ) / double ( num_adj );
        long tot_busy_time = 0;
        for ( i = 0; i < num_adj; i++ )
            tot_busy_time += a_list[ i ]->busy_time();
        cout << "Average adjuster utilization: "
            << tot_busy_time * a_factor << "%\n";

        // Determine if user wants to do more runs

        cout << "Continue (Y/N)? ";
        cin >> ch;
    } while ( ch == 'y' || ch == 'Y' );
}
```

The main program begins by declaring five variables and obtaining values for them from the user:

```
unsigned seed;
int num_mach;
int num_adj;
double m_mean;
double a_mean;
```

The value entered for `seed` will determine the sequence of random numbers generated by `rand()` (and hence by objects of class `geometric`, which use `rand()` for their underlying source of random numbers). The number of machines and number of adjusters are assigned, respectively, to `num_mach` and `num_adj`. The mean time between machine failures is assigned to `m_mean` and the mean repair time to `a_mean`.

We call `srand()` to pass the value of `seed` to the random number generator. We define `max_time`, the largest time interval the scheduler can handle, equal to 10 times the larger of `m_mean` and `a_mean`:

```
srand( seed );
int max_time =
    10 * int( m_mean > a_mean ? m_mean : a_mean );
```

Because random values of 10 times the mean or larger are very unlikely for a geometric distribution, placing this upper limit on time intervals has no noticeable effect on the simulation.

The service manager and scheduler must be declared first because the addresses of these objects must be passed as parameters to the constructors of active objects (the active objects send messages to the manager and scheduler during initialization). The size of the scheduler calendar array is set to `max_time + 1`, assuring that time intervals of up to `max_time` ticks can be accommodated:

```
manager mngr;
scheduler sch( max_time + 1 );
```

We create an array of pointers to the machine objects; the array is not used during the simulation, but the main program uses it during statistics collection to poll the machines for their uptimes. The array is referenced via the pointer `m_list`; as a pointer to an array whose elements are themselves pointers to machine objects, `m_list` has type `machine**` (pointer to `machine*`):

```
machine** m_list = new machine* [ num_mach ];
```

A `for` statement creates `num_mach` machines and assigns pointers to the machine objects to the corresponding elements of `m_list`:

```
for ( i = 0; i < num_mach; i++ )
   m_list[ i ] =
      new machine( m_mean, max_time, &sch, &mngr );
```

Note that each new machine is passed its mean and maximum time between failures along with pointers to the scheduler and manager. In like fashion, we create an array of pointers to `num_adj` adjusters:

```
adjuster** a_list = new adjuster* [ num_adj ];
for ( i = 0; i < num_adj; i++ )
   a_list[ i ] =
      new adjuster( a_mean, max_time, &sch, &mngr );
```

The program allows several simulation runs to be carried out in succession, each picking up where the previous run left off; this allows statistics to be observed at any points desired during the course of the simulation. The runs are controlled by a `do-while` statement:

```
char ch;
do {

   // Do one run and collect statistics

   cout << "Continue (Y/N)? ";
   cin >> ch;
} while ( ch == 'y' || ch == 'Y' );
```

For each run, the duration in clock ticks is obtained from the user and a corresponding `run` message is sent to the scheduler:

```
int duration;
cout << "\nNumber of time steps? ";
cin >> duration;
sch.run( duration );
```

After each run, the program computes and prints the cumulative statistics for all runs done so far. The statistics in question are the machine and adjuster utilizations, which are the average times that machines and adjusters are doing useful work.

To compute machine utilization, the program polls each machine for its up-time and accumulates the total up-time in tot_up_time:

```
for ( i = 0; i < num_mach; i++ )
        tot_up_time += m_list[ i ]->up_time();
```

To compute the utilization, the up-time is averaged over both the number of time steps and the number of machines; the result is multiplied by 100 to convert it to a percentage. Thus the value of tot_up_time must be divided (using floating-point arithmetic) by sch.time() (the number of time steps) and by num_mach; the result is multiplied by 100.0. We can convert tot_up_time to a utilization in one step by multiplying it by m_factor, which is defined by

```
double m_factor =
    100.0 / double( sch.time() ) / double ( num_mach );
```

An output statement uses m_factor to convert the total up-time to the average machine utilization:

```
cout << "Average machine utilization: "
        << tot_up_time * m_factor << "%\n";
```

The average utilization of adjusters is computed in exactly the same way except that we work with busy times rather than up-times.

Sample Run

Suppose a factory has 10 machines and only one adjuster. The mean time between machine failures is eight ticks and the mean adjustment time is three ticks. We can analyze this situation via the following interaction with the simulation program:

```
Number of machines? 10
Number of adjusters? 1
Mean time between failures? 8
Mean adjustment time? 3
Random number seed? 31416

Number of time steps? 5000
Average machine utilization: 26.608%
Average adjuster utilization: 99.98%
Continue (Y/N)? n
```

We see that the one adjuster is kept very busy, with nearly 100 percent utilization. Unfortunately, the machine utilization is low:

Table 7-1

Machine and Adjuster
Utilization for Different
Numbers of Adjusters

Number of Adjusters	Machine Utilization	Adjuster Utilization
1	26.6%	99.98%
2	50.6	96.8
3	65.8	83.3
4	71.0	66.9
5	72.2	54.6
6	72.7	45.5

machines are in service only 27 percent of the time, which means they are wasting 73 percent of their time waiting on repairs. Clearly, we need more adjusters; to determine how many, we run the simulation program for one through six adjusters, with all other input data the same for each run. Table 7-1 summarizes the results.

Four adjusters seem to be a reasonable choice, because additional adjusters yield only slight increases in machine utilization. The corresponding adjuster utilization is 67 percent, so each adjuster is idle 33 percent of the time; this adjuster idle time is the price of reasonably high machine utilization. The need for such utilization tradeoffs refutes the old "efficiency expert" approach, which strives for 100 percent utilization of all personnel and equipment.

EXERCISES

1. Define a class `uniform` that generates uniformly distributed random integers with a given range. The class defines two member functions:

```
uniform( int low, int high );
int draw();
```

The arguments of the constructor `uniform()` specify the range (`low` through `high`) in which random integers will fall; `draw()` returns the next random integer. The class should use `rand()` as its underlying source of uniformly distributed random numbers; `draw()` must scale the output of `rand()` so that it lies in the desired range. This scaling is most easily done using floating-point arithmetic. *Hint*: Let `uniform` define two instance variables,

```
double scale;
int min;
```

such that the value returned by `draw()` is computed by

```
int( scale * rand() ) + min
```

The constructor must compute values for `scale` and `min` such that the value of the above expression will range from `low` through `high` as the value of `rand()` ranges from 0 through `RAND_MAX`.

2. Define a class `deck` whose objects simulate decks of playing cards. We can represent a card by an instance of

```
struct card {
    suit_t suit;
    int rank;
}
```

where the value of `rank` ranges from 1 through 13 and the value of `suit` belongs to the enumerated type

```
enum suit_t { HEART, CLUB, SPADE, DIAMOND };
```

Class `deck` defines the following member functions:

```
deck();
card draw();
void replace( card c );
Boolean is_empty();
void shuffle();
```

The constructor `deck()` creates a deck of 52 cards ordered according to suit and rank; `draw()` removes and returns the topmost card from the deck, and `replace()` places card c on the bottom of the deck. The function `is_empty()` returns TRUE if no more cards remain in the deck and FALSE otherwise; the enumerated type `Boolean` is defined in the usual way.

The function `shuffle()` places the cards in random order. Cards can be shuffled according to the following algorithm. Pick one of the 52 cards at random and exchange it with the bottom card of the deck. The bottom card is now considered "shuffled" and the remaining 51 cards remain "unshuffled." Select one of the 51 unshuffled cards at random and exchange it with the bottommost unshuffled card. The new bottommost unshuffled card—

the card that was picked—is now transferred to the shuffled part of the deck, so that we now have 50 unshuffled cards followed by two shuffled cards. Next, pick one of the 50 unshuffled cards at random, exchange it with the bottommost unshuffled card, and so on. Continue until all cards have been transferred from the unshuffled to the shuffled part of the deck.

3. Modify the machine-adjustment simulation to compute the average lengths of the machine and adjuster queues; for this purpose the two queues should be considered logically distinct, even though the service manager uses the same queue for both machines and adjusters. The service manager is responsible for collecting the data for this computation; the basic datum required for each queue is a weighted sum of the form

```
n1*t1 + n2*t2 + n3*t3 + ...
```

where `n1, n2, n3, ...` are the queue lengths that occurred during the simulation, and `t1, t2, t3, ...` are the number of ticks for which the queue had the corresponding length. Dividing this weighted sum by the total number of elapsed ticks gives the average queue length.

4. Modify the machine-adjustment simulation to compute the average time that a machine or adjuster waits in a queue; as in Exercise 3, the machine and adjuster queues should be considered logically distinct, and separate average waiting times should be computed for machines and adjusters. Again, the service manager is responsible for collecting the necessary data; the basic datum required for each queue is the total number of ticks that objects spent waiting in that queue. Dividing this sum by the total number of elapsed ticks and the number of objects of the corresponding type yields the average time an object of that type spent waiting in the queue. When an object is removed from a queue, the service manager needs to know the time at which it entered the queue; for this purpose we can give each active object an instance variable `time_into_q` and functions `set_time_into_q()` and `get_time_into_q()` for manipulating the variable. The service manager will use the `set` function when it places an object into a queue and the `get` function when it removes the object from the queue.

5. Write an object-oriented simulation for a service counter where clerks or servers handle customer requests on a first-come-first-served basis. We assume a single queue for all servers, as in many banks and post offices, rather than a separate queue for each server, as in a supermarket. The simulation will involve two kinds of active objects: (1) a customer source ("the front door"), which places new customers in line at random intervals, and (2) the servers, which take a random time interval to serve each customer. The times between customer arrivals and the service times can have geometric distributions. The customers are represented by passive objects because customers take no actions on their own initiative but are at the mercy of the queue and the servers. Each customer object is created by the source and deleted by the server that handles the customer's request.

The customer queue can be managed by a resource-coordinator object similar to the service manager in the machine-adjustment simulation. The customer source will call the queue manager to place new customers in line, and a server will call when it is ready for the next customer. The queue manager will differ from the machine-repair service manager in the way a server is selected when several are idle: placing idle servers in a first-in-first-out queue is unrealistic, because a customer couldn't care less which server has been idle the longest. One approach is to choose an idle server at random. Another approach involves assumptions about the geometry of the queue and the service counter. For example, customers may exit from the queue at one end of the service counter; in that case, a customer is likely to choose the idle server that is closest to the queue exit point.

Useful statistics for this simulation to compute are the average queue length, the average time that a customer waits in the queue, and the average utilization of the servers.

8 _More About Input and Output_

*T*HE C++ input-output system is far too extensive to explore completely in an introductory book. Instead, this chapter provides an introduction to the input-output classes as well as to such important operations as formatting output, detecting errors, accessing named files, and direct access.

THE BASIC INPUT-OUTPUT CLASSES

The header file `iostream.h` declares the four basic input-output classes: `ios`, `istream`, `ostream`, and `iostream`. As shown in Figure 8-1, `ios` is the base class for `istream` and `ostream`, which are, in turn, base classes for `iostream`. Class `ios` must be a *virtual* base class of `istream` and `ostream` so that only one copy of its members will be inherited by `iostream`.

Class `ios` provides some basic facilities that are used by all the other input-output classes. It declares a pointer to a buffer object that provides temporary storage for input and output data; the buffer also provides the connection to the ultimate source or destination of the data, such as a disk file.* Class `ios` also declares several `state` variables, whose values govern input-

---

* Buffer objects are class objects with their own class hierarchy. For example, `iostream.h` declares `streambuf`, which is the abstract base class of all buffer objects; `fstream.h` declares `filebuf`, which is derived from `streambuf` and is the class of buffers connected to named files. Because beginners do not have to deal directly with buffer objects, the buffer classes are beyond the scope of this book.

Figure 8-1

Basic input-output classes. Class
ios *is a virtual base class of*
istream *and* ostream; *one
copy of the members of* ios *is
inherited by each of the other three
classes. Input operations are
defined in* istream, *output
operations, in* ostream. *Class*
iostream, *which supports both
input and output, inherits the
members of both* istream *and*
ostream.

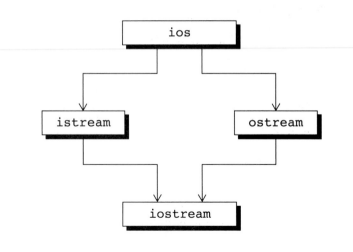

output operations. For example, the *format state* governs how output values will be printed and how input values will be interpreted. The *error state* indicates whether a previous operation on a stream object has failed; no further operations can be carried out on the object until the error indication is cleared.

Class ios defines a number of constants that help us specify the state of a stream object. For example, we can use the constants ios::dec, ios::oct, and ios::hex to specify whether integer values will be printed in decimal, octal, or hexadecimal notation.

Class istream provides facilities for formatted input. It defines the extraction operator, >>, as well as such input functions as get() and getline(). Likewise, class ostream provides facilities for formatted output. It defines the insertion operator, <<, as well as output functions such as put(), which outputs a single character.

Class iostream provides facilities for both input and output; its input facilities are inherited from istream and its output facilities are inherited from ostream. Given an iostream object, we can use both >> to input data from the stream and << to output data to the stream.

FORMAT-STATE FLAGS

The format state consists of three parameters and 15 one-bit *flags*. Each flag can be *set* (bit value 1) or *cleared* (bit value 0). All the flags are stored as bits within a `long` value. To prevent us from having to worry about the positions of the individual bits, each flag is designated by an `ios` constant. In addition, three groups of flags, called *bit fields*, are designated by the `ios` constants `ios::basefield`, `ios::adjustfield`, and `ios::floatfield`. Table 8-1 lists the `ios` constants for all the flags and bit fields.

In each of the three named bit fields, the flags are mutually exclusive—no more than one flag within the field should be set. A formatting action is also specified for the case in which none of the flags in the field are set.

The default flag settings, which apply when none of the flags have been changed by the program, are `ios::skipws` and `ios::dec` set and all the remaining flags cleared.

The remainder of this section is an overview of all the flags; the uses of some flags are illustrated in more detail later.

The flag `ios::skipws` governs whether `>>` will skip whitespace before reading a value; by default, `ios::skipws` is set and whitespace is skipped. We must use caution in reading input with this flag cleared. For example, when reading a numerical value with `ios::skipws` cleared, whitespace preceding the value is illegal and will cause an error.

The three flags `ios::left`, `ios::right`, and `ios::internal`, which comprise the bit field `ios::adjustfield`, determine how a printed value is positioned within its field—the area reserved for the value on the printed page. (Don't confuse fields on the printed page with bit fields.) Setting `ios::left` causes a value to be positioned as far to the left as possible (left alignment); setting `ios::right` causes a value to be positioned as far to the right as possible (right alignment). Setting `ios::internal` causes a sign or base indication (leading `0`, `0x`, or `0X`) to be left aligned and the rest of the number to be right aligned. If none of the flags are set (the default), right alignment is used. Typically, we use left alignment for text and right alignment for numerical values.

The three flags `ios::dec`, `ios::oct`, and `ios::hex`, which comprise the bit field `ios::basefield`, determine whether decimal, octal, or hexadecimal notation will be used for

	FLAG	BIT FIELD
	`ios::skipws`	
	`ios::left`	`ios::adjustfield`
	`ios::right`	
	`ios::internal`	
	`ios::dec`	`ios::basefield`
	`ios::oct`	
	`ios::hex`	
	`ios::showbase`	
	`ios::showpos`	
	`ios::uppercase`	
	`ios::showpoint`	
	`ios::scientific`	`ios::floatfield`
	`ios::fixed`	
	`ios::unitbuf`	
	`ios::stdio`	

Table 8-1

Format-State Flags and Bit Fields

printing integral values and will be assumed for reading them. By default, `ios::dec` is set and decimal notation is used. If none of the flags are set, values are printed in decimal notation and read according to the conventions for C++ integer constants (a leading `0` indicates octal notation and a leading `0x` or `0X` indicates hexadecimal notation).

The next four flags in Table 8-1 affect the way numerical values are printed. They do not form a named bit field, and they are not mutually exclusive: each flag can be set or cleared independently of the others. Each of the four flags is cleared by default. The following gives a brief description of each flag:

`ios::showbase`   When this flag is set, octal and hexadecimal numbers are printed in the notation used in C++ programs: an octal number begins with a leading zero and a hexadecimal number begins with `0x` or `0X`. The `ios::uppercase` flag determines whether `x` or `X` is used. Further information on octal and hexadecimal notations can be found in the glossary entries for those topics.

`ios::showpos`	When this flag is set, a positive integer is printed with a plus sign, as in +350.
`ios::uppercase`	When this flag is set, uppercase letters are used for the E in exponential notation and when printing hexadecimal numbers.
`ios::showpoint`	When this flag is cleared, trailing zeros to the right of the decimal point are omitted; the decimal point is itself omitted if it is followed only by zeros. When the flag is set, the decimal point and trailing zeros are printed. This flag applies only when both `ios::scientific` and `ios::fixed` are cleared; when one of those flags is set, the precision parameter determines how many decimal places will be printed.

The two flags `ios::scientific` and `ios::fixed`, which comprise the bit field `ios::floatfield`, determine how floating-point values will be printed. If `ios::scientific` is set, a value is printed in scientific notation; if `ios::fixed` is set, conventional fixed-point notation is used. If neither flag is set (the default), the position of the decimal point determines whether conventional or scientific notation will be used. Conventional notation is used if the decimal point is within or to the right of the number (as in `3.45`, `34.5` and `345.`) or if no more than three zeros separate the decimal point from the first nonzero digit (as in `.000345`, `.00345`, `.0345`, and `.345`). If the decimal point in conventional notation would fall outside this range of acceptable positions, scientific notation is used.

The remaining two flags do not affect formatting at all but rather control the flushing of buffers. When `ios::unitbuf` is set, the buffer of an output stream is flushed after each insertion. This prevents the programmer from having to invoke `flush` or `endl`, yet it is still more efficient than eliminating buffering altogether. Setting `ios::stdio` helps prevent certain problems when the standard output and error files are accessed via both the C *stdio* library and the C++ *iostream* library.

FORMAT-STATE PARAMETERS

In addition to the 15 flags, the format state includes three parameters: *width*, *fill character*, and *precision*. We are already familiar with the width parameter that, for output, specifies the size of the field in which a value will be printed. On input of strings, the maximum number of characters that will be read is one less than the width, thereby assuring that the string will fit in an array whose size is given by the width parameter.

The default value for the width parameter is 0, which causes the parameter to be ignored for both input and output. On output, the field width will be equal to the number of characters in the printed value; on input of strings, there is no limit on the number of characters that will be read. The width parameter is unusual in that it is reset to zero after each insertion or extraction; a nonzero width must be specified immediately prior to the input or output operation to which it applies.

When a printed value does not occupy the entire field specified by the width parameter, fill characters are printed in the unused part of the field. The default fill character is the space, which is what is normally used. Occasionally, we may wish to specify another fill character; for example, an asterisk is often used when printing the amount of a check, to help prevent the amount from being altered.

The precision parameter determines the precision with which floating-point numbers will be printed; its exact usage depends on the settings of the `ios::scientific` and `ios::fixed` flags. When one of the the flags is set, the precision parameter specifies the number of digits to the right of the decimal point. When neither flag is set (the default), the precision parameter specifies the total number of digits to be printed, regardless of the location of the decimal point.

SETTING FLAGS AND PARAMETERS

The *iostream* library provides functions `fill()`, `flags()`, `precision()`, and `width()` for accessing the components of the format state. These functions are declared class in `ios` and are inherited by all the other stream classes, such as `istream` and `ostream`.

These four functions are used in similar ways. If they are called without arguments, they return the components of the current format state without changing the state. Thus, the following statements save the components of the format state of `cout` in variables c, f, p, and w:

```
char c = cout.fill();
long f = cout.flags();
int  p = cout.precision();
int  w = cout.width();
```

Note the types of variables used for the different format-state components; as previously mentioned, the flags are stored as a `long` value.

If an argument is supplied, the function returns the current value of the corresponding component and sets that component to the value specified by the argument. We specify an argument for `flags()` with a single `ios` constant or several constants joined by the bitwise OR operators, `|`. The flags specified by the `ios` constants are set and the remaining flags are cleared:

```
char c = cout.fill( '*' );
long f = cout.flags( ios::dec | ios::showpos );
int  p = cout.precision( 5 );
int  w = cout.width( 10 );
```

After these statements, c, f, p, and w will hold the previous format state of `cout`, and the new format state will be as specified by the arguments. If later we need to restore the previous format state, we can do so as follows:

```
cout.fill( c );
cout.flags( f );
cout.precision( p );
cout.width( w );
```

The following are a few more examples of setting flags:

```
cout.flags( ios::oct );
cout.flags( ios::oct | ios::showbase );
cout.flags( ios::hex | ios::showbase |
            ios::uppercase );
cout.flags( ios::internal | ios::hex |
            ios::showbase | ios::uppercase );
```

Each function call sets those flags specified in the argument and clears the remaining ones.

The function `flags()` is sometimes inconvenient because it clears all flags not specified in its argument. The function `setf()` sets the flags specified in its argument, and the function `unsetf()` clears them; both functions leave unchanged any flags that are not mentioned in the argument. Thus

```
cout.setf( ios::showbase );
```

sets `ios::showbase` for `cout`, and

```
cout.unsetf( ios::showbase | ios::showpos );
```

clears `ios::showbase` and `ios::showpos`. In each case, the flags not mentioned in the argument are left unchanged. Like `flags()`, `setf()` and `unsetf()` return the current flag settings, so

```
long f = cout.setf( ios::showbase );
```

saves the current flags in `f` before setting `ios::showbase`.

There is a two-argument form of `setf()` especially designed for setting flags in the named bit fields. Because the flags in a bit field are mutually exclusive, only one should be set and the remainder should be cleared. The statement

```
cout.setf( ios::hex, ios::basefield );
```

sets `ios::hex` and clears the remaining flags in `ios::basefield`; flags not in `ios::basefield` are unaffected. Likewise,

```
cout.setf( ios::right, ios::adjustfield );
```

sets `ios::right` and clears the remaining flags in `ios::adjustfield`; other flags are unaffected. If the first argument is zero, all the flags in the specified field are cleared. Thus

```
cout.setf( 0, ios::floatfield );
```

clears the flags in `ios::floatfield` but does not affect any other flags.

Class `ios` provides manipulators `dec`, `oct`, and `hex` for specifying decimal, octal, or hexadecimal notation. For example,

```
cout << oct;
```

is equivalent to

```
cout.setf( ios::oct, ios::basefield );
```

and

```
cout << hex << 1000;
```

causes 1000 to be printed in hexadecimal notation.

The header file `iomanip.h` provides parameterized manipulators corresponding to `fill()`, `precision()`, `width()`, and to the one-argument forms of `setf()` and `unsetf()`. Thus, the following statements modify the format state of `cout` by setting and clearing flags and by changing the values of the three parameters:

```
cout << setiosflags( ios::showbase );
cout << resetiosflags( ios::left | ios::showpos );
cout << setfill( '*' );
cout << setprecision( 5 );
cout << setw( 10 );
```

The manipulators `setfill()`, `setprecision()`, and `setw()` set, respectively, the fill character, precision, and width. Like `setf()`, `setiosflags()` sets the specified flags and leaves the others unchanged; like `unsetf()`, `resetiosflags()` clears the specified flags and leaves the others unchanged. A drawback of these manipulators is that they cannot return the previous values of the format-state components; if the previous values need to be saved, we must use the member functions rather than the manipulators.

FORMATTING EXAMPLES

The programs in Listings 8-1 and 8-2 illustrate some common forms of formatting. To make the fields visible on the printed page, we use the period as the fill character, so that periods are printed in all unused positions of a field. Bear in mind, however, that in practical applications we usually use the space as the fill character.

The program in Listing 8-1 begins by specifying the period as the fill character:

```
cout.fill('.');
```

The string `"Example"` is then printed in a 12-character field, first with `ios::left` set and then with `ios::right` set:

```
cout.setf( ios::left, ios::adjustfield );
cout <<  setw( 12 ) << "Example" << endl;
```

Listing 8-1

```
// File iostrl.cpp
// Output formatting for strings and integers

#include <iostream.h>
#include <iomanip.h>

main()
{

    cout.fill('.');   // make fill characters visible

    cout.setf( ios::left, ios::adjustfield );
    cout << setw( 12 ) << "Example" << endl;

    cout.setf( ios::right, ios::adjustfield );
    cout << setw( 12 ) << "Example" << endl;

    cout << endl;

    cout.setf( ios::left, ios::adjustfield );
    cout << setw( 12 ) << -1000 << endl;

    cout.setf( ios::internal, ios::adjustfield );
    cout << setw( 12 ) << -1000 << endl;

    cout.setf( ios::right, ios::adjustfield );
    cout << setw( 12 ) << -1000 << endl;
}
```

```
    cout.setf( ios::right, ios::adjustfield );
    cout << setw( 12 ) << "Example" << endl;
```

The printout shows the alignment produced by each flag setting:

```
Example.....
.....Example
```

In the same way, -1000 is printed in a 12-character field, first with `ios::left` set, then with `ios::internal` set, and finally with `ios::right` set. The printout shows the alignment produced by each flag setting:

```
-1000.......
-.......1000
.......-1000
```

The program in Listing 8-2 illustrates the formatting of floating-point values. The program begins by defining a **double** constant `PI`, setting the fill character to `'.'`, and setting the precision to 4:

```
const double PI = 3.14159265;
cout.fill('.');
cout.precision( 4 );
```

The remaining statements in the program print various multiples of `PI` to illustrate the three different floating-point formats. The first group of values is printed with the default format, in which both `ios::scientific` and `ios::fixed` are cleared:

```
.....3.142e-005
......0.0003142
..........3.142
.........31.42
.........314.2
..........3142
.....3.142e+004
```

The precision determines the number of significant digits printed, which is four in each case. Note the points at which the system switches from conventional to scientific notation: 0.00003142 is printed in scientific notation but 0.0003142 is printed in conventional notation. At the opposite extreme, 3142 is printed in conventional notation but 31420 is printed in scientific notation. Note that 3142 is *not* followed by a decimal point because `ios::showpoint` is not set.

When `ios::scientific` is set, all the values are printed in scientific notation; the precision determines the number of decimal places:

```
....3.1416e+000
....3.1416e+001
....3.1416e+002
....3.1416e+003
....3.1416e+004
```

Listing 8-2

```cpp
// File iostr2.cpp
// Output formatting for floating-point numbers

#include <iostream.h>
#include <iomanip.h>

main()
{
    const double PI = 3.14159265;

    cout.fill('.');        // make fill characters visible
    cout.precision( 4 );   // set precision for entire program

    cout << "Default:\n\n";
    cout << setw( 15 ) << PI / 100000 << endl;
    cout << setw( 15 ) << PI / 10000 << endl;
    cout << setw( 15 ) << PI << endl;
    cout << setw( 15 ) << 10 * PI << endl;
    cout << setw( 15 ) << 100 * PI << endl;
    cout << setw( 15 ) << 1000 * PI << endl;
    cout << setw( 15 ) << 10000 * PI << endl;

    cout.setf( ios::scientific, ios::floatfield );

    cout << "\nScientific:\n\n";
    cout << setw( 15 ) << PI << endl;
    cout << setw( 15 ) << 10 * PI << endl;
    cout << setw( 15 ) << 100 * PI << endl;
    cout << setw( 15 ) << 1000 * PI << endl;
    cout << setw( 15 ) << 10000 * PI << endl;

    cout.setf( ios::fixed, ios::floatfield );

    cout << "\nFixed:\n\n";
    cout << setw( 15 ) << PI << endl;
    cout << setw( 15 ) << 10 * PI << endl;
    cout << setw( 15 ) << 100 * PI << endl;
    cout << setw( 15 ) << 1000 * PI << endl;
    cout << setw( 15 ) << 10000 * PI << endl;
}
```

When `ios::fixed` is set, all values are printed in conventional notation; the precision again determines the number of decimal places:

```
........3.1416
........31.4159
.......314.1593
......3141.5927
.....31415.9265
```

DETECTING ERRORS AND END-OF-FILE

Class `ios` provides the following four functions for testing the error state of a stream:

```
int good();
int eof();
int bad();
int fail();
```

Each function returns a nonzero value (*true*) if the corresponding error condition holds true and returns zero (*false*) otherwise.

Function `good()` returns *true* if no error has occurred, that is, if the other three functions return *false*. Thus if the value of `cin.good()` is *true*, all is right with stream `cin` and we can proceed to input data from it.

Function `eof()` returns *true* if the system encountered end-of-file (the end of the file attached to the stream) while attempting an input operation. Often this is not an really an error, but merely indicates that all the input data has been read.

Function `fail()` returns *true* after an input or output operation has failed. If `bad()` also returns *true*, the error was so severe as to make it unlikely that any further operations can be carried out on the stream. If `bad()` returns *false*, however, then it may be possible to recover from the error and continue using the stream.

When `good()` returns *false*, no further operations can be carried out on the stream; any attempted operations will be ignored. The function `clear()`, called with no argument, resets the error state so that further operations can be attempted.

When an input operation is attempted after all the input data has been read, the operation fails and both `eof()` and `fail()` return *true*—`eof()` because end-of-file was encountered and `fail()` because the input operation failed. When reading input, we can check the value of `fail()` after each attempted operation; if `fail()` returns *true*, we can use `eof()` to determine if end-of-file was encountered and `bad()` to determine if a fatal error occurred:

```
while ( !cin.get(ch).fail() ) {
   // Process value of ch...
}
if ( cin.eof() ) {
   // Terminate program normally...
}
else if ( cin.bad() ) {
   // Report fatal error...
}
else {
   cin.clear();   // clear error state
   // Attempt to recover from error...
}
```

The control expression in the `while` statement works as follows. The input and output functions and operators all return a reference to the stream to which they were applied. Thus, `cin.get(ch)` reads a character into `ch` (if possible) and returns a reference to `cin`. To determine if the attempted input operation failed, we apply `fail()` to the reference returned by `get()` (which is the same as applying it to `cin`):

```
cin.get(ch).fail()
```

Finally, we want processing to continue when this expression yields *false*, so we precede it with the logical NOT operator:

```
!cin.get(ch).fail()
```

The dot operator has higher precedence than `!`, so `!` is applied not to `cin` but to the logical value computed by the remainder of the expression.

We can simplify our control expressions by using two operators defined by `ios`. These operators allow a stream object `c` to be used as a control expression, as in

```
if ( c )...
if ( !c )...
```

In the first statement, the operator in question is an implicit type conversion that converts `c` to a nonzero value if `c.fail()` yields *false* and to zero if `c.fail()` yields *true*. Thus when `c` is used as a control expression, it yields *true* if no error has occurred and *false* otherwise.

Class `ios` overloads the operator `!` so that it can be applied to stream objects, as in the second `if` statement. Applying `!` to `c` yields the same result as `c.fail()`, so the value of `!c` is *true* if an error has occurred and *false* otherwise. Note that `c` (used as a control expression) and `!c` always yield opposite results.

For example, we can use the type conversion to replace

```
while ( !cin.get(ch).fail() ) {
    // Process value of ch....
}
```

with

```
while ( cin.get(ch) ) {
    // Process value of ch....
}
```

The reference to `cin` returned by `cin.get(ch)` is converted to *true* if processing can continue and to *false* if an error occurred. Because `cin >> ch` also returns a reference to `cin`, we can also write

```
while ( cin >> ch ) {
    // Process value of ch....
}
```

This `while` statement works just like the preceding one except that `>>` skips whitespace before reading a character (if `ios::skipws` is set) whereas `get()` does not.

CLASSES FOR NAMED FILES

The only files we can access conveniently with `iostream.h` are those attached to the standard streams `cin`, `cout`, and `cerr`. For accessing files designated by names, such as disk files, we use the classes declared in `fstream.h`, which are illustrated in Figure 8-2. The class `fstreambase` provides the basic facilities for working with named files. The `fstream.h` classes `ifstream`, `ofstream`, and `fstream` correspond respectively to the `iostream.h` classes `istream`, `ostream`, and `iostream`; each is derived from `fstreambase` and from the corresponding `iostream.h` class. Each inherits operators and member functions from the corresponding `iostream.h`, so,

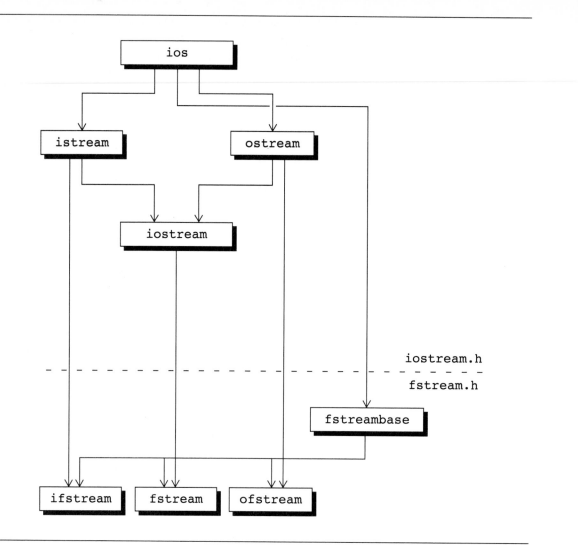

Figure 8-2

Classes for named files. The classes above the broken line are declared in
iostream.h; *those below are declared in* fstream.h. *Class*
fstreambase *provides facilities for dealing with named files. The input-output
classes for named files,* ifstream, ofstream, *and* fstream, *each inherit
from* fstreambase *and from the corresponding class in* iostream.h. *Class*
ios *is a virtual base class for* istream, ostream, *and* fstreambase;
despite the complexity of the inheritance paths, exactly one copy of the members of
ios *is inherited by each of the other classes.*

for example, we can use >> to input from `ifstream` objects and << to output to `ofstream` objects.

Class `ios` is a virtual base class of `istream`, `ostream`, and `fstreambase`. Despite the complexity of the inheritance paths in Figure 8-2, each derived class inherits exactly one copy of the members of `ios`. In particular, the functions and operators for setting the format state and accessing the error state are all inherited by `ifstream`, `ofstream`, and `fstream`.

Because the classes in `fstream.h` are derived from those in `iostream.h`, the latter header file must be included in any source file that includes `fstream.h`. Therefore, `fstream.h` contains an `#include` directive for `iostream.h`, so including `fstream.h` also serves to include `iostream.h`. All the header files use the previously discussed techniques for avoiding multiple inclusions, so it doesn't matter if other `#include` directives for `iostream.h` appear in the source file or in other header files.

INPUT AND OUTPUT WITH NAMED FILES

When we declare a stream, we can attach it to a particular file, a process known as *opening* the file. When we open a file, we give the name of the file and specify the mode in which the file is to be opened. The file name is represented by a string, which must obey whatever file-naming conventions are employed by a particular computer system. A file mode is represented by one or more `ios` constants, of which the following are the most widely used:

```
ios::in
ios::out
ios::app
ios::ate
```

Mode `ios::in` allows data to be read from the attached file; modes `ios::out` and `ios::app` allow data to be written to the file. The two output modes differ when the file name refers to a file that already exists. For `ios::out`, any existing data in the file is discarded and replaced with whatever data is written to the stream. For `ios::app`, the existing data is retained and the stream is positioned so that any new data will be appended to the end of the existing data. For both output modes, the named file will be created if it does not already exist.

Like format-state flags, the `ios` mode constants can be combined with the bitwise OR operator. Thus mode

```
ios::in | ios::out
```

allows both input and output. As is usual for `ios::out`, if the designated file already exists, any existing data in it will be discarded. However, `ios::ate` implies that any existing data will be used; therefore mode

```
ios::in | ios::out | ios::ate
```

also allows both input and output, but specifies that if the designated file already exists, any existing data in it will be retained.

When we declare a stream, we can open the corresponding file by providing the file name and mode as constructor arguments. Thus

```
ifstream input( "intext.doc", ios::in );
```

declares `input` as an `ifstream`, attaches it to the file `intext.doc`, and establishes mode `ios::in`. Likewise, the following statements declare an `ofstream` and an `fstream`:

```
ofstream output( "outtext.doc", ios::out );
fstream io( "iotext.doc", ios::in | ios::out );
```

For `ifstream` the default mode is `ios::in`; for `ofstream` the default mode is `ios::out`. Therefore, the following declarations of `input` and `output` are equivalent to the ones above:

```
ifstream input( "intext.doc" );
ofstream output( "outtext.doc" );
```

Listing 8-3 shows a simple demonstration program that opens an output file and writes four lines to it. The program begins by declaring `out` as an `ostream` and attaching it to file `test.doc` with the default mode `ios::out`:

```
ofstream out( "test.doc" );
```

Errors are not uncommon when opening a file; for example, the file name might be invalid, or a file that is supposed to already exist may not be available. After attempting to open a file, we can use the `ios` operator `!` to test whether an error occurred:

Listing 8-3

```
// File iostr3.cpp
// Writing to a disk file

#include <fstream.h>
#include <stdlib.h>

main()
{
    ofstream out( "test.doc");
    if ( !out ) {
        cerr << "Cannot open output file\n";
        exit( 1 );
    }

    out << "Now is the time\n";
    out << "for all good people\n";
    out << "to come to the aid\n";
    out << "of their country.\n";
}
```

```
    if ( !out ) {
        cerr << "Cannot open output file\n";
        exit( 1 );
    }
```

The remainder of the program writes four lines to the file. Note that the insertion operator << is used with out exactly the same way as it is used with the standard stream cout.

The program in Listing 8-4 reads the four-line file that was written by the program just discussed. The following statements declare in as an ifstream, attach it to the file test.doc with the default mode ios::in, and check for any errors that occurred in the process:

```
    ifstream in( "test.doc" );
    if ( !in ) {
        cerr << "Input file cannot be opened\n";
        exit( 1 );
    }
```

Listing 8-4

```
// File iostr4.cpp
// Reading from a disk file

#include <fstream.h>
#include <stdlib.h>

main()
{
    ifstream in( "test.doc");
    if ( !in ) {
        cerr << "Input file cannot be opened\n";
        exit( 1 );
    }

    const int SIZE = 81;
    char line[ SIZE ];

    in.getline( line, SIZE );
    cout << line << endl;

    in.getline( line, SIZE );
    cout << line << endl;

    in.getline( line, SIZE );
    cout << line << endl;

    in.getline( line, SIZE );
    cout << line << endl;
}
```

We can check our error-handling statements by attempting to run this program when the file test.doc does not exist.

The program reads each line of test.doc into the array line and then writes the line to cout. Because we want to read lines rather than words, we use getline() rather than >> to read from in:

```
in.getline( line, SIZE );
cout << line << endl;
```

When the program is run, the four lines in `test.doc` will be printed on the display.

USING COMMAND-LINE PARAMETERS

Many operating systems allow parameters to be specified on the command line that runs a program. Such command-line parameters are often used to name the files that a program is to process. For example, consider the program `iostr5`, which makes a copy of a file. We can use the command line

```
iostr5 testl.doc test2.doc
```

to run `iostr5` with instructions to copy file `testl.doc` and name the copy `test2.doc`.

Listing 8-5 shows the file-copying program `iostr5`. To access the command-line parameters, we must declare `main()` as a function with two arguments:

```
main( int argc, char** argv )
```

When the program is run, `argc` is set to the number of command-line parameters and `argv` is set to an array of strings, each element of which is a command-line parameter. (Why is `char**` an appropriate type for an array of strings?)

The name of the program is considered to be the first command-line parameter. Thus for the command line given above, the value of `argc` is 3, and the elements of `argv` are as follows:

Element	Value
argv[0]	"iostr5"
argv[1]	"testl.doc"
argv[2]	"test2.doc"

Error checking is very important when using command-line parameters, for many errors can be made in typing the command line. Our copying program begins by checking that the number of parameters is correct:

```
if ( argc != 3 ) {
   cerr << "Incorrect number of parameters\n";
   exit( 1 );
}
```

Listing 8-5

```
// File iostr5.cpp
// File copying; source and target files are specified
// via command-line parameters

#include <fstream.h>
#include <stdlib.h>

main( int argc, char** argv )
{
   if ( argc != 3 ) {
      cerr << "Incorrect number of parameters\n";
      exit( 1 );
   }

   ifstream in( argv[ 1 ] );
   if ( !in ) {
      cerr << "Input file cannot be opened\n";
      exit( 1 );
   }

   ofstream out( argv[ 2 ] );
   if ( !out ) {
      cerr << "Output file cannot be opened\n";
      exit( 1 );
   }

   char ch;
   while( out && in.get(ch) )
      out.put( ch );
}
```

Next, the value of argv[1] is used to open for input the file that is to be copied:

```
ifstream in( argv[ 1 ] );
if ( !in ) {
   cerr << "Input file cannot be opened\n";
   exit( 1 );
}
```

Finally, the value of argv[2] is used to open for output the file that is to receive the copy:

```
ofstream out( argv[ 2 ] );
if ( !out ) {
   cerr << "Output file cannot be opened\n";
   exit( 1 );
}
```

The following code copies the input file to the output file:

```
char ch;
while( out && in.get(ch) )
   out.put( ch );
```

The program uses get() to read each character from in, and put() to write it to out. (We could just as well have used << instead of put().)

Type conversions are used to check both the input and output streams. The stream out is converted to *true* if no output error has occurred so far. The value of in.get(ch) is a reference to in, which is converted to *true* if no input error occurred while reading ch. These two truth values are combined with the logical AND operator, so copying will continue as long as both the input and output streams are error free. When get() encounters the end of the input file, the input operation will fail, the value of in.get(ch) will convert to *false,* and the while statement will terminate.

DIRECT ACCESS

So far we have employed only *sequential access,* in which we read or write a file from beginning to end, with all data items being read or written in the same order in which they occur in the file. C++ also allows *direct* or *random access,* in which items can be read or written at any specified position within a file.

For each file, the system maintains a current position—the position at which the next item will be read or written. We can access the current position with the function tellg(). A position is stored as a value of type streampos, so

```
streampos p = direct.tellg();
```

sets p to the current position in the file attached to stream direct. If we later wish to return to this position, we can use

```
direct.seekg( p );
```

to set the current position to the value of **p**.

The program in Listing 8-6 provides a brief introduction to direct access. The program begins by declaring the `fstream` object `io` and attaching it to the file `test.io` with mode `ios::in | ios::out`:

```
fstream io( "test.io", ios::in | ios::out );
if ( !io ) {
    cerr << "File cannot be opened\n";
    exit( 1 );
}
```

With mode `ios::in | ios::out`, any existing contents of `test.io` are discarded; thus `test.io` is initially empty and the current position is at the beginning of the file. If we had used mode `ios::in | ios::out | ios::ate`, any existing contents of `test.io` would have been retained, and the initial position would have been at the end of the file.

The program next writes the string

```
"The quick brown fox jumps over the lazy dog.\n"
```

in four segments. Before writing each segment, it assigns the current position to a `streampos` variable. These variables then point to various positions within the file and can be used later to return to those positions. For example, after

```
streampos p1 = io.tellg();
io << "The quick ";
```

the value of **p1** is the position of the **T** in **The**. After

```
streampos p2 = io.tellg();
io << "brown fox ";
```

the value of **p2** is the position of the **b** in **brown**, and so on.

We have written the file sequentially, saving certain positions by assigning them to variables **p1** through **p4**. We can now demonstrate direct access by reading the word that begins at each of the saved positions. For example,

```
io.seekg( p4 );
```

sets the current position to **p4**, which is the position of the first letter of **lazy**. The statement

```
io >> setw( 6 ) >> word;
```

reads one word, beginning at the current position; it thus reads `lazy` into the array `word`. Finally, the statement

```
cout << word << endl;
```

prints `lazy` on the display.

Similar groups of statements read and display the words beginning at positions `p3`, `p2`, and `p1`. When the program is run, it outputs the following to the display:

```
lazy
jumps
brown
The
```

Listing 8-6

```cpp
// File iostr6.cpp
// Random access

#include <fstream.h>
#include <iomanip.h>
#include <stdlib.h>

main()
{
    fstream io( "test.io", ios::in | ios::out );
    if ( !io ) {
        cerr << "File cannot be opened\n";
        exit( 1 );
    }

    streampos p1 = io.tellg();
    io << "The quick ";

    streampos p2 = io.tellg();
    io << "brown fox ";

    streampos p3 = io.tellg();
    io << "jumps over the ";

    streampos p4 = io.tellg();
    io << "lazy dog.\n";
```

(continued)

```
        char word[ 6 ];

        io.seekg( p4 );
        io >> setw( 6 ) >> word;
        cout << word << endl;

        io.seekg( p3 );
        io >> setw( 6 ) >> word;
        cout << word << endl;

        io.seekg( p2 );
        io >> setw( 6 ) >> word;
        cout << word << endl;

        io.seekg( p1 );
        io >> setw( 6 ) >> word;
        cout << word << endl;
    }
```

EXERCISES

1. Write a program that reads a text file and writes a file that is identical except that every sequence of consecutive spaces has been replaced by a single space. The names of the input and output files are provided as command-line parameters.

2. Write a program to read a text file and write it with every line preceded by a line number. Each line number should be right-aligned in a four-character field and followed by a colon, two spaces, and the remainder of the line. The names of the input and output files are provided as command-line parameters.

3. Write a program to read a file, each line of which consists of a one-word item name and a price, the two separated by whitespace, as in:

```
Computer  1935.75
```

The program should output the names and prices in two columns, with the names left aligned and the prices right aligned; each price should be printed with two decimal places. The columns should have column headings `Item` and `Price`, which should be centered over their respective columns. To center a column heading, left-align the corresponding string, but include at the beginning of the string enough spaces to achieve centering.

4. Write a program that reads a text file and formats it into lines that do not exceed a given maximum length. Each line should contain as many words as possible, but no word should be broken between lines. Adjacent words on a line are separated by a single space. The program should prompt the user for the names of the input and output files and for the maximum line length. *Hint:* Use >> to read the input file one word at a time.

1 C++ *Keywords*

asm	float	signed
auto	for	sizeof
break	friend	static
case	goto	struct
catch*	if	switch
char	inline	template*
class	int	this
const	long	typedef
continue	new	union
default	operator	unsigned
delete	private	virtual
do	protected	void
double	public	volatile
else	register	while
enum	return	
extern	short	

* The keywords catch and template are reserved for future extensions to the language.

Operator Precedence and Associativity

The following table lists all C++ operators grouped according to precedence and associativity. The groups are listed in order of decreasing precedence, and the column at right gives the associativity of the operators in each group. Chapter 1 explains how precedence and associativity govern the grouping of operators and operands in expressions.

In the table, the labels *prefix* and *postfix* distinguish the uses of ++ and −− as prefix operators (++n, −−n) and as postfix operators (n++, n−−). The symbols +, −, *, and & are used for both unary (one operand) and binary (two operand) operators; the former are distinguished with the label *unary*. Unary + and − are the plus and minus operators in expressions such as +x and −m*n. Unary * is the indirection operator, and unary & is the address-of operator.

Table A2-1	OPERATORS	ASSOCIATIVITY
Operator Precedence and Associativity	::	left to right
	-> . ( ) [ ] *postfix* ++ *postfix* --	left to right
	prefix ++ *prefix* -- ~ ! *unary* + *unary* - *unary* * *unary* & *(type)* sizeof new delete	right to left
	->* .*	left to right
	* / %	left to right
	+ -	left to right
	<< >>	left to right
	< <= > >=	left to right
	== !=	left to right
	&	left to right
	^	left to right
	|	left to right
	&&	left to right
	||	left to right
	? :	left to right
	= *= /= %= += -= <<= >>= &= ^= |=	right to left
	,	left to right

3 Turbo C++

Turbo C++ is an implementation of C++ for MS-DOS computers. Its *integrated development environment* (IDE) simplifes compiling, linking, executing, and debugging programs with one or several source files. As the first C++ implementation from a major supplier of microcomputer software (Borland International), Turbo C++ is expected to garner a substantial share of the market for MS-DOS C++ implementations. Ultimately, its strongest competition will probably come from Borland's arch rival, Microsoft, whose anticipated C++ implementation has not been released at the time of this writing.

This appendix is a brief introduction to Turbo C++ and the integrated development environment. Also included are workarounds for a few problems that were encountered in compiling and running the example programs under Turbo C++ Version 1.00.

INSTALLATION

Turbo C++ requires an IBM PC, XT, AT, or PS/2, or a compatible computer, running MS-DOS or PC-DOS 2.0 or higher; 640K of RAM and a hard disk are also required. A full installation — one that does not omit any optional files — requires about 6 megabytes of disk space.

Installation — transferring files to your hard disk from the diskettes in the software package — is carried out by the program

INSTALL.* You *must* use this installation program to install Turbo C++. Most of the files are delivered in a special compressed or *packed* format and must be unpacked before installation. For this reason, and because of the number of diskettes, files, and disk directories involved, manual installation is impractical.

Fortunately, the installation program is easy to use. Insert Disk 1 in drive A and enter the following command:

```
A:INSTALL
```

On-screen instructions will guide you through the remainder of the installation process.

The installation program allows you to choose the path names for the eight directories in which the implementation will be stored. A default is proposed for each path name, and we recommend that you accept the defaults. All references to directories in this appendix assume that the default path names were accepted.

You will be asked whether to install the Tour, which is an online introduction to the integrated development environment. We recommend that you install this helpful program, which is discussed further in the next section.

You will be asked whether to unpack the example program files that come with the implementation. These files will be easier to access, but will take up more disk space, if they are unpacked.

You will be asked which of five memory models to install; by default, all five are installed. Memory models, which are characteristic of MS-DOS implementations, determine the amount of RAM available for code and data. Because each memory model requires a separate copy of the library, some disk space can be saved by not installing all five models. The small memory model, which allows up to 64K of code and 64K of data, is sufficient for almost all the exercise and experimental programs that students are likely to write.

TOURING THE IDE

The Tour mentioned earlier is provided by the program TCTOUR. The following commands run this tutorial program:

```
CD \TC\TOUR
TCTOUR
```

---

* In this appendix we follow the MS-DOS and Turbo C++ convention of displaying program, file, and directory names in all uppercase letters. When entering these names into the computer, however, you can type them in either uppercase or lowercase, the latter usually being more convenient.

The Tour is far easier to learn from than any printed description of the integrated development environment. The program illustrates its instructions with IDE screens, and it mimics the responses of the IDE when the user carries out practice commands. In this appendix we will not go into such basic matters as pulling down menus, selecting commands, and using dialog boxes, because such skills are far better acquired from the TCTOUR program.

Like many other interactive programs, the IDE has a menu bar listing the menus from which commands can be selected. In printed explanations, the Turbo C++ manuals use a notation of the form *menu | command* to indicate that a particular command is to be selected from a particular menu. For example, to choose File | Open means to pull down the File menu and select the Open command. To choose Edit | Paste means to pull down the Edit menu and select the Paste command.

The symbol ≡ represents the system menu, which can be pulled down by typing Alt-Spacebar. Thus to choose ≡ | Clear desktop means to pull down the system menu and select the Clear desktop command.

The menus also list shortcut *hot keys* that can be used to execute commands directly, without selecting from the menus. From the File menu, for example, we see that pressing F3 is equivalent to choosing File | Open, pressing F2 is equivalent to choosing File | Save, and pressing Alt-X is equivalent to choosing File | Quit.

RUNNING THE IDE

We run the IDE by executing the program TC, which is in the directory \TC\BIN. We *could* work with \TC\BIN as our current directory, in which case our C++ program files would be placed in \TC\BIN along with the implementation files. Usually, however, it is better to place our program files in a separate *working directory*. We can use different working directories for different programming projects, and if more than one person uses the computer, each person can use a different set of working directories.

Suppose that our working directory is \CPPWORK, which we can create with an MS-DOS MD (Make Directory) command:

```
MD \CPPWORK
```

To run the IDE with \CPPWORK as the current directory, we

must (1) change the current directory to `\CPPWORK` with a CD (Change Directory) command, (2) specify `\TC\BIN` in a `PATH` command so that the system can find the `TC` program, and (3) run the `TC` program. Thus the following MS-DOS commands run `TC` from the working directory `\CPPWORK`:

```
CD \CPPWORK
PATH \TC\BIN
TC
```

THE DESKTOP

When the IDE is running, the screen usually shows a menu bar and usually one or more windows. A window is *opened* when it is created on the screen and *closed* when it is removed. Turbo C++ allows overlapping windows, so an open window may be hidden by other windows. The window in which you are currently working is the *active window*, which is designated by a bright double-line border.

Most of your work will be done in *edit windows*, each of which is labeled with the name of the file being edited. Turbo C++ has a multiple-file editor, so several files—and hence several edit windows—can be open at the same time. Some other important windows are the *Output window*, which is used to view program output, and the *Message window*, which is used to view compiler and linker error messages.

A particular configuration of open windows is called a *desktop*. When you exit from the IDE, it saves your current desktop, and restores it the next time the IDE is run. (If, as described below, you specify a project when you run the IDE, then the desktop last used *on that particular project* is restored.)

When you run the IDE for the first time, or when for some other reason there is no previously saved desktop, the IDE starts out with a default desktop containing a single, blank edit window labeled `NONAME00.C`. `NONAME00.C` is recognized as a dummy file name; the name of the first actual file that you open will replace `NONAME00.C` and the file will be loaded into the renamed window.

When you run the IDE, it may present you with an old desktop in which you are no longer interested. In that case, you can clear the desktop—close all open windows—by choosing ≡ | Clear desktop.

COMPILING A PROGRAM WITH ONE SOURCE FILE

As an introduction to the IDE, we will see how to enter, compile, link, and execute the hello-world program in Listing 1-1 (page 2).

Run the IDE from your working directory as described above. If the initial desktop contains anything other than the `NONAME00.C` window, clear it by choosing ≡ | Clear desktop.

We now need to choose a file name for the hello-world program. Turbo C++, which can compile both C and C++ programs, uses the file name extensions `.H` for header files, `.C` for C source files, and `.CPP` for C++ source files. The `.C` or `.CPP` extension determines whether the file will be compiled as a C or C++ source file. Because the hello-world program is written in C++, we give its source file the name `HELLO.CPP`.

To open a file for the hello-world program, choose File | Open or press F3. Enter `HELLO.CPP` in the dialog box that appears. If a blank `NONAME00.C` window is present, its name will change to `HELLO.CPP`; otherwise, a new window named `HELLO.CPP` will be opened. If the file `HELLO.CPP` already exists in your working directory, it will be loaded into the `HELLO.CPP` window. If no such file exists, the window will remain blank, and you can proceed to type in the desired text.

Assuming that you are creating a new file, type the text of Listing 1-1 into the `HELLO.CPP` window. When you are finished, choose File | Save or press F2 to save the file in your working directory.

To compile, link, and execute the hello-world program, choose Run | Run or press Ctrl-F9. A Compiling window and later a Linking window will open and keep you informed as to which files are being compiled or linked. Note that most of the compile time is spent compiling the large `IOSTREAM.H` header file, which the hello-world program includes with an `#include` directive.

When the hello-world program executes, the output that it produces will flash on the screen too quickly to be seen. To study the output at leisure, open the Output window by choosing Window | Output. The Output window shows a segment of recent output to the display; if you scroll to the bottom of this segment you should find the message `Hello, world!` printed by the hello-world program. You can return to the edit window by pressing F6 until the edit window is active.

If your program contains errors, the IDE will aid you in locating and correcting them. To demonstrate this, let's introduce two errors into the hello-world program: delete the closing parenthesis in "`main()`" and delete the semicolon at the end of the output statement. Again choose Run | Run or press Ctrl-F9 to try to compile and run the program. After a while, a message at the bottom of the Compiling window will inform you that there are errors and instruct you to press any key.

When you press a key, the Compiling window will close and you will see that a Message window has opened. The Message window contains two error messages that correctly diagnose the two errors we introduced into the program. You can use the up and down arrow keys to move a highlight to each of the error messages; a corresponding highlight in the edit window indicates approximately where each error occurs. Note that for both the errors in our example, the highlight in the edit window indicates the line following the one on which the error actually occurs.

Pressing Enter will return you to the edit window so you can correct the errors. Once in the edit window, you can move the cursor to the approximate positions of the errors by typing Alt-F8 to go to the next error and Alt-F7 to go to the previous error. When you go to the location of an error with Alt-F7 or Alt-F8, the corresponding error message will appear highlighted at the bottom of the edit window.

The following three hot keys are useful for compiling, linking, and executing programs:

Alt-F9	Compile only; produces object file
F9	Compile and link; produces executable file
Ctrl-F9	Compile, link, and execute

Note that none of these keys does any more work than necessary. If a program has already been compiled, F9 will just link it and Ctrl-F9 will just link and execute it. If a program has already been compiled and linked, then Ctrl-F9 will just execute it.

COMPILING A PROGRAM WITH SEVERAL SOURCE FILES

Turbo C++ allows you to define a *project* consisting of all the source files that must be compiled and linked to produce a given executable file. Once you have defined a project, a program with several source files can be compiled and linked as easily as one with only a single source file. For example, typing Ctrl-F9 will compile all the source files in the project, link them, and execute the resulting program.

As mentioned, projects are also useful for managing desktops. If you specify a project when you run the IDE, the current desktop for that project will be restored. Because of this, it may be convenient to use projects even for programs with only one source file.

For example, let's create a project for our simulation program in Chapter 7. This program consists of a header file REPAIR.H and five source files: GEOMETRC.CPP, ACTIVE.CPP, MANAGER.CPP, SCHEDULE.CPP, and SIMULATE.CPP. Assume that these six files have been copied into your working directory. Run the IDE with the TC command; if the desktop contains anything other than the NONAME00.C window, clear it by choosing ≡ | Clear desktop.

To begin, choose File | Open (or press F3) six times, and each time enter into the dialog box the name of one of the above six files. When you are through, your desktop should contain six overlapping windows, each labeled with the name of one of the six files.

Next, you must create a *project file*, which specifies the source files that belong to the project; project files have the extension .PRJ. Open a project window by choosing Project | Open project. A dialog box will appear for you to enter the name of the project file you are creating; let's call the file for the simulation project SIMULATE.PRJ. When you have entered this name, an empty project window labeled Project: SIMULATE will appear on the desktop.

You must now enter the name of each of the five source files in the project window. Choose Project | Add item; a dialog box will appear for you to enter the name of the first source file (the names can be entered in any order). When you have done so, that name will appear in the project window and the dialog box will reappear. Continue until you have entered the names of all five source files, then press Esc to cancel the dialog box. When you are finished, the names of all five source files should be listed in the project window (you may have to scroll up and down to see them all).

Setting up the project has been a bit tedious, but we are now ready to reap the benefits. Press Ctrl-F9 and watch as the IDE automatically compiles each of the five source files, links them, and executes the resulting program.

For projects, the three hot keys mentioned above work as follows:

Alt-F9   Compile only source file in active window

F9   Compile and link all files in project

Ctrl-F9   Compile and link all project files, then execute

As before, F9 and Ctrl-F9 do not do any more work than necessary. To see an example of this, make a small change in one of the source files and press F9 or Ctrl-F9. Observe that only the source file you changed is recompiled; the existing object files are used for the source files that have not been changed.

Exit the IDE with Alt-X. Information about the project will be stored in the project file SIMULATE.PRJ, and a description of the current desktop will be stored in a file SIMULATE.DSK. To work further on the project, run the IDE and specify the project file as a command-line parameter:

```
TC SIMULATE.PRJ
```

The IDE will restore the desktop to its previous state and load any other needed information about the project. In particular, it will recall which source files are part of the project, so that you can still compile and link the entire project with F9 or Ctrl-F9.

If your working directory contains only one project file, then you need not specify that file when you run the IDE. The project will be loaded automatically when you run the IDE with the command

```
TC
```

PROBLEMS AND WORKAROUNDS

It is unfortunately normal for Version 1.00 of a software product to suffer from a certain number of bugs, and Turbo C++ is no exception. We do not attempt to present a complete bug list here, but confine our attention to four problems that affect the example programs in this book. If you are using a later version of Turbo C++, you should check whether these problems have been corrected. You can determine the version number of Turbo C++ by choosing ≡ | About.

Delimiter Handling by `ignore()`

In Release 2.0, a statement such as

```
cin.ignore( 80, '\n' );
```

extracts and discards all characters up to *and including* the delimiter character \n (assuming the 80-character limit is not exceeded). In Turbo C++, however, only the characters preceding the delimiter are discarded; the delimiter is left in the input stream. A workaround is to follow the above statement with the call `cin.ignore( 1 )`, which ignores one character (the delimiter):

```
cin.ignore( 80, '\n' );
cin.ignore( 1 );
```

This change must be made in Listing 3-3 (page 151), which uses `ignore()` to discard the rest of a line, including the terminating newline. The program will malfunction if the terminating newline is not extracted and discarded.

Delimiter Handling by `getline()`

In Release 2.0, a statement such as

```
cin.getline( line, 80, '\n' );
```

extracts all the characters preceding the delimiter \n and stores them in the array `line` (assuming the 80-character limit is not exceeded). The delimiter is extracted from the input stream and discarded. In Turbo C++, however, the delimiter is stored in the array `line` rather than being discarded. Thus every string read with the above statement ends with a newline, which is not what we normally desire.

As a workaround, we can use the function `get()` instead of `getline()`. We are familiar with the one-argument version of `get()` as a function for reading a single character. The two- and three-argument versions of get() work like the corresponding versions of getline() except that the delimiter is *not* extracted from the input stream. We can use a call to ignore() to extract and discard the delimiter:

```
cin.get( line, 80, '\n' );
cin.ignore( 1 );
```

In some programs it will not matter if the delimiter is left in the input stream, in which case the call to ignore() can be omitted.

The problem with getline() has at least minor effects on every example program that calls the function. For example, newlines stored at the ends of strings will produce unexpected blank lines in the output when the strings are printed.

Only one program, however, suffers a serious malfunction. The program in Listing 6-10 (page 317), which counts words and sequences of punctuation marks, uses the statement

```
cin.getline( buffer, SIZE, '$' );
```

to read a block of text into the array buffer. The dollar sign that signals the end of the text is not to be counted and so should not be read into the array. However, the Turbo C++ version of getline() *does* place the dollar sign in the array, where it is treated as a punctuation mark. If the dollar sign is not absorbed into another punctuation mark sequence, the count of such sequences will be too large by one.

The fix is to replace getline() with get(). Because nothing further is read from the input stream after the delimiter is encountered, we do not need to use ignore() to discard the delimiter.

Nested for Statements

In Listing 6-3 (page 286), the following code from function box::hide() does not compile:

```
for ( int i = 0; i < height; i++ )
    for ( int j = 0; j < width; j++ )
        if ( i == 0 || i == imax || j == 0 || j == jmax ) {
            set_cur_pos( row + i, col + j );
            cout << " ";
        }
```

executable file	A file containing machine code that is ready for execution by the computer. An executable file is produced by *linking* code from one or more object files and from the library.
expression statement	A statement consisting of an expression followed by a semicolon; when the statement is executed, the expression is evaluated and its value is ignored. Thus the expression is evaluated only for its side effects; if the expression has no side effects, the expression statement has no effect.
extraction operator	The operator >>, which is used to read input data from a stream.
formal argument	A data object that receives a value passed to a function. When a function is called, each formal argument is initialized with the value of the corresponding actual argument.
format state	For a stream, flags and parameters that determine how output values will be printed and (to a lesser extent) how input values will be read.
friend	A function or operator that has access to the private members of a class but is not itself a member of the class.
function declaration	Provides the information needed to call a function. The declaration gives the name of the function, its return type, and the type of each argument.
function member	See *member function*.
function prototype	A function declaration.
header file	A file containing declarations that are to be used in one or more source files. A header file is normally included in a source file with an #include directive.
heterogeneous list	A list of class objects, which can belong to more than one class. Processing heterogeneous lists is an important application of *polymorphism*.
hexadecimal notation	A notation for bit patterns that uses the 16 digits 0 through 9 and a through f (or A through F). In C++ integer constants, hexadecimal notation is signaled by a leading 0x (or 0X). Thus 0x135 is in hexadecimal notation whereas 135 is in decimal notation.
homogeneous list	A list of class objects, all of which belong to the same class.
indirection operator	The operator *, which is used to access a value referred to by a pointer.
inheritance	A relationship between classes such that some of the members declared in one class (called the base class) are also present in the second class (called the derived class). We say that the derived class inherits the members in question from the base class.
inheritance path	A series of classes that provide a path along which inheritance can take place. For example, if class B is derived from class A, class C is derived from class B, and class D is derived from class C, then class D inherits from class A via the inheritance path ABCD.
initialization list	In the definition of a constructor, the function heading can be followed by a colon and a list of calls to other constructors. This initialization list can contain calls to (1) constructors for base classes and (2) constructors for class members that are themselves class objects.
inline function	A function such that each call to the function is, in effect, replaced by the statements that define the function.
insertion operator	The operator <<, which is used to send output data to a stream.

instance	An instance of a class is a data object whose type is the class in question.
instance variable	A data member that is not designated as static. Each instance of a class contains a corresponding data object for each nonstatic data member of the class. Because the data objects are associated with each instance of the class, rather than with the class itself, we refer to them as *instance variables*.
integral promotion	Some types, such as `char`, are intended only for storing values in memory. When such values appear in expressions, they are promoted (converted) to type `int` (or `unsigned int`) before any operations are carried out on them.
intermediate base class	A class that lies on an inheritance path connecting a base class and a derived class. For example, if class `C` is derived from class `B` and class `B` is derived from class `A`, then `B` is an intermediate base class lying on the inheritance path between the base class `A` and the derived class `C`.
lifetime	The lifetime of a data object is the time period from when the data object is created to when it is destroyed.
linkage	The property of an identifier that governs its accessibility in different source files. An identifier with *internal linkage* is accessible only in the source file in which it is declared; an identifier with *external linkage* is accessible in all the source files of a program.
linking	Combining object files with one another and with library code to produce an executable file.
lvalue	A name of a data object. The name can be a simple identifier, such as `n`, or a more complicated expression, such as `a[ i ]`, `b.m`, or `*p`.
macro	An identifier that is defined to represent a segment of program text. Subsequent occurrences of the identifier (except inside string literals) are *macro calls*, which the preprocessor *expands* by replacing each call with the corresponding text. Some macros can be called with *parameters*, which the preprocessor inserts in the text at specified positions before using the text to replace the macro call.
manipulator	A data object that is used with the insertion and extraction operators *as if* it were a value to be inserted into a stream or a data object whose value is to be extracted from a stream. In fact, however, a manipulator causes a specified operation to be performed on the stream; this operation may or may not cause insertions or extractions.
member	A data object, function, or operator declared in a class declaration and (for a function or operator) not designated as a friend. See *data member, member function*.
member function	A function or operator declared in a class declaration and not declared as a friend. In C++, we send a message to an object by applying a member function to an instance of the class. A member function has access to a class's data members and so can manipulate the instance variables of any instance to which the function is applied.
member pointer	A pointer that designates a member of a class. Member pointers are distinct from, and must not be confused with, pointers that designate data objects.
member variable	See *data member*.

message	Information sent to an object. A message generally produces an internal change in the object that receives it, and the object may respond to the message by returning a reply. In C++, we send messages by applying member functions to class objects.
method	The means by which an object receives and responds to a particular kind of message. In C++, a method is a member function.
modifiable lvalue	The name of a data object whose value can be changed by assignment. Most lvalues are modifiable; some that are not are array names and the names of constant data objects.
multiple inheritance	A language feature that allows a derived class to have more than one base class.
newline	The character that causes a printer or display to go to the beginning of a new line.
null character	The character whose integer code is 0. The null character is used for terminating strings.
null pointer	A pointer that does not point to any data object. In C++, the null pointer can be represented by the constant 0.
object	In object-oriented programming, an entity that can store data and can send and receive messages. In this book, we use the word *object* for class objects, which are objects in the sense of object-oriented programming. Some books, however, use the term for data objects, which are just regions of memory. Therefore readers must take care to determine how each author uses this important term.
object file	A file containing the machine code produced when a source file is compiled. Before the code in an object file can be executed, it must be *linked* with code from the library and possibly from other object files.
octal notation	A notation for bit patterns that uses the eight digits 0 through 7. In C++ integer constants, octal notation is signaled by a leading 0; thus 0135 is in octal notation whereas 135 is in decimal notation.
overloading	A language feature that allows a function or operator to be given more than one definition. The types of the arguments with which the function or operator is called determines which definition will be used.
pointer	The address of a data object of a particular type. Pointer types always specify the type of data object that can be designated by a pointer, as in pointer-to-int, pointer-to-double, and so on.
pointer arithmetic	Adding or subtracting a pointer and an integer; the pointer must point to an element of an array. The integer determines the number of elements by which the pointer value is moved forward or backward in the array. For example, p + 5 points to the element that is five elements beyond the one pointed to by p, and p − 3 points to the element that is three elements before the one pointed to by p.
polymorphism	A language feature whereby we can send the same message to objects of several different classes, and each object can respond in a different way depending on its class. We can send such a message without knowing to which of the classes the object belongs. In C++, polymorphism is implemented by means of virtual functions.

preprocessor	A part of the compiler that manipulates the program text before any further compiling is done. Three important tasks of the preprocessor are (1) to replace each `#include` directive with the contents of the designated file, (2) to replace each escape sequence with the designated character, and (3) to process macro definitions and expand macro calls.
private base class	A base class such that public and protected members of the base class are inherited as private members of the derived class. Thus the inherited members are accessible to the members and friends of the derived class, but they are not accessible to users of the derived class.
private member	A class member that is accessible only to the class's member and friend functions. A private member of a base class is *not* inherited by a derived class.
protected member	A protected member is the same as a private member *except* a protected member of a base class is inherited by a derived class, whereas a private member is not. For details of inheritance see *public base class* and *private base class*.
public base class	A class such that public and protected members of the base class are inherited as, respectively, public and protected members of the derived class. Thus members that are accessible to users of the base class (public members) are also accessible to users of the derived class. Also, protected members retain their protected status so that they can be inherited in turn by classes derived from a class that itself inherited them.
public member	A class member that is accessible to all users of the class — access is *not* restricted to the class's member and friend functions. A public member of a base class is inherited by a derived class; for details of inheritance see *private base class* and *public base class*.
pure virtual function	A virtual function that is declared in a base class but not defined there; responsibility for defining the function falls on the derived classes, each of which generally provides a different definition. It is illegal to create instances of a class that declares a pure virtual function, so such a class is necessarily an abstract base class.
qualified name	An identifier is qualified by adjoining it to the name of a class or class object; the resulting qualified name refers to a member of the corresponding class. We use the dot operator, `.`, to qualify an identifier with the name of an object; for example, `acct.balance` designates the instance variable `balance` of the object `acct`. We use the scope resolution operator, `::`, to qualify an identifier with the name of a class; for example, `account::balance` refers to the member `balance` of class `account`.
reference	An identifier that serves as an alternate name for a data object; a reference is defined in terms of an existing name for the data object and becomes an alias of that name. References provide a means whereby the names of data objects can, in effect, be passed to and returned by functions and operators.
side effect	Evaluating an expression normally computes the expression's value; any other effect of the evaluation is called a side effect. The most common side effect is assigning a new value to a variable.
single inheritance	The situation in which every derived class has only one base class.
scope	The scope of an identifier is the portion of the program text in which that identifier is accessible.

scope resolution operator	The operator `::`, which is usually used to indicate the class in which an identifier is declared. Thus `account::balance`, `account::rate`, and `account::deposit` are all identifiers declared in class `account`. See *qualified name*.
source file	A file containing program text.
static member	A class member designated as static. A static data member declares a *class variable*—a variable associated with the class itself rather than with any instance of the class. A static member function has two distinctive properties: (1) A static member function has access to only the *static* data members of its class (whereas a nonstatic member function has access to all data members). (2) A static member function can be called independently of any instance of the class (whereas a nonstatic member function is always applied to a particular class instance). Indeed, a static member function can be called even if no instances have been created.
stream	A source from which input data can be obtained or a destination to which output data can be sent.
string	A sequence of characters terminated by a null character. A string is represented by a pointer to its first character.
string literal	A series of characters enclosed in quotation marks; a string literal represents a string consisting of the enclosed characters followed by a terminating null character. When a string literal occurs in an expression, it is replaced by a pointer to the first character of the corresponding string.
type	A classification of data values according to the way they are stored in memory and the operations that can be carried out on them. The type of a value must be known to interpret properly the bit pattern that represents the value in memory.
type cast	A unary operator for converting values to a given type; the operator is formed by enclosing the type name in parentheses. Thus `(int)` is an operator for converting values to type `int`, `(double)` is an operator for converting values to type `double`, and so on.
type conversion	A conversion of a value from one type to another. When converting, we normally wish to retain the underlying mathematical value but to change the way it is represented in memory. Sometimes, however, we may wish to change the underlying value, as when we convert a floating-point number to an integer for the purpose of discarding its fractional part. A pitfall of type conversion is that it may sometimes produce an unexpected and undesired change in the underlying value.
typedef name	A name given to a type via a type-name definition introduced by the keyword `typedef`. A type-name definition allows us to give a name to a type that would otherwise be represented by a combination of symbols, such as `void (*)()`.
unary operator	An operator that takes only one operand.
virtual base class	In multiple inheritance, a derived class can inherit the members of a base class via two or more inheritance paths. If the base class is not virtual, the derived class will inherit more than one copy of the members of the base class. For a virtual base class, however, only one copy of its members will be

inherited regardless of the number of inheritance paths between the base class and the derived class.

virtual function   When a virtual function is called via a pointer or reference, the class of the object pointed or referred to determines which function definition will be used. (For nonvirtual functions, the type of the pointer or reference rather than the class of the target object determines which definition will be used.) Virtual functions implement polymorphism, whereby objects belonging to different classes can respond to the same message in different ways.

whitespace   A sequence of characters containing only spaces, tabs, newlines, and form feeds.

For Further Study

Dewhurst, Stephen C. and Kathy T. Stark. *Programming in C++*. Englewood Cliffs, N.J.: Prentice Hall, 1989.

Dlugosz, John M. "The Secret of Reference Variables." *Computer Language,* August 1989, pp. 83–87.

—— "Member Pointers in C++." *Computer Language,* January 1990, pp. 79–87.

—— "Debugging in C++." *Computer Language,* February 1990, pp. 33–41.

Gorlen, K. *Data Abstraction and Object-Oriented Programming in C++*. New York: Wiley, 1990.

Lippman, Stanley B. *C++ Primer*. Reading, Mass.: Addison-Wesley, 1989.

Miller, William W. "Multiple Inheritance in C++." *Computer Language,* August 1989, pp. 63–71.

Stroustroup, Bjarne. *The C++ Programming Language*. Reading, Mass.: Addison-Wesley, 1986. (This classic book by the developer of C++ has, as of this writing, not yet been revised to reflect the changes in Release 2.0. Readers may wish to wait for a revised edition.)

—— and Margaret A. Ellis. *The Annotated C++ Reference Manual*. Reading, Mass.: Addison-Wesley, 1990. (This reference manual reflects the changes in Release 2.1 and has been chosen as the base document (starting point) for development of a C++ ANSI standard.)

Wiener, Richard S. and Lewis J. Pinson. *The C++ Workbook*. Reading, Mass.: Addison-Wesley, 1990.

Index

Abstract base class, 278–280
Accessibility in derived classes, 228
Active simulation objects, 325, 334–345
Actual arguments, 32, 110–111
Addition of vectors, 179, 181
Address, 15, 102, 107, 109–110
Address-of operator (*see* Operator &)
Adjusters, 323–324
  utilization of, 323
Alias, 110
ANSI escape sequence, 282–283
Argument passing, 110–111
Arguments, 31–33
  actual, 32, 110–111
  default, 81, 87–88
  formal, 32–33, 110–111
  pointer, 110–111
Arithmetic operators, 22–23
Arithmetic types, 10–15
Arity, 166–167
Array assignment forbidden, 104
Array declaration, 103
Array initialization, 103, 106–107, 123–124
Array processing, 104–105
Arrays, 102–107
  char, 123, 125
  of class objects, 105, 107
  and pointers, 113–115
Assignment, 17–18, 23–24
  of strings, 197, 203, 205, 207, 208
  of vectors, 181–183
Assignment operators, 23–24
  for strings, 197, 203, 205, 207, 208

for vectors, 181, 183
Associativity, 21–22, 166
Automatic storage class, 20–21, 102

Backslash, 5–6
bad() function, 378–380
Base class, 221–264
  abstract, 278–280
  private/public, 227–228
Bit fields, 368–370
Bitwise OR operator (*see* Operator |)
Block, 4, 19–20, 42–43
Branch, 299
break statement, 57, 58
Buffer, 371
  objects, 367
  output through, 51
  overflow, 156
  programmer defined, 156

Calendar queue, 351–357
Call, 4, 7, 31–32, 89
Case label, 56–58
char type, 10–13
Character constants, 12–13
Children, 299
cin stream, 5, 40
Class
  account, 64–81, 84–86, 91–94, 162–163, 168–170, 221–224
  active, 331, 334–336
  adjuster, 331, 335, 339–340, 342–345
  base, 221–264
  base, 271–272
  block, 280–281, 284–286

box, 280, 282, 287–289
boxer, 274–277
calendar, 258–260
child, 269–271
chk_acct, 222, 224, 230–231
clock, 257–260
clock_calendar, 258–260
clock_time, 165–166
cocker, 274–277
constant, 301
counter, 261–263
deque, 234–242
derived, 221–264
derived, 271–272
difference, 302–304
disp_c, 261–263
dog, 273–280
expr, 301, 303–304
figure, 280–284
fstream, 383
fstreambase, 381–382
geometric, 328–330, 333–334
giant_schnauzer, 274–277
ifstream, 381–384
ilist, 250–252
incr_c, 261–263
incr_disp_c, 261–263
inode, 249–250, 252
ios, 367–368
iostream, 367–368, 381–382
istream, 367–368, 381–382
itable, 254–256
label, 280, 282, 288, 290–291
list, 245, 249
machine, 331, 335–342

manager, 332, 335, 347–351
miniature_schnauzer, 273–277
node, 245, 249
ofstream, 381–384
ostream, 367–368, 381–382
parent, 269–271
product, 302–305
quotient, 302–305
queue, 236–238
sav_acct, 221–222, 224, 227–230
scheduler, 332, 335, 351–357
schnauzer, 273–277
stack, 236–238
standard_schnauzer, 274–277
state, 308, 310–317
state_P, 310–317
state_S, 310–317
state_W, 310–317
string, 191–218
sum, 301, 303–304
table, 139–149, 159–160, 254–256
time_acct, 222, 224, 232–233
triangle, 280, 282, 287–290
vector, 171–191
Class hierarchy, 222, 257
class keyword, 64, 70, 73–74
Class network, 257
Class objects, 62ff.
  arrays of, 105, 107
  pointers to, 112–113
Class variables, 309–310
Classes 61–81
  input-output, 367–368, 381–382
Clipping, 285
Clock ticks, 323, 325
Comma operator, 30–31, 34, 47–48
Command-line parameters, 386–388
Comments, 1–2
Comparisons of strings, 208–209
Compiling, 74–80
Concatenation of strings, 205, 207, 208

Conditional expression, 29–30, 34, 166
const keyword, 18
  in function declaration, 94–96
  in pointer declaration, 120–122, 158
Constant data objects, 18–19, 94–96
Constant functions, 94–96
Constructors, 70–72, 84–86
  for array elements, 106, 107
  calling for virtual base class, 263
  copy, 177, 199, 201
  initialization list, 229–230, 258–259, 262–263
  strings, 197, 199, 201
  for vectors, 175
Control expression, 42, 46, 52, 56–57
Control statements, 42–56
Coordinating resources, 345–351
Copy constructor, 177
  for strings, 199, 201
Copying strings, 192–195
cout stream, 5, 51

Data abstraction (see Data hiding)
Data hiding, 63
Data member, 65
  static, 309–311
Data object, 15–16, 62
  lifetime, 20–21
dec manipulator, 374
Declaration, 97–98
  array, 103
  function, 7, 33, 87–88, 94–96
  pointer, 108–109, 120–122
  variable, 16–18, 46, 153–154
Decrement operator
  (see Operator −−)
Default arguments, 81, 87–88
default: label, 57–58
#define directive, 189–191
Definition, 97–98
  function, 7, 31–32
  variable, 17
Deques, 234–243
Derived class, 221–264
  accessibility in, 228
Descendants, 299

Destructors, 72
  for strings, 197, 201, 203
  virtual, 272–273
Direct access, 389–391
Discrete simulation, 323
do statement, 43–44
double type, 14–15
Dynamic memory allocation, 102, 134–137

Elements of array, 102–103
Encapsulation (see Data hiding)
#endif directive, 189–191
endl manipulator, 51, 156
enum keyword, 14
Enumeration types, 13–14
eof() function, 378–380
Equality operators, 27–29
  for vectors, 181
Error state, 368
Escape sequence, 5, 6, 13
  ANSI, 282–283
  \", 6
  \', 13
  \0, 123
  \\, 6
  \a, 6
  \n, 6
  \t, 6
  \xhhh, 283
Event-driven simulation, 323, 325
Event message, 325–326, 334–336, 351–357
Executable file, 75–76, 78
exit() function, 151
Explicit conversion, 36–37, 39
Expression evaluation, 21–22, 33–35, 299–305
Expression statement, 6
Expression tree, 299–305
Extending existing class, 254–256
extern keyword, 97, 155
External linkage, 96–97
Extraction operator
  (see Operator >>)

F suffix, 15
fail() function, 378–380
false, 27
File modes, 383–384

File scope, 20
Fill-character parameter, 371
`fill()` function, 372–373
Finite automata (*see* State machine)
Finite state machine (*see* State machine)
`flags()` function, 372–373
`float` type, 14–15
Floating-point constants, 14–15
Floating types, 10, 14–15
`flush` manipulator, 51, 371
`for` statement, 46–51
Formal arguments, 32–33, 110–111
Format state, 368–374
  flags, 368–374
  parameters, 371–374
Friend, 163, 168–170
Function
  arguments, 31–32, 87–88, 110–111
  call, 4, 7, 31–32
  declaration, 7, 33, 87
  default arguments, 81, 87–88
  definition, 7, 31–32
  overloading, 81–87
  prototype, 7
  return, 31–32
Function-call operator (*see* Operator `()`)
Functions, string, 125–131

Geometric distribution, 327–330, 333–334
`get()` function, 368
`getline()` function, 157–158, 368
Global identifier, 19, 20
`good()` function, 378–380
Greatest common divisor, 219–220
Grouping, 22

Header files, 3, 75, 98
  `iomanip.h`, 214, 374
  `iostream.h`, 3, 5, 189, 190, 367
  `stdlib.h`, 151, 326
  `stream.h`, 3
  `string.h`, 125, 191
Heterogeneous list, 266–273

`hex` manipulator, 374

Identifier, 9–10
  scope of, 19–20
`if-else` statement, 52–55
`#ifndef` directive, 189–191
`if` statement, 52–55
`ignore()` function, 155–156
Implicit conversion, 36–37
`#include` directive, 3, 75, 223
Increment operator (*see* Operator ++)
Indirection operator, 107–108, 118–119
Inheritance, 62, 221–264
  multiple, 221, 257–264
  single, 221–257
Initial state, 306
Initialization
  array, 103, 106–107, 123–124
  variable, 17–18
Initialization list, constructor, 229–230, 258–263
Inline expansion, 81, 88–90
`inline` keyword, 90
Input, 4–5, 367–392
  of characters, 155–156
  of vectors, 186–187
  of strings, 155–157, 213–214
Input-output classes, 367–368, 381–382
Insertion operator (*see* Operator <<)
Instance, 62
Instance variable, 64–65, 309–310
`int` type, 10–12
Integer constants, 12
Integer types, 10–14
Intermediate base class, 260–262
Internal linkage, 96–97
`iomanip.h` file, 214, 374
`ios` constants (`ios::` prefix omitted)
  `adjustfield`, 368–369
  `app`, 383
  `ate`, 383
  `basefield`, 368–369
  `dec`, 368–369
  `fixed`, 369–372
  `floatfield`, 368–370
  `hex`, 368–369

`in`, 383–384
`internal`, 369
`left`, 369
`oct`, 368–369
`out`, 383–384
`right`, 369
`scientific`, 369–370, 372
`showbase`, 369–370
`showpoint`, 369–370
`showpos`, 369–370
`skipws`, 368–369
`stdio`, 369, 371
`unitbuf`, 369, 371
`uppercase`, 369–370
`iostream.h` file, 3, 5, 189–190, 367
Iterator, 159–160, 254–256

L suffix, 12, 15
Leaves, 299
Length of string, 210
Library, 3
Lifetimes of data objects, 20–21
Limited-access sequence, 234–243
Linear search, 146–147
Linkage, 96–98
Linked lists, 244–254
Linking, 74–76, 78
Listing, 2
Local identifier, 19–20
Logical operators, 28–29
`long double` type, 14–15
`long` type, 10–12
Lvalue, 16, 19, 102–103, 107–109

Machine-adjustment problem, 323–325
Magnitude of vector, 172, 185–186
`main()` function, 4, 386–388
Manipulator, 51, 156–157, 214, 371, 374
Math library, 3
Mean time between failures, 327
Member, 64
Member function, 66–72, 81–86, 162–163
  static, 310–311, 313
Member name, 64
Member variable, 65
  static, 309–311

Memberwise assignment/ initialization, 175, 177
`memcmp()` function, 208–209
`memcpy()` function, 199
Message, 62–63
Method, 63
Mixed-mode expressions, 36
Modifiable lvalue, 19, 103
Multiple definitions error, 98
Multiple inclusions, 189–191
Multiple inheritance, 221, 257–264
Multiplication, of vectors, 179

Names of data objects, 16, 19, 102–103, 107–109
Nested blocks, 19–20
Nested `if` statements, 54–56
`_new_handler` variable, 137–138, 153–155
Node, 299
Null character, 122–123
Null pointer, 120, 243

Object file, 75–78
Object-oriented programming, 61–63
Objects, 61–63
`oct` manipulator, 374
Opening file, 383
Operator
  , (comma), 30–31, 34, 47–48
  !, 28–29, 380
  !=, 27–29, 120
  %, 23
  %=, 25
  & (address-of), 109–110, 114
  &&, 28–29, 34, 388
  ( ), 166, 212
  (*type*), 37, 39, 166
  * (**indirection**), **107**–108, 118–119
  * (multiplication), 21–23
  *=, 25
  +, 21–23
  ++, 26–27, 118–119
  +=, 24–25, 168
  –, 21–23
  ––, 26–27, 118
  –=, 25
  –>, 112–113
  . (dot), 65, 67–69, 166

/, 21– 23
/=, 25
::, 68, 166
<, 28–29
<<, 5–6, 164–167, 186–187, 213–214, 368
<=, 28
=, 17–18, 22–25, 27–28, 166
==, 27–29, 120
>, 28
>=, 28
>>, 40, 155–157, 186–187, 213–214, 368
?:, 29–30, 34, 166
[ ], 166, 184, 211–212
`delete`, 134–137, 166
`new`, 134–137, 166
`sizeof`, 166
unary +, 23
unary –, 23
|, 372
||, 28–29, 34
`operator` keyword, 163, 168
Operator overloading, 163–168
Output, 4–6, 367–392
  of vectors, 186–187
  of strings, 213–214
Overloading
  function, 81–87
  operator, 163–168
Overriding
  inherited functions, 232–233, 259–260
  virtual functions, 271–272

Parent, 299
Passive simulation objects, 325
Pointer arithmetic, 116–120
Pointers, 107–122
  and arguments, 110–111
  arithmetic with, 116–120
  and arrays, 113–115
  to base and derived classes 264, 268
  to class objects, 112–113
  comparison of, 120
  declaration of, 108–109, 120–122
  null, 120, 243
  and subscripts, 115–116
  and virtual functions, 267–273

Polymorphism, 63, 266–273
Position of substring, 209–210
Precedence, 21–22, 166
Precision parameter, 371–372
`precision()` function, 372–373
Preprocessor, 3
Preprocessor directives, 3
Private base class, 227–228
`private` keyword, 73–74, 227–228
Private members, 73–74
Program
  breeds of dogs, 273, 277–280
  command interpreter, 54–58
  compute balance, 76–80
  compute discounts, 38–41
  compute interest, 48–51
  copy file, 386–388
  count words, 316–318
  direct access demo, 389–391
  expression evaluation, 301–305
  format floating-point numbers, 376–378
  format strings and integers, 375–376
  heterogeneous linear list, 292–295
  heterogeneous linked list, 295–298
  linked-list demo, 250–254
  machine-adjustment simulation, 357–363
  phone book, 149–153
  print "Hello, world!", 1–6
  print greeting, 7–9
  rabbit problem, 44–46
  read file, 385–386
  string demo, 214–218
  vector demo, 187–190
  write file, 384–385
`protected` keyword, 222–223, 228–229
Public base class, 227–228
`public` keyword, 73–74, 227–228
Public members, 73–74
Pure virtual function, 278–280

Qualified names, 66, 68–69
Queues, 234–243

rand() function, 326–327
Random access (*see* Direct access)
Random numbers, 326–327
Rational numbers, 219
Redefining inherited functions,
    232–233, 259–260
Redefining virtual functions,
    271–272
Reference counts, 192, 194–195,
    210–211
Reference, passing by, 111, 131–133
Reference types, 111, 131–133
    and virtual functions, 267–273
Relational operators, 28–29
Repetition statements, 42–51
resetiosflags()
    manipulator, 374
Resource coordination, 345–351
return statement, 31–32
Root, 299

Scalar, 171
Scalar multiplication, 171
Scalar product, 171–172, 179
Scheduler, 324–325, 351–357
Scope of identifier, 19–20
Scope resolution operator (*see*
    Operator : :)
seekg() function, 389–391
Selection statements, 52–55
Separate compilation, 78–80
Sequence points, 34–35
Sequential access, 389
Sequential search, 146–147
Service manager, 323–324
Set, 160–161, 218–219
setf() function, 373–374
setfill() manipulator, 374
setiosflags() manipulator, 374
setprecision() manipulator,
    374
setw() manipulator, 156–157,
    214, 374
short type, 10–12
Side effects, 25–26, 34–35
signed char type, 11–12
Signed integers, 11
Simula, 322
Simulation
    and object-oriented program-
        ming, 322

case study, 322–363
discrete, 323
event driven, 323–325
Simulation event list, 351–357
Single inheritance, 221–257
Smalltalk, 322
Source file, 2, 75–76, 78
srand() function, 326
srcpy() function, 126
Stacks, 234–243
State diagram (*see* State graph), 321
State graph, 306–308, 321
State machine, 305–318, 320–321
State variable, 337
Static data member, 309–311
Static keyword, 20, 97
Static member function, 310–311,
    313
Static member variable, 309–311
Static storage class, 20–21, 102
stdlib.h file, 151, 326
Storage class, 20–21, 102
str... functions, 191
    strcat(), 159
    strchr(), 158
    strcmp(), 130–131, 208
    strcpy(), 125, 127–128, 199
    strlen(), 129, 191, 199
    strstr(), 159
stream.h file, 3
streampos type, 389–391
Streams, 5
    end-of-file detection, 378–380
    error detection, 378–380
String literal, 5, 124–125
String representation, 192–195
string.h file, 125, 191
Strings, 5, 122–125
    class string, 191–218
    functions for, 125–131
struct keyword, 64–65, 73–74
Subscripting operator (*see also*
    Operator [ ])
    for strings, 211–212
    for vectors, 184
Subscripts 103, 117
    and pointers, 115–116
Substring extraction, 212–213
Subtraction, of vectors, 179
Subtree, 299
switch statement, 56–58

tellg() function, 389–391
Tree, 299
true, 27
Type cast, 37, 39, 166
Type conversions, 35–37, 39
Type of data object, 16
Type-safe linkage, 96–97
typedef keyword, 138–139,
    154–155
Typedef name, 138–139
Types, 10–15
    arithmetic, 10–15
    class, 61–81
    enumeration, 13–14
    floating, 10, 14–15
    integer, 10–14
    pointer, 107–109
    reference, 111, 131–133, 267–273

U/UL suffix, 12
unsetf() function, 373–374
unsigned char type, 11–12
unsigned int/long/short
    types, 11–12
Unsigned integers, 11

Value
    classified by type, 10
    of data object, 16
    passing by, 110
    of variable, 17
Variable, 16
    class, 309–310
    declaration, 16–18, 46, 153–154
    definition, 17
    instance, 309–310
Vector, 171
Vector arithmetic, 171
Virtual base class, 260–264
    calling constructor for, 263
Virtual destructor, 272–273
Virtual function, 266–273
    pure, 278, 279, 280
virtual keyword, 269

while statement, 42–43, 45–46
Width parameter, 371
width() function, 372–373